The Landscape of
THOMAS HARDY

The Landscape of
THOMAS HARDY

—— DENYS KAY~ROBINSON ——

With photographs by Simon McBride

Salem
House

First published in Great Britain 1984 by
Webb & Bower (Publishers) Limited
9 Colleton Crescent, Exeter, Devon EX2 4BY

Published in the United States
of America by
Salem House Limited
99 Main Street
NH 03079

Designed by Vic Giolitto

Text Copyright © Denys Kay-Robinson 1984
Photographs Copyright © Simon McBride 1984
Design Copyright © Webb & Bower (Publishers) Limited 1984

British Library Cataloguing in Publication Data

Kay-Robinson, Denys
   The landscape of Thomas Hardy.
   1. Hardy, Thomas, *1840–1928*—Homes and haunts
   —England—Wessex
   I. Title
   823'.8   PR4753

ISBN 0 906671 72 8

Typeset in Great Britain by Keyspools Limited
Golborne, Warrington WA3 3QA

Printed and bound in Hong Kong by Mandarin Offset International Limited

Half-title page:
Culliford Tree

Title page:
Dorchester: Colliton Walk.

The flat summit of Batcombe Hill.

Contents

They are great trees, no doubt, by now
That were so thin in bough—
That row of limes—
When we housed there; I'm loth to reckon when;
The world has turned so many times,
so many, since then!

THOMAS HARDY

Preface

Eleven years have passed since the publication in 1972 of *Hardy's Wessex Reappraised*, the first book devoted exclusively to a detailed survey of the Hardy Country since Hermann Lea's classic *Thomas Hardy's Wessex* of 1913. In those eleven years changes in the Wessex scene have not only continued but in many cases accelerated, and it was high time to make a further series of journeys through the region in order to bring the information up to date. Simultaneously it was decided to expand extensively the pictorial side of the book, mainly with colour photographs; and to this end Simon McBride and his equipment joined me in my travels so that I could point out exactly what subjects best fitted the text. As a result, the McBride photographs form the largest collection taken specifically to illustrate Hardy's Wessex locations since Hermann Lea's pioneer work—and the largest colour collection ever.

In addition to modernizing my earlier book by taking note of physical changes, I have revised certain passages in the light of later information, repaired a number of omissions, particularly in respect of the poems, and corrected all errors known to me, including one or two in the maps. I have also taken advantage of the greatly increased number of photographic captions to include in them as much information as possible that is not given in the text. Where Hardy varied his own texts in later editions I have continued the policy of generally confining myself to his final version.

Once more I have met with kindness and helpfulness from nearly everyone I have had occasion to approach, whether for assistance in academic research or for on-the-spot information, and to all of them I offer my own and Simon McBride's warmest gratitude.

Burbage, Wiltshire   D.K-R.

I SOUTH WESSEX
CASTERBRIDGE
Dorset: Dorchester

And midnight clears High Street of all but the ghosts
    Of its buried burghees,
From the latest far back to those old Roman hosts
    Whose remains one yet sees,
Who loved, laughed, and fought, hailed their friends, drank their toasts,
    At their meeting-times here, just as these!

AT CASTERBRIDGE FAIR

Most of the characters introduced to 'Caster-bridge' from outside approached it over Grey's Bridge; and the panorama they saw before descending from Stinsford Hill ('Mellstock Hill', 'Mellstock Rise') or Rushy Pond is astonishingly little changed. A 'new' spire here and there, a late-Victorian mock-keep in the background, the vast red bulk of the 1884–5 prison toward the right: not much else would puzzle those Hardy ghosts. Only on the flanks of the town and in the foreground—alongside the road linking the two bridges, and where 'Mixen' Lane was—are modern buildings conspicuous.

The spread of houses out to the nearer bridge, Grey's, means that the avenue of trees bordering the main road now stops short of this point instead of continuing more than halfway to Town or Swan Bridge. The descendants of the romantic young ladies in the poem 'Sitting on the Bridge'—Grey's, that is—very seldom sit on it today, and even the bench now provided alongside it is patronized mainly by the heirs of the 'Crusted Characters'. But an iron notice on the new wall (the bridge was widened in 1927) still threatens with transportation for life anyone found causing damage. Of the 'dace, trout, and minnows' noted by Parson Maybold among the 'long green locks of weed' below, only the dace, I am told, have ceased to be evident.

To the north of Grey's Bridge Ten Hatches still stands, in good repair but with the five westernmost hatches removed from their frames. Ten Hatches Hole in which Henchard was so narrowly prevented from drowning himself has barely altered, nor has the Blackwater (still willow-fringed) further upstream. (Earlier in *The Mayor of Casterbridge* the prison reach of the Frome is misleadingly termed *Schwarzwasser*.) It was by the 'eve-lit weir' of Ten Hatches that Hardy sat, as he recalled in the lines 'Before My Friend Arrived', on the day before the body of Horace Moule was brought back from Cambridge for burial in Fordington churchyard. And in widely different mood, here the disgusted candidate for the workhouse in 'The Curate's Kindness' wished he could do away with himself on finding he was not after all to be rid of his wife. Between the mainstream of the Frome that flows under Grey's Bridge and the minor arm that flows under Swan, only a strip of allotments hugging the latter today lessens the extraordinary desolation that still characterizes the marshy expanse, a fit setting yet for 'The Fight on Durnover Moor'.

There are now public conveniences beside Swan Bridge, and the parapet on which Sergeant Troy sat to await Fanny Robin is not the one there today, for in 1954 the old bridge collapsed

Casterbridge and Durnover (circa 1848)

─────── Key ───────

1 Alternative house in *The Burghers*
2 Gaol entrance arch and gallows site
3 Water mill
4 Theatre (replaced High W. St theatre 1828)
5 Laura Maumbry's uncle's house
6 No 51 (the house with the oriel)
7 Shire Hall
8 Seedsman's shop
9 Holy Trinity church
10 The George Inn
11 St Peter's church
12 Town Hall
13 King's Arms Hotel
14 The Three Mariners Inn
15 The Ship Inn
16 The Antelope Inn
17 Hardy's site for High Place Hall
18 Waggon Office (?) (No 21)
19 Town Pump
20 All Saints church
21 The Phoenix Inn
22 Dorford chapel
23 Cottages probably including Susan
    Henchard's
24 Museum 'in a back street'
25 Henchard's house
26 Henchard's corn-store
27 Durnover old vicarage and garden

28 Church of St Geroge, Durnover
29 Durnover Barton
30 William Barnes's house
31 John Hick's house
32 Napper's Mite almshouses
33 Hardye's Grammar School
34 Cottages probably including Abe
    Whittle's
35 Site of priory or friary
36 Section of Roman wall
37 Durnover Mill
38 Old Greyhound Inn (site)

i Glyde Path Hill
ii Colliton Row
iii Shire Hall Lane
iv Bull Stake (North Square)
v Grey's School Passage
vi Top o' Town
vii The Bow or Crossways
viii Town or Swan Bridge
ix Cornhill
x Durnover Green
xi Durnover Cross
xii Church Lane
xiii Old Gool Lane
xiv Charles Street
xv Bowling Green Lane

xvi Standfast or Prince's Bridge
xvii Standfast Road
xviii Mixen (Mill) Lane
xix Trinity Cottages

Key to Hardy names
'High Place Hall' = Colliton House
'Chalk Walk' = Colliton Walks
'Chapel of Ease' = Christ Church
'Durnover Moor' = Fordington Field
'Durnover Green, Cross, Hill' =
    Fordington Green, Cross, Hill
'Pummery' = Poundbury
'Corn Street' = South Street and
    Cornhill
'Bowling Walk' = Bowling Alley
    Walks

9

The Hangman's Cottage, 'Casterbridge' (Dorchester), appears in more than one of Hardy's works, but most prominently in the long short story 'The Withered Arm'. Today a private house (and what a sensational address!), its external appearance is little different from when the young Thomas once climbed the railings on the eve of an execution and saw the Hangman eating his supper.

and had to be rebuilt. Up-river, on the right bank, is the site of the Priory Mill. The walls of one of the mill buildings have been left standing up to garden-wall height, with a small modern house looking somewhat out of place inside them. Outside, the noise of the 'cascade which had raised its terrific roar for centuries', is today reduced to a gentle murmur, and the Priory (or Friary) ruins on which Henchard looked out from Jopp's cottage, are no more. Indeed, the cottage itself, so rich in 'scraps of tracery, moulded window-jambs' and other stones from the Priory, has vanished as though it never existed—which perhaps it did not.

Somewhat to the west, and above the cliff,

towers the large factory-like brick façade of the 'new' prison. One feature of the older building is left, the 'classic archway of ashlar' prominent in 'The Withered Arm', and through which Bold-wood passed after shooting Troy. But the words 'County Jail 1793', once incised over the doorway, are now missing; possibly they were removed when the government took over prison administration from local authorities in 1877. The other entrance mentioned in 'The Withered Arm', fronting the Bull Stake (now North Square), was replaced by the present iron gate in 1899.

Hangman's Cottage, in which the resident executioner still lived during Hardy's boyhood, is today a very neatly kept private residence. The outside staircase noticed by Gertrude Lodge has been removed, and there is a garage, but otherwise, despite some enlargement, the only conspicuous external change is a large area of new brickwork repairing the front wall. The wicket in the prison wall, pointed out by the

Ten Hatches, 'Durnover Moor' – recently shorn of five of the hatches – where the already divided 'Froom' (Frome) further divides. The solitude of the area, close on the main part of the town, is manifest. The trees on the skyline are the scattered successors of the once fine avenue lining the 'Weatherbury' (Puddletown) road.

hangman to Gertrude, has so completely disappeared that it is difficult to judge where it was, for the cottage is not really opposite the prison. The steep rise in front of the cottage, reached by a bridge across the stream, is Glyde Path Road, formerly divided into Glyde Path Hill—the 'Glyd'path Rise' of 'The Burghers'—Colliton Row, and Shire Hall Lane. The poem mentions a pleasaunce, a door in an outer wall, and an arch. The house was therefore probably Colliton House, the door the arched one with the mask above it described in *The Mayor of Casterbridge*.

Colliton (or Colyton) Park is now given over to the buildings and car-parks of the new county administrative headquarters. Lengths of the old boundary wall and a few trees, surrounded by new lawns and flowerbeds, alone remain from the past. Colliton House is the 'High Place Hall' occupied by Lucetta Templeman; Hardy varied its position, however, not merely with each new edition, but within any single edition. The 'little-used alley' to which the door with the mask gave access must surely have been Glyde Path Road, and the allusion to 'the Town Hall *below* Lucetta's house' [my italics] also suggests this site. On the other hand, the reference to the house overlooking the market, and to the nearness of the Town Hall archway where Henchard's waggon upset, seem to suggest a position in Cornhill. Windle* identifies 'High Place Hall' with great precision as the corner building at the junction of Cornhill and Durngate Street, maintaining that the gateway with the mask was 'borrowed' from Colliton House. But all the Cornhill houses formed then, as now,

* For full details of all authors and works mentioned in the text see bibliography on pages 229–30.

a continuous terrace, and that makes nonsense of Hardy's remark that Lucetta's house 'had the characteristics of a country mansion' and 'dignity without great size'. These epithets, however, apply perfectly to Colliton House.

The mansion is now part of the County Council offices, but has been left freestanding, and cleaning of the stonework has restored its original tone. On the south side a one-storey canteen has been added—fortunately where it is not too conspicuous, except to those looking for the original site of the door with the mask. This door once stood in a stone wall that ran alongside Glyde Path Road from the corner where the canteen now obtrudes, past the forecourt of the new brick County Laboratory to the back of the nearest house in High West Street. Today the arch and mask frame the library doorway in the County Museum.

The north-west corner of the park is formed by two of the tree-lined walks that mark the line of the ancient town walls: North Walk and Colliton ('Chalk') Walk. Here Henchard made his fateful plea to Farfrae not to leave the town; and after more than a century the only difference in the scene is the asphalt underfoot. In the angle between the Walks, excavation within the last decade has exposed the remains of the only complete Roman town-house to be seen in Britain. Just beyond the southern end of Colliton Walk, almost at Top o' Town, stands Eric Kennington's memorial statue of the seated Hardy.

West of Colliton Walk and the Yeovil road (the Grove) Fordington's great vicar Henry Moule built in 1846 a small chapel of ease, Christ Church, to spare his parishioners in this outpost of his sprawling parish the necessity of tramping to Fordington St George. This is the chapel of ease alluded to in 'A Changed Man'. It has recently been demolished, together with some cottages, to make room for the residential part of the Grove Trading Estate; but it had already outlived its purpose with the formation in 1910 of St Mary's parish out of north Fordington and the building of St Mary's, Victoria Park.

The barracks in which Captain Maumbry was quartered before he exchanged his cuirass for a cassock, where the narrator in 'The Revisitation' lay sleepless, and from which the 'King's-Own Cavalry' sallied forth to hold their memorable 'Dance at the Phoenix', were mainly on the south side of a huge grassed square, the Barrack Green. Here, in the opening pages of 'A Changed Man', the band played on Sunday afternoons. This green survived, its grass long and untended, well into the 1970s, but is now covered by an enormous glass-and-concrete block housing a miscellany of government offices, and by its attendant asphalted car-park. The buildings themselves, later called the Marabout Barracks, have survived in part, one large section being now occupied by the sorting department of the Post Office. Some of the cookhouses, storehouses, and part of the hospital are among the units still standing. The Riding School, where Moule preached before he built Christ Church, is now a garage. The Infantry and Militia Barracks, south of Poundbury Road, including the keep or gatehouse that now harbours the regimental museum, were all built after the events in Hardy's relevant works.

North of the barracks the development of the trading estate means that once-isolated Poundbury ('Pummery', 'Pummerie') has become virtually part of the town, though the earthwork itself has not altered perceptibly since the last of the sheep marts evoked in 'A Sheep Fair'. Southwest of it, too, the solitude melts as the space between Poundbury and the Bridport road becomes filled in with new streets and houses. The railway (Great Western, 1857) is another intruder since the period of Henchard and Maumbry; thanks to Brunel it passes through a tunnel under the great square mass instead of cutting across it.

The residential development flanking the Bridport road has obliterated Damer's Barn which, together with its 'slimy pond', used to stand opposite the junction of Damer's Road and this thoroughfare. One or two fine water-colour sketches of the barn are to be seen in the

Dorset County Museum. 'Dammer's Crest', referred to in 'The Burghers', is where the road breasts the top of the hill a furlong or two farther west.

The trees that once gave the principal approaches to Dorchester the longest tree borders in Wessex, with the exception of one or two roads near Wilton, have suffered sadly in the past two decades. Already by the turn of the century—long before the advent of Dutch Elm Disease—the elms bordering the Puddletown road had experienced many casualties, and the avenue has never recovered. In 1969 it became necessary to fell the trees along Weymouth Avenue, and more recently it has been the turn of Bridport Road. The best surviving border is along Alington Avenue (Wareham Road) leading to and past Max Gate—and even here the trees are on only one side. Alternatively one may study the various Walks, whose borders have fared far better.

Looking down the two High Streets, East and West, one sees few buildings that would be unfamiliar to the characters in any of the later-set works, and many that would be recognized by the protagonists in those set earlier. Hardy's principal allusion to this view occurs at the beginning of 'A Changed Man', in the description of what the invalid saw from his first-floor oriel window. Some have fancied the 'old, substantially built house' with the oriel to be Top-o'-Town House, but Hardy himself revealed that he had in mind 51 High West Street. This stands on the north side, quite a distance down from Top-o'-Town; but the oriel, rather deceptively, did command approximately the view ascribed to it. Unfortunately for Hardy lovers a change of ownership in 1973 resulted in the new proprietors deciding to restore the original façade of the house, a procedure that involved discovering that the oriel was a later addition and removing it. On the same side, the uppermost house in High West Street appears from Hardy's rather odd description to have been the residence of Laura and her uncle in 'A Changed Man'.

'Casterbridge' (Dorchester), looking up High East into High West Street. 'Corn Street' (Cornhill, which continues as South Street) turns off on the left, just short of the nearest car. The building on the right is The King's Arms (its real name), showing the bow window through which, from the other side of the road, Susan and Elizabeth-Jane watched Henchard presiding over the mayoral dinner.

At the corner of the former Shire Hall Lane there stood, until the 1840s, the Trenchard mansion so much admired by Hardy. This may have been the 'noble pile' of the poem 'A Man'. The short length of stone balustrade at first-floor level on the west side of Glyde Path Road is perhaps a surviving fragment. The grey Shire Hall, scene until 1955 of the Assizes and Quarter Sessions (but not Petty Sessions, which were held in the Town Hall), is also outwardly unaltered. Hardy wrote in *The Mayor of Caster-*

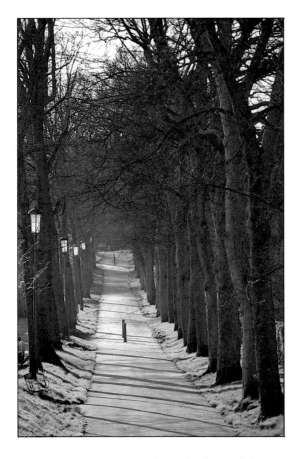

One of 'Casterbridge's' most distinctive features is its graceful tree-lined pedestrian 'Walks', laid out and planted in the eighteenth century along the lines of the vanished Roman walls. Here is West Walks (there is only one, despite the plural), where in *The Mayor of Casterbridge* Farfrae set up his entertainment to rival Henchard's.

bridge that sheep could be heard bleating without the Shire Hall while a sheep-stealer was being sentenced within; these sheep must have been in Colliton Park—for Fordington Field, the nearest extra-mural pasturage, would even in the pre-motor age have been out of earshot. Now we have the court (from 1972 a Crown Court), not the sheep, in Colliton Park, and the Shire Hall is, mainly, a quiet memorial to the Tolpuddle Martyrs.

Between the hall and Holy Trinity church was the little seed shop that housed Henchard's last business in Dorchester, and himself and

Elizabeth-Jane overhead. This is borne out by the following details. When Henchard decided to leave Casterbridge, Elizabeth-Jane accompanied him down to Grey's Bridge, and while returning from there met Farfrae, with whom she walked up High East Street as far as the Bow. Here she turned off with him into South Street instead of going 'straight on to her own door'. This places the shop firmly in or just off High West Street. Elsewhere we are told that the shop occupied a 'pleasant, sunny corner', and that it stood 'overlooking the churchyard'. In fact at the period of the novel there really was a seedsman's shop in just such a situation. It lay down Grey's School Passage, which flanks the west side of Holy Trinity churchyard. At the far end of the churchyard, facing its north side, is a little branch passage, Trinity Cottages. The seedsman's shop occupied the ground floor (recently reconstructed) of the corner building at the junction of the two passages.

East of Holy Trinity—which was rebuilt in 1875 and has recently been acquired by the Roman Catholic Church—stands the Dorset County Museum, built in 1881 (with galleries added in 1903) by Hardy's then recent employer G. R. Crickmay, on the site of the George Inn. This was therefore not the museum recommended to Elizabeth-Jane by Lucetta, though the great mahogany table still in its library is probably the one around which Hardy envisaged the narrators of the stories in *A Group of Noble Dames*. In 1969–71 the museum was enlarged and a Rural Life section added.

St Peter's Church features in *The Mayor of Casterbridge*, *The Trumpet-Major*, and the poems 'The Dance at the Phoenix' and 'The Peace Peal'. The tower has long since recovered from the dilapidated state described in *The Mayor*. The whole church was restored in 1856 by John Hicks (apprentice-assistant, Thomas Hardy), and again before the end of the century by C. F. Ponting. There were repairs in 1961, and a further repointing in 1967. The tenor bell that so pleased the Trumpet-Major is still there, more than a ton of it, along with its seven colleagues, three of which were recast during the nineteenth century. The 8 o'clock curfew mentioned in *The Mayor* continued to sound, except for an interval during the First World War, until the outbreak of the Second World War. The chimes that 'stammered out' the Sicilian Mariners' Hymn were not, despite the implication in some versions of *The Mayor*, those of another building— no other building within earshot had the eight bells needed; they were the chimes of St Peter's itself, as is borne out by the poem 'The Chimes'.

In front of the church, the curve of the 'Crossways or Bow' was not long ago flattened for road improvement and the wall taken back some five feet nearer the church. The railings that topped the wall during most of the nineteenth century were removed and not subsequently replaced, since it was felt they would look wrong so much nearer the building. The gate and pillars, however, have been resited. The plate bearing the name of The Bow was put on the wall at Hardy's expense after the council had refused to affix one. It was here that the long-suffering woman in 'A Wife Waits' (part of 'At Casterbridge Fair') waited for her husband to emerge from 'the Club-Room below'— according to Hermann Lea, a building facing into the Bull Stake and already demolished.

Until 1847 the old Town Hall abutted on to the wall surrounding St Peter's and an arched throughway under it gave access to the 'large square called Bull Stake'. Here stood the post to which bulls were tied and baited by dogs to make the meat tender—in those unenlightened days calves were not yet reared in little dark boxes. The stake has long since vanished, and the square (North Square) has been mostly rebuilt. It was by the church wall at the entrance to the archway that Henchard's waggon capsized after the clash with Farfrae's. When the present Town Hall was erected in 1848 a narrow road was left between it and the church. At first there was no clock turret at the corner, but a small cupola in the centre of the roof ridge. The cupola was removed and the corner tower added in 1864, and a new Corn Exchange was built at

the back of the building in 1867. The Gothic entrance was constructed in 1876, since when the Town Hall has remained externally unchanged. Hardy probably thought of the Town Hall and the Corn Exchange in their present form when he put Bathsheba Everdene among the corn merchants, and also in writing 'After the Fair' with its reference to 'Clock-corner steps'.

In Hardy's poem 'The Garden Seat' the seat (at Max Gate) was already old and frail. In a letter referring to the decay of the garden seats in general, Florence Hardy wrote of their 'wooden' legs. But not all had such legs; the magnificent cast-iron ends of the bench shown here were rescued from oblivion only a few years ago and the bench was restored.

Externally unchanged over a somewhat longer period is the King's Arms in High East Street, which was last rebuilt between 1800 and 1820. The front room in which the commissioners dealt with Henchard's bankruptcy may have been either the front bar now on one side of the entrance or the coffee lounge on the other. In the room behind the first-floor bow Henchard himself, dining with the other dignitaries in his heyday as mayor, had been seen through the opened sash by Susan and Elizabeth-Jane, amid the crowd, from the waggon office steps opposite. These steps, as old photographs show, used to jut out from the doorway of 21 High East Street, now a branch of the Wessex Trustee

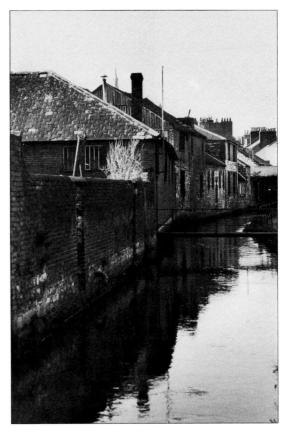

The original Three Mariners Inn, familiar to readers of *The Mayor*, disappeared, much to his regret, well within Hardy's lifetime, and now its successor is an inn no more. But those passing the site in High East Street can still see this reminder over the old entrance to the yard.

'Durnover's' once notorious 'Mixen Lane' (Mill Street) slums have today given place to houses and flats as demure as a church fête. Among the few old buildings left are these, separated by the river from the 'Lane' itself. It was a narrow branch-stream (now covered over) that the poachers used to cross by planks put out for them.

Savings Bank. There appears to be no record of a genuine waggon office, although it turns up again in 'The Waiting Supper' as the place where Nicholas saw Christine.

In his speech on being presented with the freedom of Dorchester Hardy named various buildings, once known to him, whose disappearance he particularly lamented. Among them was the Three Mariners Inn of *The Mayor* (in earlier editions the King of Prussia). This seemingly most agreeable Elizabethan stone building with mullioned bow windows was pulled down, and its successor of the same name built on the site, before the end of the last century. It is now a British Legion club, but the rectangular stone entry-arch alongside still carries the incised legend 'PALE ALE BREWERY'.

Hard by Swan Bridge is the White Hart where Sergeant Troy and Pennyways discussed their plans, but it has been so extensively redecorated within and without that all sense of antiquity has gone. It stands well back from the road, leaving a forecourt for customers to park their cars where once the carriers' carts loaded up with their goods and passengers, including the story-tellers of *A Few Crusted Characters*, and where

Gertrude Lodge dismounted from her carthorse at the end of her ride over the heath.

The third bridge within the town limits is Standfast or Prince's Bridge in Fordington, mentioned in 'the Dance at the Phoenix'. It belongs to an area much redesigned, that of the once notorious Mill Street ('Mixen Lane'). The original bridge remains—with repaired parapets—but it has lost its importance, for most vehicles now cross by the newer bridge a few yards downstream. The adjacent confluence of roads formed Standfast Cross. Fordington Cross is rather more than a cross, being the point south-east of Fordington Green where King's Road is converged upon by High Street, Fordington, Alington Road, St George's Road and Little Britain. Many street names in the area have been changed since Hardy wrote. The stretch of the present High Street between Holloway Road (formerly Cuckolds Row) and Fordington Cross was Fordington Hill. North of the cross the present King's Road was called Standfast Road; south of the cross it was King Street. Between Standfast Bridge and Grey's Bridge the present King's Road was called Tubb's Road.

Although it still contains a few fine old houses and streets of Victorian cottages, Fordington has altered much more than Dorchester. Not only have the low-lying slums vanished, but the 'congeries of barns and farmsteads' on Fordington Hill has now been transformed for the most part into a region as urban as the rest of Dorchester. It is therefore fortunate for us that in a tiny rural pocket east of the churchyard a muddy rustic enclosure containing pigsties and a small shed (thatched until 1971) can reasonably be regarded as the remnant of the 'Durnover Barton' that Hardy bestowed on Henchard, and where Susan arranged for Farfrae to meet Elizabeth-Jane.

The church of St George in Fordington has had a curious history during the last 200 years, for it has regained in the twentieth century the medieval outline it lost in the eighteenth when the old chancel was pulled down and a new and much smaller one built in the Georgian style.

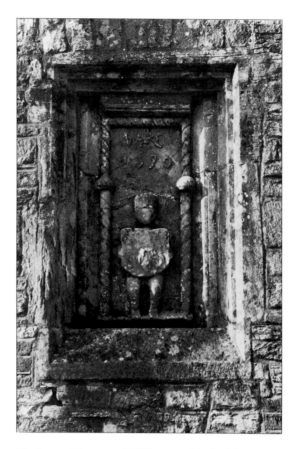

The former 'Durnover Mill' became a block of flats as long ago as 1891, but round by the entrance (away from Mill Street) there are still some vestiges of the older era, including this stone-carved figure, dated 1590, that used to be set above a mill window.

This was the chancel that existed during the period of *The Dynasts* and 'Enter a Dragoon', the poem 'No Bell-Ringing', the comings and goings of Lucetta and Elizabeth-Jane, and the activities of the Reverend John Maumbry in 'A Changed Man'. It was pulled down and rebuilt in the old proportions by the Reverend Richard Bartelot shortly after he became vicar in 1906. Hardy strongly opposed the plan to rebuild and was greatly distressed by the removal of the Georgian structure. He agreed with Bartelot, however, about the demolition of another addition, a galleried aisle put up alongside the nave in 1831; and when the same vicar went on to enlarge and improve the nave, Hardy himself designed new Gothic pillars for the north aisle. In the churchyard the principal changes are the disappearance of the thatched wall (or at least the thatch) and promenade noted in *The Mayor*, and the comparatively recent removal of nearly all the tombstones, including some of considerable interest; only the far enclosure where the Moules lie has been left undisturbed. This was the area where, in 'Enter a Dragoon', Sergeant Clark's two 'wives' met one another at his grave.

Fordington Green has been preserved, and indeed improved, Bartelot having planted a septet of trees to which the borough council has added. There is a scene in *The Dynasts* in which Napoleon's effigy is merrily burnt on 'a patch of green grass on Durnover Hill'. This refers not to

A stretch of 'Durnover Moor'. This curious horseshoe of land nearly surrounding 'Casterbridge' belongs to the Duchy of Cornwall. Building is inexorably encroaching, but in parts the transition from town to country is still as dramatic as when Hardy marvelled at its abruptness in *The Mayor of Casterbridge*.

Churchyard and pigyard – a strange juxtaposition, especially on the fringe of a town. The church is St George, 'Durnover'; the pigstyes are the remains of what may be taken as 'Durnover Barton', where Susan arranged the meeting between Farfrae and Elizabeth-Jane.

'Casterbridge' from the east, seen across one of the several channels of the 'Froom' (Frome) and part of 'Durnover Moor' (Fordington Field). The spire is that of All Saints, the tower St Peter's. The bulky building toward the right is the Prison.

Fordington Green but to Fairfield, formerly Salisbury Field, close by, on to which the garden of the Old Vicarage abuts: the vicar watched the burning from the garden gate. The old house, outwardly little altered, is now converted into flats. On the western side of Fairfield the tree-lined path—Salisbury Walk—that leads down to the Town Bridge is the 'deserted avenue of chestnuts' into which Fanny Robin turned to reach

the Union without going through the town.

Maumbry, we are told, lived at or near Fordington Cross. The Mill Street ('Mixen Lane') of his day, so graphically conjured up in *The Mayor*, where its squalor is in no degree exaggerated, has now given place to demure squares and blocks of council flats. Nothing remains to suggest the former overcrowding in this little island of 'free' land in the midst of the

Map of the Principal Towns and Villages
of
SOUTH WESSEX
BASED ON THE WORKS OF THOMAS HARDY

UPPER WESSEX

Stapleford Park

VALE OF
LITTLE DAIRIES

Stourcastle

Hambledon Hill

Trantridge

Chaseborough

Knollingwood Hall

Nuttlebury

Tranton

Lornton Inn

Lornton Copse

Hintock Ho.

Shottsford
Forum

Stagfoot Lane

Yewsholt Lodge

Warborne

Middleton Abbey

Millpond
St Jude

King's Hill Speer

Tower

Welland Ho.

Elm Cranlynch

Chene Manor

erbury

Tolchurch

Kingsbere

Greenhill

Flytchett

Wyndway Ho.

Sandbourne

Stickleford

East Egdon

Alderworth

VALLEY OF THE
GREAT DAIRIES
Talbothays

EGDON HEATH

Holmstoke?

Havenpool

Springham

Wellbridge

Black Dog
Inn

Anglebury

HAVENPOOL
HARBOUR

Nether
Moynton

Bindon Abbey

Chaldon

Dagger's Grave

Corvsgate

Bollard
Head

Kingworth
Shore

Lulstead Cove

Kingscreech

Little Enkworth

Luworth Cove

St Alban's Head

Enkworth Ho.

Knollsea

Scale
in Miles

0 ½ 1   2   3   4   5

Key to the Map of South Wessex

Hardy's names in italics

Abbot's Beach, Abbotsea: Abbotsbury
Abbot's Cernel: Cerne Abbas
Alderworth: Brickyard Cottage
Black'on: Blackdown Hill
Bollard Head: Ballard Point
Broad Sidlinch: Sydling St Nicholas
Budmouth Regis: Weymouth and
    Melcombe Regis
Casterbridge: Dorchester
Catknoll: Chetnole
Chaldon: East Chaldon
Chalk Newton: Maiden Newton
Chene Manor: Canford School
Cloton: Netherbury
Corvsgate: Corfe Castle
Creston: Preston
Damer's Wood: Came Wood
Dead Man's Bay: West Bay
East Egdon: Affpuddle
East Quarriers: Easton
Elm-Cranlynch Corfe Mullen
Emminster: Beaminster
Enkworth House: Encombe House
Estminster: Yetminster
Evershead: Evershot
Faringdon Ruin: Winterbourne Farringdon church
Flintcomb-Ash: Plush
Flytchett: Lytchett Minster
Froom-Everard: West Stafford
Greenhill: Woodbury Hill
Haggardon Hill: Eggardon Hill
Havenpool: Poole
Higher Crowstairs: Hog Hill (but see page 105)
Higher Jirton: Higher Forston (?)
Hintock House: Turnworth House
Holmstoke: Hethfelton (?)
Isle of Slingers: Portland
Kingsbere: Bere Regis
Kingscreech: Steeple
King's Hintock: Melbury Osmund
Knollingwood Hall: Wimborne St Giles
    House
Knollsea: Swanage
Little Enkworth: Kingston
Little Welland: Roger's Hill Farm (?)

Lornton Copse: Horton Wood
Lornton Inn: Horton Inn
Lower Longpuddle: Piddlehinton (also
    Puddletown)
Lower Mellstock: Lower Bockhampton
Lulstead Cove: Lulworth Cove
Mai Dun: Maiden Castle
Marshwood: Middlemarsh
Melstock: Stinsford
Middleton Abbey: Milton Abbas
Moreford Rise: a hill near Moreton
Nether Moynton: Owermoigne
Newland Buckton: Buckland Newton
Nuttlebury: Hazelbury Bryan
Overcombe: Sutton Poyntz
Owlscombe: Batcombe
Oxwell Hall: Poxwell Manor
Port Bredy: Bridport
Po'sham: Portisham
Pummery: Poundbury
Revellers' Inn: Revels Inn Farm
Ringsworth Shore: Ringstead Bay
Roy Town: Troy Town
Sandbourne: Bournemouth
Scrimpton: Frampton
Shottsford Forum: Blandford Forum
Springham: Warmwell
Stagfoot Lane: Hartfoot Lane
    (now Melcombe Bingham)
Stickleford: Tincleton
Street of Wells: Fortuneswell
Sylvania Castle: Pennsylvania Castle
Tolchurch: Tolpuddle
Upper Longpuddle: Piddletrenthide
Valley of the Great Dairies:
    the Frome Valley
Vale of Little Dairies: Blackmoor Vale
Warborne: Wimborne Minster
Weatherbury: Puddletown
Welland House: Charborough House
Wellbridge: Wool
Wyndway House: Upton House (site
    only)
Yalbury Wood: Yellowham Wood
Yewsholt Lodge: Farrs House

huge Duchy of Cornwall estate. Even the mill has given place to a block of flats, its pool partly overgrown. Near the entrance, however, is an old effigy, once over a mill window, and several millstones and pieces of the old wall can be seen.

But the river continues to flow, and those who recall how the poachers, on their return across Fordington Field, would whistle to those in the houses to bring out their plank bridges, must often be puzzled by the modern scene; for the river is, and clearly must always have been, on the wrong side of the street: beyond the water lies, not the open moor, but Fordington village on its height. The explanation is that the back gardens and courts of the Mill Street houses, all of which were on the north side of the road and river, were divided from the stretch of moor that lay between them and the London road by a lesser channel of the Frome, forcing the poaching fraternity, if they wished to enter their houses from the back, to call for some means of crossing. The channel was covered over at the beginning of this century. Lea's photograph of the Mill Street backs was taken either after this or from inside the islanded area: some of the back courts were very long.

With the destruction of the slum dwellings went also the tavern immortalized in *The Mayor*, the 'Peter's Finger'. Its real name was the King's Head, but the more colourful title was borrowed by Hardy from an inn, still extant, at Lytchett Minster ('Flytchett', page 57), near Poole. Peter's Finger is a corruption of St Peter ad Vincula—St Peter in Chains.

On the Fordington–Dorchester boundary, close to the Town Bridge, a building now used by the Jehovah's Witnesses is the former 'Dorford' Baptist Church, the setting for the factually based poem 'The Chapel-Organist'; and a short way up High East Street from the Fordington turning is the Phoenix, of 'The Dance at the Phoenix' fame. In spite of its distance from the barracks, the Phoenix was a favourite with the military. It still stands, but is now occupied by a stationer's. Only the sign still hangs out in evidence that it was once a tavern.

All Saints church, also mentioned in 'The Dance at the Phoenix' and in *The Mayor*, has a curious association with the poem 'The Casterbridge Captains'. The sub-title of the poem is 'Khyber Pass, 1842', and it tells of three lads who had carved their names on the back of one of the All Saints pews. All three become soldiers and fight in India, where two are killed. The survivor returns to Dorchester and finds the names still on the pew. But between 1842 and 1845 the seventeenth-century church was pulled down and a new one built—Dorchester's finest piece of Victorian architecture. Contrary to nineteenth-century practice, the pulpit, choir stalls, and some of the pews from the old church were retained; so that the soldier who, with his friends, had carved his name in one church, returned to find the carvings in another. They were still there for Hardy to sketch for the first edition of *Wessex Poems*, but during subsequent repairs the panel was removed. All Saints is now deconsecrated and used as an annexe to the Museum.

In the centre of Cornhill the town pump manages to survive, though no longer operative as in Henchard's day. Just beyond Durngate Street is the site of the Greyhound Inn, where in *The Trumpet-Major* Bob Loveday waited for Matilda Johnson. One fragment of the inn remains, the sixteenth-century arched stone doorway. Preserved and reset, at Hardy's suggestion, in the new building on the site, it was again reprieved when that building was in turn demolished, and today it spans the passage connecting South Street with the municipal car-park that has replaced Old Greyhound Yard.

At the back of the car-park is a group of stone buildings, now occupied by Ling's printing works but which originally housed a brewery; the actual brewing was done in the low structures beside Acland Road, and the long, very tall building next to them was the malthouse. It originally had only two storeys, a lofty ground floor and an attic level reached by a wooden staircase in one corner. Near the centre of the attic floor was a large trapdoor, through which

23

an apprentice once fell—luckily, on to a pile of shavings. In the east wall of the attic a doorway, surmounted by what Hardy called a cat's-head, opened into the void. In spite of some discrepancies (Hardy put in extra floors, for instance) there can be no doubt that the malthouse was the model for Henchard's corn-store in which he had the fight with Farfrae. After it had ceased to be a malthouse the building was taken over by a building company, and later by a heating-appliance firm which inserted an extra floor and modified the doors and windows. But the filled-in attic doorway remains visible, facing Acland Road. In the magazine version of the story an illustration of the fight shows, through the doorway, a roof strongly resembling that of Wollaston House opposite.*

Until less than a decade ago it was possible to identify the site of Henchard's long garden by two lime-trees still growing before one of the high brick backs of the South Street shops, but today the trees have been removed to make way for a parking-space. The house itself, now a branch of Barclay's Bank, fronting South ('Corn') Street, is one of the finest and best-kept mid eighteenth-century buildings in Dorchester, and externally lacks only a balcony to accord with Hardy's description; the green railings were removed for salvage during the Second World War. 'Back Street', in which lay the commercial entrance to Henchard's premises, and in which Abe Whittle lived, is now called Charles Street. Much of it has been rebuilt—some of the South Street shops extend right through to it—but toward the lower end there are still some small terraced cottages that pre-

serve the atmosphere of a residential street for the community's humbler members.

A short distance below Barclay's Bank is Napper's Mite, now a café and offices, but almshouses when Hardy referred in both *The Mayor* and *Far from the Madding Crowd* to the striking of the ancient clock over the entry. The clock is still going, though at present its voice is silent. In contrast to the survival of Napper's Mite is the fate of its neighbour, Hardye's Grammar School, which after various re-buildings—the last by Hardy's early employer, Crickmay—was finally demolished in 1966 in favour of a shopping arcade. This was the school attended by Frank Troy, who would have been there during its pre-Crickmay phase. The school is now established in the south-eastern suburbs.

Opposite the Hardye Arcade and next to each other are two buildings that played an important part in Hardy's early years, and about which he wrote in *The Life*. These are the former home and offices of the architect John Hicks, and the house in which William Barnes lived and taught before he exchanged a pedagogue's life for a parson's. On each house a plaque beneath the first-floor window records the historic importance of these otherwise insignificant terrace structures. The Hickses' house became a small temperance hotel; then the ground floor was occupied by a bicycle shop; and today, the final indignity, it is a snack-bar. Barnes's house has fared rather better, and is now an estate agent's offices.

Returning to Cornhill, the Antelope Hotel, where Henchard waited to return Lucetta's letters, has hardly altered since it acquired its twin-bow frontage early in the nineteenth century. The yard goes right through to Trinity Street, where from 1851 to 1883 the museum occupied a handsome house (number 3) still very little changed within or without, except for the upper part of the façade. Today it is a dentist's premises.

The china shop over which were 'the only lodgings fit' for Susan and Elizabeth-Jane was either at the corner of Trinity Street and High

* According to a strong tradition in the family that for more than a century has owned Upwey Mill (see p 128), near Weymouth, the mill building was the model for Henchard's granary. Hardy, a frequent visitor, is said to have pointed to a lofty trapdoor and said it was the one beside which Henchard and Farfrae fought. However, apart from the fact that they fought beside the door in the wall, not the trapdoor, there seems no reason why Hardy should have gone to Upwey for a setting when one that exactly fitted his needs stood exactly where he needed it. I suspect that in fact on one occasion he indicated the Upwey Mill trapdoor and remarked on its similarity to the one in the building he had used for the fight scene. But the millowners' belief is held in very good faith.

West Street (the site of the former theatre, now a restaurant called 'The Horse with the Red Umbrella'), or a short distance along High West Street, where Mabb's the men's outfitters now stands. Along here too are Judge Jeffreys' House, the first home of the museum, and today a fashionable restaurant and tea-room; and further west, the Old Ship Inn, where Norbert told his story of the great battle in the poem 'Leipzig'. Only the stone-mullioned first-floor windows remain from the original building; any picturesqueness, however, has been completely destroyed by clumsy refacing earlier in the present century and rather styleless redecoration within. Which of the bars was the 'Mastertradesmen's Parlour' no one now seems to know.

One can place only approximately the cottage that Henchard procured for Susan 'in the upper or western part of the town, near the Roman wall and the avenue which overshadowed it'. The reference is to West Walks and the surviving length of Roman city wall near the northern end. But the nearest houses are large town houses, and nothing else in the area qualifies fully as the cottage Hardy had in mind. It is certain, however, that Susan would no longer be able to look through the trees of the West Walks at the 'tumuli and earth-forts of the distant uplands'—the open country west of Dorchester—because the view has been closed by much red-brick residential development in Cornwall Road and beyond. Furthermore, between the avenue and Cornwall Road there has existed since 1900 a small and leafy public park, the Borough Gardens.

It was amid the trees of the West Walks that Farfrae organized the entertainment that proved so much more successful than Henchard's at Poundbury. Regular and straight-boled, the sycamores would serve him today as they served him then.

After the junketings Farfrae escorted Elizabeth-Jane home (she was then living at Henchard's house) down West Walks and round the corner along Bowling Alley Walks ('the Bowling Walk') to the Junction, as the point is now known where South Street, Trinity Street, and several other roads meet. The southern part of West Walks, together with Bowling Alley, were also known as the Old Walk, the term used by Benjamin Grower when directing the two constables during the skimmington affair. In Bowling Alley Walks there are now lamps, but Farfrae escorted his partner through darkness to the first street-lamp in South Street. Buildings hereabouts have altered considerably, and some of the trees have been removed. South Walks, the tree-lined footpath alongside South Walks Road, is the 'chestnut-walk' where Henchard informed Farfrae of his offer of marriage to the 'second woman' (Lucetta).

Westward from the Junction runs Damers Road, in which, on the north side, stand the buildings of the Damers Road Hospital. This was formerly the Union or workhouse in which Fanny Robin died, and to which went the ancient protagonist of 'The Curate's Kindness'. Built in 1836, it has had some additions, but the principal block, of brick and pale grey rubble, differs from the building seen by Fanny only in lacking the ivy that made it 'look like an abbey'.

The Damers Road area was once on the brink of the town, and it is here, to westward and southward, that the greatest modern spread shows. The urbanization has meant an immense change in the surroundings of the two railway stations, Maumbury Rings, the cemetery, and even Max Gate.

The first railway station, built in 1847 by the Southampton & Dorchester Railway Company (soon bought up by the L & SW), is substantially as it was at first, but the need for up-trains from Weymouth to reverse on to a spur line in order to reach the platform has been eliminated by the construction of a passenger causeway from the old up-platform to a new one beside the up-line itself. The old arrangement, however, is plainly to be traced. Maumbury Rings ('the Amphitheatre', 'the Ring'), once as solitary as it was sinister, became not only surrounded by roads and houses, but very nearly enclosed by railways. The Great Western line—then the Wiltshire, Somerset & Weymouth—was originally planned to pass through the Maumbury earthwork as through the Poundbury, but here too, public pressure and Brunel's enlightened policy saved the day.

Notwithstanding its changed environment, Maumbury must remain the grimmest spot in Dorchester, its black story culminating in 1706 in the hideous execution of nineteen-year-old Mary Channing. Hardy used this event in his poem 'The Mock Wife', and recorded some of the grislier details in his notebooks. But his chief use of Maumbury is in *The Mayor*, where he makes it the meeting-place of Henchard and Susan, and in 'Her Death and After', where it is the scene of the interview between the lover and the husband. Except that the earthwork is no

Came Rectory – a rectory no longer – the delightful little 'doll's house' just outside 'Casterbridge', whose most famous incumbent was Hardy's friend and mentor, the Dorset dialect poet William Barnes.

Designed by himself and built by his brother Henry, Max Gate was Hardy's home from 1885 to his death in 1928. From the outset the design aroused much criticism, not least from first wife Emma. Today the growth of the surrounding trees (many planted by Hardy in person) has softened the harshness of the exterior, and the interior has been lightened and beautified by the present tenants. Though a National Trust property, Max Gate is not open to the public.

longer lonely, Hardy's detailed pictures of it remain completely valid. Long thought to have been built by the Romans, it was proved by excavations begun in 1908 to date from the New Stone or Early Bronze Age; the Romans merely adapted it. The corner in which, as Hardy confirms, the gallows stood, was the south-west; earlier it had stood in the centre. Ironically, the entrance to the Rings now faces, at short range, the regional headquarters of the Dorset police.

Earliest of the gallows sites was in Gallows Hill, the old name for the Icen Way. The gibbet stood halfway along, at the intersection with South Walks Road, in the angle formed by the latter's eastern section and Salisbury Walk; Buzzford, in *The Mayor*, refers to the Monmouth rebels hanged there 'in the times of the Romans'. Before the new prison was built the old one stood at the foot of High East Street, and the whole of Icen Way was called Gallows Hill; the gallows themselves stood at the corner where Salisbury Walk meets the eastern section of South Walks Road.

South of Maumbury Rings lies the municipal cemetery, the setting, with its gates and lodge, of 'The Supplanter'; it is also 'the Field of Tombs where the earthworks frowned' in 'Her Death and After'. It looks what it is, a large well-kept town burial-ground, with little new about it except the latest graves. East of it, and of the railway, is a labyrinth of new residential streets; east of these again, an expanse still unbuilt on; and then Alington Avenue, notable now for the new inn called The Trumpet Major. In the angle between the avenue and Syward Road is Max Gate, Hardy's home from 1885 until his death, and the setting of a number of poems. The house is named after Mack's Gate, a turnpike cottage formerly on the site and mentioned as 'Max Turnpike' in *The Dynasts*.

Now a National Trust property, it remains structurally very much as he left it, if somewhat mellower: from afar, hardly visible behind its much-needed screen of tall trees, the planting of which is recorded in the poem 'Everything Comes'. The last of the three studies he occupied there has been recreated, with the original fireplace and furniture, in the Dorset County Museum, but it is not clear whether this is the room referred to in 'An August Midnight'. Sad to say, Emma's piano on which—in a last-minute attempt to re-establish an under-standing—she played the old tunes of their early years just before she died (as related in 'The Last Performance' and used for the theme of 'Lost Love'), has vanished. Was it in prophecy or to record what had already happened that in 'The Strange House' Hardy wrote of the ghostly piano-playing:

> There's no piano to-day;
> Their old one was sold and broken:
> Years past it went amiss . . .?

This piano is also the instrument in 'At the Piano' and one of the household features alluded

to in 'Ten Years Since'. 'The Little Old Table' is the one now in the replica of Hardy's study at the museum.

'The Spell of the Rose' is another poem inspired by the Hardys' estrangement. If what it tells us be true, the rose could conceivably be a pink, sweet-scented one, clearly of great age, that continues to flourish beside the house; this is the only old rose in the garden. Not far away the 'Druid' stone of 'The Shadow on the Stone' is still to be seen, and the tenants of Max Gate until 1971 recalled the disintegration of what seems to have been the original 'Garden Seat'. (But see photograph and caption on page 15.) Other survivals are the headstoned graves of Moss, the black labrador, and Wessex, Florence Hardy's terrier, who may have moved Hardy to eulogize him as 'A Popular Personage at Home', but who was singularly unpopular outside it and with visitors. His passing is commemorated in 'Dead Wessex, the Dog to the Household'.

Further afield, to the west, Conquer Barrow—scene of 'The Death of Regret' and 'Evening Shadows', in which it is the 'Pagan mound'—swells majestically under its dense cover of bushes and tall trees on the very edge of a newish residential estate. A short way further still, where the West Stafford road breasts Frome Hill, the Frome Hill tumulus rises as conspicuously as when Angel Clare looked across the vale from it (for surely this was the 'detached knoll a mile or two west of Talbothays'), and the companions walked thither in 'Seeing the Moon Rise'.

Less than a mile south of Max Gate stands Conygar Hill, the excavation of whose two known barrows in 1922 is thought to have inspired 'The Clasped Skeletons', though Pinion assigns this poem to a barrow at Bincombe (see page 133). Down the Wareham road (A352) stands the little pink-and-thatch doll's house, Came Rectory, that was the last home of William Barnes. Hardy used to walk to the Rectory from Max Gate by a path—it is still usable—that cut off the sharp elbow in the highway; and he was taking this route to his fellow-poet's funeral when he saw a sudden gleam of sunlight on the distant coffin as it was borne to the church. He commemorated the incident in the poem 'The Last Signal'. Came Rectory, just after Barnes's successor had moved in, is the scene of 'The Old Neighbour and the New'. The nearer water-meadows in the vale, with their tracks and weirs, are those of the poem 'Paths of Former Time'.

Came House, home of the Damers, the un-named evil family in 'The Doctor's Legend', stands south of the Rectory, off the main road, with the church close by; and at a little distance to the west of it, in a meadow, is all that is left of St German's church at Winterborne Farringdon, the 'Farringdon Ruin' of *The Trumpet-Major*. The remnant is still as Hardy described it.

A mile to the west lies Maiden Castle ('Maidon', 'Mai Dun'), from whose 'many ram-parts' Henchard, with his telescope trained on the Weymouth road, watched Farfrae's meetings with Elizabeth-Jane and saw the return of Newson. But the finest picture of the huge fortress occurs in—indeed, *is*—the short story 'A Tryst at an Ancient Earthwork'. As an evocation of place and mood this is unsurpassed by any of Hardy's descriptions in the great novels. Safe under the protection of the Depart-ment of the Environment, Maiden Castle today conforms to his word picture in every respect save one—there is no longer a notice board

warning of prosecution for removing relics or cutting up the ground. Despite the nearness of Dorchester and the main road, within the 60ft-high multiple rampart complete quiet reigns, save for the occasional lowing of the cattle pastured there and (on my last visit) the singing of an exceptionally large exaltation of skylarks. Harper states that at the beginning of the century the place swarmed with rabbits. With the com-ing of myxomatosis this ceased to be so, but nowadays the rabbits, here as elsewhere, are returning.

The huge ramparts thrown up to replace a previous single earth-wall were stormed, prob-ably in AD 45, by the famous Second Legion. Nearly 2000 years later, well after the date of Hardy's story, excavations have revealed (by chance) a huge cemetery containing the bodies of men and women killed in this contest. But it was the earlier discovery of a Roman temple that apparently inspired Hardy's slight tale. Today the Dorset Museum contains, if not the bronze-gilt figure of Mercury in the story, at any rate a number of figurines in silver-bronze and other materials, found on the site.

Inside Maiden Castle itself all trace of the British cemetery and Roman temple have now vanished again beneath the grass, and the great green expanse belongs once more to the cattle and the larks.

2 SOUTH WESSEX
MELLSTOCK
Dorset: Stinsford

And then, when the night has turned twelve the air brings
From dim distance, a rhythm of voices and strings
'Tis the quire, just afoot on their long yearly rounds,
To rouse by worn carols each house in their bounds;
Robert Penny, the Dewys, Mail, Voss, and the rest; till anon
Tired and thirsty, but cheerful, they home to their beds in the dawn.

WINTER NIGHT IN WOODLAND

Stinsford is a curious entity, being made up of three distinct hamlets, four large houses, several riverside and downland farms, and not a shop nor tavern to the entire parish. Hardy's description of 'Mellstock' in *Under the Greenwood Tree* shows that its component hamlets have altered very little. Nor has the air of remoteness been lost, a phenomenon the more remarkable because the parish boundary actually marches with that of Dorchester.

Stinsford Farm, between the church group and the Tincleton road, has acquired the familiar quota of concrete and steel modernization. Behind it a cluster of cottages now occupies the 'green-wooded meadow' known as Boucher's Close, across which, as he records in *The Life*, Hardy used to walk home from Dorchester to his birthplace, pausing on the farther side to sit on the now vanished stile where on one occasion he read *The Spectator's* crushing review of *Desperate Remedies*.

Close to the church is a very modern glass-and-timber structure, a new addition to the special school at present occupying Stinsford House. This house (almost wholly a reconstruction, following the fire of 1892 recorded in *The Life*) was the setting for the poem 'The Widow Betrothed', but the lodge has been replaced by a villa and the drive is disused. Stinsford House,

the terrace along its south front, the single wall separating the grounds from the churchyard, and the overlooking church tower, may well have been the real setting, transferred many miles east, for the scene in *Two on a Tower* in which Swithin, inside the belfry, sees Viviette on the terrace while her brother and the Bishop play bowls nearby. In another scene Swithin overhears the two men talking on the other side of the wall. In Stinsford House too lived Lady Susan, *née* Strangways, and her actor husband, William O'Brien, whose memorial with two overlapping hearts can be seen on the south chancel wall in the church. Nearby is the vault built for the O'Briens, at Lady Susan's order, by Hardy's grandfather. In *A Pair of Blue Eyes* Hardy transfers this to Cornwall, making it the prototype of the Luxellian family tomb (see page 216).

Stinsford church has changed much since the days of the 'Mellstock quire' (disbanded about 1841) and Hardy's own boyhood. Some of the changes, such as the replacement of the fine barrel roof to the nave by one of plain deal, occurred in the 'normal' course of restoration; but many have been made in commemoration of Hardy himself. Another of the more regrettable 'improvements' was the removal of the musicians' gallery pictured in 'A Church Romance',

Part of the path or 'drong' trodden so many times by the young Hardy between his parental home and 'Mellstock' (Stinsford), as often as not *en route* for 'Casterbridge'.

and the stage for the 'Mellstock quire'.

Noting in *The Life* the installation in 1902 of a brass tablet celebrating his family's forty years' service in the Stinsford 'quire', Hardy states that the gallery had been removed some sixty years earlier. This date is supported by Beatty—with reservations in his 1963 thesis, with none in the 1971 *Thomas Hardy Year Book*. On the other hand the Reverend G. H. Moule, in his *Stinsford Church and Parish* (1940) says 'it appears that the gallery was removed before the end of the nineteenth century', which certainly does not imply the early 1840s, and is echoed in the church brochure published anonymously, also about 1940, where the removal is placed 'some sixty years ago'. In support of the earlier date Beatty quotes a number of notes and letters by Hardy, in which, however, Hardy nowhere

states expressly that the gallery was dismantled in the 1840s. In support of the later date is the testimony (given to the Reverend L. J. Medway) of a former churchwarden, who died in 1968 aged ninety-five, that he had watched the removal of the gallery when he was a small boy. This too would bring the date to about 1880. If it is correct, Hardy's failure to record any contemporary comment on the removal is strange, though it must be remembered that for several years before and after 1880 he was not living in the Dorchester area. The tall box pews, already twice patched, were removed in 1911, the best panels being saved and incorporated in the present wall-panelling. In the porch there is a copy of a sketch-plan by Hardy himself showing the shape of the gallery and where each singer and player sat. The porch walls have been enriched with Tudor panels taken from Kingston Maurward Old Manor, and seats have been made from oak brought in 1911 from sixteenth-century Parnham House, near Beaminster. The bells (mentioned in *Desperate Remedies*) were rehung and the treble recast in 1927.

A visitor to the church can still see in the north aisle the elaborate monument to the Greys of Kingston Maurward, with the skull that so deeply impressed Hardy as a child and is referred to in both *Desperate Remedies* and *An Indiscretion in the Life of an Heiress*. But that other cause of childish fear, the nearby entrance to the vaults, has been sealed since the renewal of the flooring in 1911. In the south aisle the most conspicuous change is the memorial window to Hardy, inserted in 1930 and incorporating the passage from I Kings 19 alluded to in the poem 'Quid Hic Agis?'.

The chancel shows two important innovations: the memorial reredos given in 1939 by Mrs Weber, and the organ presented in 1931 by Hardy's sister, Kate. The old musicians were first replaced by a barrel organ operated by Hardy's uncle, James, who continued in this role for forty years until he died at the task. The barrel organ was then replaced by a harmonium and lost sight of, though a similar instrument, in working order, stands in the Dorset County Museum. After the harmonium (played by James's daughter, Theresa) had been discarded in favour of the organ, it lay forgotten in a vicarage outhouse until the 1960s, when it was rescued and taken home for resuscitation by a resident of Lower Bockhampton. The rescuer fell ill, however, and passed the harmonium to another proposed restorer. But he left the district before he had carried out the work, and it seems that the harmonium has finally disappeared. The museum also contains examples of the home-made instruments used by the 'Mellstock'-type musicians, and copies of their hand-written music.

A number of other alterations were made, mostly in 1911, but all to features not referred to in Hardy's work. His only other allusion in print to an interior feature is to one that never existed. In *Under the Greenwood Tree* he writes of the 'little world of undertones and creaks from the halting clockwork, which never spread further than the tower they were born in'. In reality the church never had a built-in clock, as Hardy admitted long afterwards in a letter; though he did not disclose whether he had based his description on some account of a free-standing clock that perhaps had stood in the gallery.

The churchyard receives frequent mention in his poems, including several that do not specify it by name. On entering through the gateway, still adorned with the absurdly large urns (sketched by him for the first edition of *Wessex Poems*), the first thing that takes the eye is the row of Hardy graves. The lettering on all these can be easily read, which is more than can be said for the fast-vanishing inscriptions on the many gravestones referred to in 'Voices from Things Growing in a Churchyard' and several other poems. Among more recent graves is that of Cecil Day Lewis, the poet (*d.* 1972).

The two yew trees cited by Dairyman Crick to indicate the grave of William Dewy are still there, though not much ivy now covers 'the wall that the ivies bind' ('The Dead Quire'). The whole of this last poem can be followed on the ground. The 'dormered inn' where the revels were being held is said to have been the southernmost cottage on the east side of Lower Bockhampton's ('Lower Mellstock's') main street, close to the bridge. No vestiges of an inn are traceable in this now skilfully restored house, although there are plenty of signs that it used to be a smithy; nor does the existence of an inn here appear among the records. However, it may have been an unregistered beerhouse— blacksmiths often ran these—in which illicit drinking on the premises took place (did it perhaps give Hardy his cue for 'Rolliver's' in *Tess of the D'Urbervilles*?), or Hardy could simply have 'promoted' it. The same cottage seems to have served him for Mop Ollamoor's home in 'The Fiddler of the Reels'.

The pursuers of the ghostly music followed it across the bridge—unaltered save for the tarmac on the roadway—and turned through the 'Bank-walk wicket, brightly bleached' along the Frome Path ''twixt the hedges twain'. This path, still a favourite walk, is entered now through an opening in a short length of tubular steel railings set in white wooden posts. The 'hedges twain' have become ragged and gapped, while in contrast there is a far greater number of large trees. In this age of polluted streams the 'crystal Froom' (or, to be exact, a minor branch of it) still 'crinkles' on both sides of the path. The northern arm borders the grounds of Kingston Maurward ('Knapwater') House, and it is not difficult to visualize Edward and Cytherea, in *Desperate Remedies*, seeing one another's reflections in the clear, shallow water before (not, it would appear, without considerable stretching) they clasped hands across it in melancholy farewell. At the 'bottom of Church Lane' the spectral 'quire' turned to go up 'Moaning Hill' to the churchyard. Church Lane is a wideish, gravelled way (once wider still) connecting the Frome path with the church, and 'Moaning Hill' is Hardy's name for the area on the right of the ascending lane, where the tall trees inside

Kingston Maurward grounds catch the winds blowing across the Frome valley.

Near the top of Church Lane a gate on the east side opens into a small secluded burial ground, the Cecil Hanbury Memorial Garden cemetery. The Hanburys were the last private owners of Kingston Maurward House; the poem 'To C.F.H.' was written for Cecil Hanbury's daughter Caroline. Just beyond this quiet place is the former Stinsford vicarage, Parson Maybold's home, externally plain but with rather a charming interior. The short drive and circular turning-space in front of the house are still enclosed by a shrubbery, as in Maybold's day.

The brief hill leading north from the church

No wonder this stone skull, at the foot of the wall-monument to the Grey family in 'Mellstock' Church, terrified Hardy as a small boy, and that much later he mentions it in more than one work. 'Knapwater' (Kingston Maurward) Old Manor was built in 1591 for a Grey owner, and the Greys remained in ownership until the last heiress married a Pitt in the eighteenth century.

opens into one of the most prominent roads in Hardy's pages, the Stinsford–Wareham ('Anglebury') road through Tincleton ('Stickleford'). This—the scene, with Stinsford Hill, of 'Your Last Drive'—is today a smooth, tarred thoroughfare, the Stinsford sector of it bounded by orderly hedges. But well within living memory it was white, rough, and rutted, and bordered by trees close and thick enough to give the name of Dark Hill (still sometimes used) to the part west of Bockhampton Cross. The church lane itself is described by Harper (1904) as overhung by enough trees to cause 'a midday twilight'. The description in the opening chapter of *Under the Greenwood Tree*, therefore, is correct,

and remained so for many years. The trees were cleared only when it became essential to improve visibility for motorists; some of the trunks are still rotting behind the hedges.

Between the church turning and the Cross is the entrance to Kingston Maurward Park, in which stand Kingston Maurward House and its predecessor, the Old Manor. Hardy knew Kingston Maurward House very well from early childhood through his 'romance' with its chatelaine, Mrs Martin. His failure to describe the interior in *Desperate Remedies* is consequently not due to lack of knowledge; indeed, some see certain of Kingston's internal features in Encombe ('Enkworth') House in *The Hand of Ethelberta* (see page 144). His enforced separation from Mrs Martin is the theme of 'In Her Precincts', but again the interior is not pictured. The harvest supper that saw their reconciliation provided the factual material, even to the presence of the soldiers, for the harvest supper in *Far*

The 'Froom Path' between 'Lower Mellstock' (Lower Bockhampton) and 'Mellstock' (Stinsford) church area, with 'crystal Froom' rippling along on not just one side, but both. Along this path in 'The Dead Quire' the ghostly singers and players led the sobered roysterers that Christmas morn from tavern to churchyard.

from the Madding Crowd; and it inspired the poem 'The Harvest Supper' as well as Hardy's various laments for the passing of the old country songs. The barn that was the scene of the real supper (as distinct from the barn described in the novel, for which see page 99) was still standing, just to the north of the Old Manor, until the 1970s, but after the roof had inexcusably been allowed to fall in, the walls were reduced to half-height and now enclose an area for which no use has so far been found.

The main entrance to the park is still through gates beside a lodge, but bronze bitterns no longer perch on the piers. The drive, now tarred, crosses grounds that fully match Hardy's description. The northern part of the park is Kingston Maurward Eweleaze, the roadside fringe of which is now occupied by a group of workers' cottages. Near the house there are one or two prefabricated buildings, discreetly sited.

In spite of the chequered recent history of the house—occupied during the Second World War by the army, then sold by the Hanburys in 1948 to Dorset County Council which transformed it into the Dorset Farm Institute, now renamed the Dorset College of Agriculture—it has not changed externally to any degree since Miss Aldclyffe was its fictional chatelaine in *Desperate Remedies*. Most of the ancillary buildings alluded to in the novel have also survived reasonably intact, even if their functions have changed. The grounds and lake, after deteriorating progressively during the present century, were given a gratifying clean-up when it was decided to make them one of the focal points of the 1968 Hardy Festival, and there was boating again. The Georgian temple ('the Fane') was restored at the same time.

'Mellstock' Church and churchyard, a focal point in *Under the Greenwood Tree* and the setting for many poems, also appear in several lesser prose works. In the foreground are two of the Hardy family tombs.

The barn at 'Knapwater' in which the boy Hardy attended the Harvest Supper he described later in *Far From the Madding Crowd* was still standing less than a decade ago. The roof, however, was then quite unnecessarily allowed to fall in, and all we are now presented with is this curious and (so far) useless enclosure.

That it is not possible to follow Miss Aldclyffe's route from the new manor to the old is due to Hardy's licence in describing it rather than to change. The waterfall that was 'enough to drive anybody mad' in the Old Manor is an inoffensive cascade, even now that weed and other obstructions have ceased to hinder its flow. The other source of auditory vexation, the water pump, was modernized in 1925 and abandoned on the introduction of mains water after the council purchase of 1948. But the pump-house and some of the machinery, original as well as of 1925, is still to be seen.

Until a few years ago the Old Manor remained in every respect as dilapidated as Hardy indicated. Becoming successively a home for poor widows, a Second World War evacuation centre, and a nest for squatters, it was saved from demolition only by public agitation and the intervention of a lessee of the County Council pledged to restore it, which he did, in somewhat

controversial style, by 1968. Beatty argues that the architecture of the fictional building more nearly resembles the probable design of old Clyffe House (demolished 1842) at Tincleton. One may note the name Ald*clyffe*, and certainly no 'old arched gateway with its flanking tower-bases' ever stood 'ten or twenty yards' from the Kingston mansion. But the *history* of Hardy's manor, the division into cottages, the debasing of the fine windows (now restored) and the use of the top floor (a single huge attic) as a warehouse, is unquestionably that of Kingston.

East of the Old Manor a colony of bungalow houses for the elderly has recently been built, but the large high-walled garden now used by the horticultural section of the College remains intact, and so does the thatched cottage adjoining its eastern end, the 'Peakhill Cottage' lived in by Adelaide Hinton. Pleasantly restored and modernized, it has risen in status since Lea wrote that it had 'little else to commend it' but the thatch. A long drive connects the cottage with the main street of Lower Bockhampton. There is also a back drive from the park into this street. At the junction of street and drive stands the former school built at the instance of Mrs Martin, attended for one year by the eight-year-old Hardy, and enshrined in due course in his fiction as the academy at which Fancy Day taught. Also the subject of the poem 'He Revisits His First School', it has now undergone some modification to turn it into a private residence. The school bell still hangs over the porch, but the windows on either side, with their stone mullions, diamond-leaded panes, and high sills 'of Ham Hill stone' on one of which Fancy Day sat to look out across the little green patch called the Grove, have very lately been replaced by modern 'picture' windows, doubtless much improving the light in the rooms within, but externally totally inappropriate to the style of building.

The Grove remains, and south of it stands a long, low building, Riverside House, at right angles to the village street. Lea gives this as Farmer Shiner's house in *Under the Greenwood Tree*. Hardy's description runs:

> Farmer Shiner's was a queer lump of a house, standing at the corner of a lane that ran into the principal thoroughfare. The upper windows were much wider than they were high, and this feature, together with a broad bay window where the door might have been expected, gave it the aspect of a human countenance turned askance, and wearing a sly and wicked leer.

Beatty terms this 'Hardy's propensity for distortion'. Riverside House was never at the corner of a lane, has original upper windows that are higher than wide (see Hardy's sketch in the County Museum), shows no trace of a ground-floor bay past or present, and is unlikely to strike many people as sly, wicked, or a queer lump. But in the small area between it and the still extant withy bed by the Frome there was once a lane, a short cul-de-sac not displayed on early printed maps, but unmistakable on an undated MS estate map in the county archives. The sketch based on this map and reproduced here shows that where the lane left the 'main thoroughfare' it had a house at either corner, the more northerly being quite distinct from the present so-called Shiner residence, which is seen between it and the school.

Hardy's first school at 'Mellstock', which he later made Fancy Day's in *Under the Greenwood Tree*, has long been just a private house. But the school bell still hangs in its niche over the porch.

What sort of houses were they along this lane? The last buildings hereabouts were two or three brick cottages, not long demolished; but in *The Life* Hardy notes that the area used to contain 'several old Elizabethan houses, with mullioned windows and doors, of Ham Hill stone. They stood by the withy bed'. They were pulled down by Morton Pitt, of Kingston Maurward—some before Hardy's birth, but others long enough afterwards for him to recall their appearance. Was it in one of these at the corner of the lane (which probably vanished when they did) that Hardy installed his peppery farmer? He can hardly have failed to remember that some of them still existed at the time of the story.

The southern end of the village, including the thatched former post office (said by Bailey to be

On the right, 'Lower Mellstock' Bridge spanning one of the 'Froom' channels alongside the 'Froom Path'. Immediately beyond the river, the Withy Bed. In the centre distance, the house dubiously called 'Farmer Shiner's'. Between it and the Withy Bed there used to run, across the scene, a lane bordered by stone houses one of which seems more likely to have been Hardy's model in *Under the Greenwood Tree*.

the post office in the poem 'The Thing Unplanned') and many mellow old cottages, mostly thatched, must look much as Hardy knew it in later life if not at the time of 'The Passer-by'. Farther north various unsuitable new villas and bungalows wreck the harmony. 'Martins', the best of the new houses, stands on the site of Robert Penny's boot emporium—the probable scene, according to Bailey, of 'The Night of the Dance'. There is a pretty sketch of the shop—its real owner was Robert Reason—in the County Museum. After the First World War a memorial clubroom-cum-reading room was put up on the site, and opened by Hardy himself. This later became redundant, and was succeeded by 'Martins'.

Beyond Bockhampton Cross the road—the 'lane' of 'To Louisa in the Lane'—shorn of its trees, continues toward Higher Bockhampton ('Upper Mellstock'). On the right is an elongated coppice of hardwoods, the Thorncombe Wood of the poem 'She Hears the Storm'. The same poem mentions 'Mellstock Leaze' (Stinsford Leaze, to the west of the lane). This is also the 'pasture' of 'Her Immortality'. East of the lane, between it and Thorncombe Wood, lies Middle Field, commemorated in 'At Middle-Field Gate in February'. There is still a gate, though now a broad iron one, leading from the lane.

At Higher Bockhampton an inexcusably vile untarred track, mercifully with a car-park leading from the near end, branches off toward Hardy's birthplace, which stands at the far end, at right angles to the other houses. The Hardy house and its next-door neighbour are all that is left of the original buildings in the lane. The other cottages are brick replacements (and in some instances replacements of replacements) of

Lower Bockhampton. The vanished lane and stone houses, one of which may have been the model for Farmer Shiner's. From a MS estate map.

the old cob-and-thatch structures there at the time of Hardy's birth, and pulled down as the lifeholds fell in. A good idea of these original cottages is to be had from a sketch by James Sparks (1902), reproduced in the *Thomas Hardy Year Book* no 10, page 88. The cherry trees that once lined the route have also gone, but the well from which the community drew its water—mentioned in the story 'Enter a Dragoon'—survives, with part of its superstructure. It

stands about halfway down the lane, adjoining the roadway and the grounds of a house called Greenwood, and is still officially a public well.

The Hardy house never had a name, though as the Dewys' house in *Under the Greenwood Tree* Hardy called it 'Lewgate', a title that also crops up in *A Few Crusted Characters*. The Dewys, in fact, were modelled on the Dart family who lived in the house already mentioned, at right angles to the Hardys'. This, formerly subdivided into several cottages, is a place of many dormers, as may be seen in a watercolour that hangs in the hallway of the Dorset County Museum. It has now been given a new porch and metal casements.

Hardy's home, as he recorded in his 'Notebooks', was used as a change-over point in the northward conveyance of smugglers' goods. There is a tiny window in the porch said to have been inserted for the purpose of watching for excise officers. Once certain deliberately misleading phrases in the first edition of *Under the Greenwood Tree* had been amended, the description of the Dewys' home became a faithful portrait of the Hardys' house as Hardy knew it in childhood. In less detail, it appears in several other works. Pinion argues that it is the 'cottage-residence' of 'Enter a Dragoon'; the description in the story does not entirely fit, but this could be another instance of deliberate disguise. The house also figures, anonymously, in a crop of poems, including 'On One who Lived and Died where he was Born' (Hardy's father), 'The Alarm' (about his grandfather), 'The Self-Unseeing', 'Concerning his Old Home', and—quoted in *The Life* but not included in any collection until 1976—'Domicilium'.

From 1913 to 1921 this was the home of Hermann Lea, who assented to Hardy's request and somewhat disguised the house in his Wessex volume as Hardy had done in the earlier version of *Under the Greenwood Tree*. In his closing years Hardy was distressed by the shabbiness of the house, but since 1948 house and garden have been National Trust property and excellently tended.

There have been changes since the days of Dick Dewy, of which the more important are that the cob walls are now protected by bricks or cement, the parlour chimney has lost the bread oven and inglenook-seat it had when the Dewys held their Christmas party, and the central staircase has been removed, involving also the removal of the cache for smuggled liquor. In 1980, in a delicate operation, the bricks were removed from the frontage, the cob, which had begun to slip, was strengthened by the insertion of foundations, and the bricks were replaced. Among improvements already made by the Trust was the reopening of a blocked-up doorway mentioned by Hardy. General renovation and redecoration became annual. Outside, the stables have been pulled down and the small orchard abandoned, together with some of the garden. In 1969 there was a project to restore the original appearance of the house, and in 1974 the National Trust made a start by opening up the inglenook in the living-room.

On every side except that of the lane the cottage and garden are bounded by the trees of present-day 'Egdon Heath'. This part of the heath was in fact always well-wooded, the trees formerly encroaching more upon the house than they do now:

It faces west, and round the back and sides
High beeches, bending, hang a veil of boughs.

Near the back of the building a granite monument to Hardy was set up in 1931 by 'a few of his American admirers'.

At the other (Bockhampton Lane) end of the miserable track stood Elizabeth Endorfield's cottage, one of those later pulled down and not replaced. The northern part of Bockhampton Lane, between this point and what is now the A35, retains its old name of Cuckoo Lane. Like the southern part, however, it is a good deal less leafy than when Fancy encountered Dick upon it, the big hedgerows having been much reduced to improve visibility. It was a few paces up Cuckoo Lane from the main road that Farfrae drew rein on seeing Henchard after the latter's

pursuit to tell him of the skimmety-ride. Close to where the roads meet is the 'Snail-Creep' alluded to in *Under the Greenwood Tree*—a footpath which leads directly over the hill from Hardy's cottage, crosses the A35, and continues on the north side. But unlike its larger neighbour Yellowham ('Yell'ham', 'Yalbury', 'Great Yalbury') Wood (see page 49), Grey's Wood, which used to run alongside the Snail-Creep and in which Dick Dewy went nutting, has recently and regrettably been felled almost in its entirety. North of it Stinsford parish extends as far as Waterston ('Climmerston') Ridge, thus including much of Slyre, Slyre's or Slyer's Lane. The latter turns off the A35 a few hundred yards east of Grey's Bridge, and for the first quarter-mile at least is the route taken by Carrier Burthen to convey his passengers to Piddletrenthide ('Upper Longpuddle') in *A Few Crusted Characters*. See page 94.

The Hardcomes, whose sad fate was recalled by one of the storytellers, lived at 'Climmerston', and past 'Climmerston Ridge' the sporting Parson Toogood and his clerk followed the hunt. The 'rugged ridge of Waterston' and the 'grey, gaunt, lonely lane of Slyre' lay also on the cavalryman's route in 'The Revisitation'. The description of Slyre Lane still fits. Almost devoid of bordering trees or houses, its tarred surface now makes it literally grey, and only the grid wires crossing it strike a modern note.

Waterston Ridge is similarly devoid of buildings, most of this stretch of the Ridgeway consisting of a grass ride between hedges that in parts nearly choke it. The 'Sarsen stone' of 'The Revisitation', alongside the Ridgeway half a mile east of Slyre's Lane, is in reality a rough slab of naturally fused flints from which the surrounding chalk has been washed away.

In the western angle formed by the lane and the A35 stood the turnpike house to which the coachman drove after his vain wait on Stinsford Hill for Lieutenant Vannicock and Laura Maumbry; the traces of its garden are just discernible. All along the A35 hereabouts (extending further on the south side) straggle,

Another focal point in *Under the Greenwood Tree*: Hardy's birthplace, again the subject of many a poem. His great-grandfather built the house in 1801, but omitted to give it a name, nor has subsequent world-wide fame remedied the omission.

battered and bent, the iron railings by which Fanny Robin supported herself on her journey to the Union. Nearly opposite Slyre Lane they are interrupted by a kissing-gate, the first of the succession in 'The Third Kissing-Gate'. The topography of this poem is hard to follow, for there were in fact four gates, of which the second also survives. The 'gray garden wall' (actually lichen-covered red brick) belongs to Stinsford House, and fringes the path (with the stream in between) before the last gate is reached. Close to this gate was the 'waterfall', formed by the descent of the stream over a low stone ledge before it entered a culvert under the foot of Church Lane (page 33). Ledge and culvert are still there, but except in spate the water now passes through a newer culvert alongside. The path, which remains in regular use, is also the one by which the fleeing Manston in *Desperate Remedies* reached Tolpuddle ('Tolchurch').

To the east, where the A35 climbs out of the Frome valley toward Yellowham, it becomes Stinsford ('Mellstock') Hill. Wider and busier now, with a parking-bay and stone-built conveniences at its summit, it is in other respects still the green-verged, unbuilt-on slope with 'high-banked hedges' (*The Mayor of Casterbridge*) where the narrator in 'On Stinsford Hill at Midnight' encountered the strange singer, and Hardy had his blood-chilling vision of the two unknown men seated on chairs as recalled in *The Life*. Not far from where the Tincleton road forks off, standing in the bank as Hardy states, is the first milestone out of Dorchester, on which the defeated Henchard rested his basket at the beginning of his retreat.

The 'lone copsewood' that Fanny entered in order to make herself a pair of crutches was either some small wood that has vanished or the copse still adjoining Birkin House. Before this she had paused to rest against the second milestone from the town, now, like the first, restored to its proper place after both had spent the Second World War lying discreetly buried under the turf.

3 SOUTH WESSEX
EGDON HEATH
Dorset: the heath

... The outlook, lone and bare,
The towering hawk and passing raven share,
And all the upland round is called 'The He'th'.

BY THE BARROWS

'Egdon Heath' is such a useful collective name for the multitude of heaths between Stinsford and Bournemouth that one forgets it is only a Hardy coinage. 'Egdon' was never the huge, wild moor that he depicted, and the dual encroachment of cultivation and building has since reduced it, while the Forestry Commission has changed its appearance and many of its paths and tracks, though not altogether its character. When the implements of the foresters are stilled and dusk creeps over the plantations, the atmosphere is not very different from that conjured up in *The Return of the Native*, and the heath (especially if you happen to have lost your bearings) suddenly seems as vast as Hardy drew it.

There are still unforested tracts covered only by heather and bracken, as well as areas cleared temporarily by felling. Except for the wild ponies, the 'heath-croppers', all the Egdon fauna mentioned by Hardy survive, with the addition of deer. The human population, if we discount the areas lost to town-spread or military camp, is actually less. Not only have nearly all the isolated cottages and groups of dwellings such as 'Mis-

tover Knap' disappeared, but many of the heathside villages have shrunk. The population of Puddletown ('Weatherbury') at the 1961 census was 795; by 1971 it had risen to 1020, but in 1981 it had dwindled again to 949. At the time of *Far from the Madding Crowd* it had been around 1250.

After his own birthplace, the feature of the heath made most famous by Hardy is 'Rainbarrow'—properly Rainbarrows: *The Dynasts* refers rightly to three tumuli. It is said that in *The Return* Hardy moved 'Rainbarrow' much nearer the centre of 'Egdon'. A careful reading of the novel does reveal a modest shift eastward, but not nearly as much as is suggested. The path down to the 'Quiet Woman' (the Traveller's Rest, now Duck Dairy Farm), followed by Olly Dowden and Mrs Yeobright in the opening scene, has no factual basis according to the maps of the period, which show the only path to emerge near the inn running well *west* of the barrows, even in their true position. Bracken-covered and hollowed into a cup at the top, the larger of the two tumuli now visible supports a hollybush on its western rim, with another

'Egdon Heath' in the nineteenth century.

To Puddletown

Troy Town

Beacon Plantation

Stafford Park Copse

Kite Hill

Yellowham Wood

Bucks Head Inn

Greenwood Tree (alleged)

Troy Town Copse

Beacon Corner

Keeper's House

Beacon Hill

Coombe Plantation

Toppuddle Hollow

Green Hill

Greenhill Pond

Grey's Wood

Mistover Knap

Small Creep

To Dorchester

Ilsington Wood

Dart's House

Birthplace

TRACK OF ROMAN ROAD

Higher Bockhampton

Rushy Pond

Lane, later Rhododendron Mile

Rainbarrows

Cuckoo Lane

Thorncombe Wood

fence

To Tincleton

'Blooms-End' Valley

Bockhampton Cross

Headless William's Pond

Pond House

To Stinsford

'Quiet Woman' Inn

Cottages in enclosure

Norris Mill

cottages

_ _ _ _ _Forest tracks and footpaths

To Lower Bockhampton

Bhompston Farm

Duddle Farm

growing near its base. Self-sown conifers have encroached very close.

Rainbarrows stand on the eastern escarpment of a wide basin, the western side of which is separated by a twin-backed ridge from a valley that broadens from north to south. This is the westernmost valley of 'Egdon' and has Thorncombe Wood extending along its western edge. Not far from the head of both depressions is a small round pool, Rushy Pond, near which, in 'The Paphian Ball', the Mellstock quire met the Devil, and which is the subject of another poem, 'At Rushy Pond'. The poem, 'I Said and Sang her Excellence' bears the words 'At Rushy-Pond' at its foot. Here, too, Gertrude in *The Withered Arm* paused on her macabre ride to the hangman's cottage, and it is in this tale that the pond is said to be bisected by a railing linking the ends of two hedges. Old maps bear out the truth of the description, though no trace of hedge or fence remains.

Farther down the valley the scrub and rhododendrons give way to cultivated pasture, except on the east flank, and the pasture continues south of the Dorchester–Tincleton road until it merges into the Frome meads between Bhompston Farm and Duddle Farm. In the field immediately north of the road lies a large irregular pool, much encroached upon by undergrowth and rushes, but retaining enough clear water to support a few ducks. Here, many years ago, a drunken mail-van driver ran off the highway (not hedged then), overturned his vehicle, and was drowned, so giving his name to Heedless William's Pond. Hardy mentions it only in 'The Fiddler of the Reels', though in 'A Tragedy of Two Ambitions' he turned to account the legend that William's whip stuck in the ground, took root and became an ash tree. Today an old ash stump and several younger ashes border the pool.

The valley itself I believe to be the one Hardy called 'Blooms-End'. Others maintain that 'Blooms-End' is the valley immediately behind the Birthplace. Certainly, on his own curious map to illustrate *The Return*, where North is on

the left of the sheet and East at the top, 'Rainbarrow' becomes a mysterious 'Black Barrow', and 'Shadwater Weir' (see page 62) appears to be a few yards from the Tincleton road, 'Blooms-End' *house* is marked where the Birthplace stands. This, as Millgate points out in his impressive biography of Hardy, ties in with the strong autobiographical elements in the novel. But what even Millgate overlooks is that the position of the house on the map is totally inconsistent with the majority of descriptive indications scattered through the text. In these it is made clear that the house faced from the widening mouth towards the head of the valley, that the front entrance lay on the north side (the setting winter sun threw the shadow of the building across the gate and front palings), and that it also faced toward 'Mistover Knap'. In another place Hardy states that the mummers walked to 'Blooms-End' from the Vyes' 'Mistover' home by going down the valley west of 'Rainbarrow'. None of these pointers is relevant to the Birthplace, nor are the several references to the great age of 'Blooms-End'; at the time of the novel's action the Birthplace had been in existence little more than fifty years. Less unequivocal but still favouring the more southerly valley is the assertion that from the 'lofty ridge' dividing 'Blooms-End' valley from the next the 'Quiet Woman' could be seen in one direction and 'Mistover Knap *afar off*' (my italics) in the other.

The description of the building also fails to apply to the Birthplace, except for the 'heavy thatchings, which dropped between the upper windows'. In a letter to a friend Hardy admitted that he had based 'Blooms-End' on 'vague recollections of Bhompston farmhouse', though the position was 'a little shifted'. Bhompston lies just over a mile due south of the Birthplace, beyond the Tincleton road. To the former farmhouse (now undergoing conscientious renovation to restore it as far as possible to its original appearance) belonged originally the white palings of 'Blooms-End', the white exterior walls, the outside door leading straight into a low-pitched, slightly sunken kitchen, and the situation relative to the compass. But where did the 'little shift' imagined by Hardy place it? 'Blooms-End' is referred to once in *The Dynasts* (where Granfer Cantle of *The Return* appears as a young man), and once in the poem 'In Weatherbury Stocks'. But the only reference outside *The Return* that affords us any help is the allusion in 'The Fiddler' to 'Heedless William's Pond, the familiar landmark by Bloom's End (*sic*)'. Thus Bhompston seems to have been shifted to the position of Pond House, a mansion described as 'old and rambling' that stood, before its destruction by fire at about the turn of the century, where the bungalow called Pond Cottage stands today.

However, this position is really too near the road, for every time a character in *The Return* wished to travel between 'Blooms-End' and the 'Quiet Woman' he or she took, not the road as would have been natural to or from the Pond House site, but a path over the heath—the southernmost, in fact, of the three paths mentioned by Hardy. These are shown on his map radiating from the Birthplace; but if the Birthplace as 'Blooms-End' on the map is a red herring in terms of the text, so may the paths be; for my conclusion is that Hardy imagined

Rushy Pond (real name), on the 'Egdon' heights near Hardy's birthplace, was familiar to him from early childhood, and he afterwards brought it into several poems and stories. A number of legends are attached to it, among them that it was dug out by fairy people.

An 'Egdon Heath' panorama looking east from the high ground separating the valley containing Heedless William's Pond from that immediately west of Rainbarrows. The latter can be seen against their modern background of trees toward the left; on the right are the buildings of Duck Farm, occupying the site of the 'Quiet Woman' (The Travellers' Rest).

47

'Blooms-End' house to be situated in the same valley as Heedless William's Pond, but probably a few hundred yards or so north of the pond. This would still justify the definition in 'The Fiddler', but also the use of a heath path to reach the 'Quiet Woman'.

Duck Dairy Farm (or Dairy House), Hardy's 'Quiet Woman', was originally the Traveller's Rest—mentioned as such in the poem 'Weathers'—and later became the Duck. Most of the old buildings were pulled down, and a new farmhouse erected, in the 1930s. Only one or two outhouses survive, and none of the old inn trappings. Nor can 'Wildeve's Patch' be traced, for the heath, which formerly extended a short way south of the Tincleton road at this point, has now been pushed back a meadow's depth to the north of it. A footnote in *The Return of the Native* tells us that the real Quiet Woman lay 'some miles to the north-west'—in fact at Halstock, where it still flourishes, adorned with a modern sign faithfully bearing out Hardy's description. The same footnote states that the fictional 'Quiet Woman' was partly modelled on the Red Lion at Winfrith. Some years ago a fire so severely damaged the Red Lion that in its new and enlarged form only one or two unexpectedly thick internal walls—the old outer walls—are left of the building known to Hardy.

A quarter of a mile east of Duck Dairy Farm a branch lane leads north-east to Puddletown. Since the era of Hardy's prose writings, more than a mile at the southern (Tincleton road) end of the lane has been bordered on both sides with rhododendrons. At this end, in its pre-floral days, first Wildeve and then Venn saw the carriage containing Clym and Eustacia pass, for the road forms the lower part of the route that 'ascended to Mistover by a circuitous and easy incline' and was the only approach to the Vyes' home suitable for vehicles.

The 'easy incline' is not continuous, the early part of it being broken by a number of dips, the first of which is the 'Draats'-Hollow' of the poem 'The Sheep Boy'. Properly called Draats (pronounced Drahts) Bottom, the shallow de-

pression extends for some distance west of the road through an area cleared of trees in 1968. North of the rhododendron avenue the lane bends west, then at Beacon Corner turns sharply east, making for Puddletown. The sharp turn really constitutes two arms of a cross, the other arms being unmetalled tracks. The westward track ascends a shallow vale called Tolpuddle Hollow, between Beacon Hill and Green Hill, until these unite to terminate it. The tableland thus formed is the likeliest candidate for 'Mistover Knap'. To reach the Vyes' home it was probably necessary to fork left again a short way from Beacon Corner, on to a track still extant over the summit of Green Hill. Beside the track lies a large circular pond, now much overgrown. This is Green Hill or Greenhill Pond, the original of the 'large pool' by Captain Vye's cottage. Rushy Pond and even Heedless William's Pond have been named as the prototypes of this famous spot; but Heedless William is both too low-lying and too far to the south-west, and Rushy is too far west. To the watchers at the 'Quiet Woman' Eustacia's signal fire on the bank by the pool appeared to the *right* of 'Rainbarrow'. A fire near Rushy Pond would have been visible, if at all, to the *left*, even without allowance for Hardy's eastward shift of the barrow. Lea, though not naming Green Hill, says the Vyes' pool lay north of 'Rainbarrow'. Afforestation eliminated a number of ponds on the heath, but Green Hill was always the only large one, and the only one with vehicular access.

The 'two converging bank fences', like the house itself, have disappeared, probably when the Forestry Commission prepared the area for the conifers that now cover it. Gone too is the ruined brick-kiln noted by Lea; and understandably the heather has been replaced by bracken and pine needles.

A sketch made in 1901 shows 'Mistover Knap' with fir trees on the skyline at the head of an irregular valley. This view, like the reverse one several times mentioned in *The Return*, was for a long time obscured by the Forestry

Commission's work, but since the clearance in 1968—and until the replacement saplings grow up—it has come back into being. The trees shown in the sketch were there before the Commission took over, and according to Lea they perished in a fire. Another disappearance is that of the 'very curious Druidical stone' that Clym told Eustacia about, and which is mentioned in Llewellyn Powys's *Dorset Essays*. Powys quotes an elderly relative of Hardy's as stating that the 'huge monolith' stood in the bracken not far from Hardy's birthplace, and was much beloved of him as a child. Its long existence ended when it was smashed up for building-stone by some vandal.

'Mistover Knap' also figures in 'The Fiddler of the Reels', where its firwoods are described as 'backed by the Yalbury coppices'. The 'Yalbury coppices', otherwise 'Great Yalbury Wood' or Yellowham Wood, formerly extended farther south of that part of the Dorchester–Puddletown road known as Yellowham ('Yalbury') Hill. Over this rise Dick Dewy, Fancy Day and the rest of the party walked on their way to the wedding, which was not at Stinsford but at Puddletown (here called 'Lower Longpuddle', but see page 51), Keeper Day's house being just over the parish border. Here too Fanny Robin on her last journey met Bathsheba and Frank Troy. At the foot of the hill is Yellowham Bottom or Plain, haunt of the ghost in 'Wessex Heights' and the point where Henchard paused to listen for Farfrae during the pursuit that followed the skimmety-ride.

At least four poems allude to Yellowham Hill: 'The Comet at Yellowham', 'Old Excursions', 'Ice on the Highway', and the delightful 'The Milestone by the Rabbit-burrow'. This last refers to the third milestone out of Dorchester, near the foot of the western slope. The milestone, like its fellows, was buried in 1940, but unlike them was never dug up, and there is now no official record of its whereabouts. Unofficially, however, the burial was watched by the father of the present occupant of 'Keeper Day's Cottage', who always maintained that he could still point to the exact spot.

Strictly speaking, most of Yellowham Wood is not part of Egdon Heath at all, but it has far greater affinities with the heath than with the country to the north of it. It figures in fewer poems than the hill, but is much more prominent in the novels and stories, especially, of course, in *Under the Greenwood Tree*. Yellowham remains a wood of pleasantly mixed timber, still conforming to Hardy's description of it as the route of the wedding party; the 'dark perpendicular firs' are also the 'Yell'ham-Firs' of the poem 'The Mother Mourns'. There are still foxes about, as in *Under the Greenwood Tree*, and pheasants, as mentioned in *Far from the Madding Crowd*.

The one house in the wood is that of 'Keeper Day'. In real life he was Keeper Browne; his daughter Elizabeth was the young woman of the poem 'To Lizbie Browne'. I found the house less altered than implied by Lea. It stands precisely where Hardy indicates; the front window is still set with thickly leaded diamond glazing, in which one can detect a number of the original thin bottle-glass panes. Inside, the window-bench has been removed. The 'huge inglenooks' and the little window in the chimney-back, on the other hand, are not to be seen because they never existed. The ceilings are beamed. A lean-to extension has been built on, but otherwise the house has scarcely been altered. There is still a side-wicket to the garden, and a flourishing piggery.

Finally, the Greenwood Tree itself, after another century and a quarter, still flourishes— or so one is assured. Hardy refers to it as 'already ancient' and 'horizontally of enormous extent', and pictures it surrounded by a 'carefully-tended grass plot'. Today the tree pointed out is all but invisible amid the bushes and other trees that have grown up over the 'grass plot' about it. What can be descried certainly does not suggest a magnificent, or even once-magnificent, veteran. But tradition in the cottage maintains that this is the tree indicated by Thomas Hardy himself, long years ago: an authority not lightly to be challenged. Perhaps we may compromise

by considering the designated tree as a scion of the original.

Less than half a mile from the eastern fringe of Yellowham Wood, on the main road, lie a farmhouse and its attendant buildings. These are the modern representatives of Troy Town ('Roy Town'), site of the Buck's Head in *Far from the Madding Crowd* and 'The Waiting Supper'. Once an important coaching stage, the inn's decline was piecemeal. When Nicholas Long in 'The Waiting Supper' stayed there it was 'rather cavernous and chilly', the stable-roofs were 'hollow-backed', and the traffic had gone. When Joseph Poorgrass met Jan Coggan and Mark Clark there the old stabling had been pulled down, and 'little remained besides the habitable inn itself'. Harper, writing in 1904, describes the place as not yet pulled down but no longer an inn. And Lea (1913) says it was pulled down a few years previously. It stood on the opposite side of the high road to the present farm. One rather nondescript building still on the site is said to have belonged to it; the cottages nearby were built later.

Greenhill Pond on 'Egdon Heath', now hidden among the Forestry Commission's conifers and much undergrowth, was fairly certainly the pond beside which Hardy imagined Captain Vye's cottage in *The Return of the Native*.

Today embowered in shrubs and small trees, Heedless William's Pond lies a short distance north of the 'Casterbridge–Stickleford' (Tincleton) road, in the mouth of the valley identified by many with the elusive 'Blooms-End'.

A mile east of Troy Town the Wareham and Blandford roads part company, and here is Puddletown, the 'Weatherbury' of *Far from the Madding Crowd*. Pinion, evidently relying on a phrase in the novel (last paragraph of Chapter 7) and a reference in *Under the Greenwood Tree*, asserts that Puddletown is also 'Lower Long-puddle', the villages of Piddletrenthide and Piddlehinton together forming 'Upper Long-puddle'. All other authorities identify Piddle-trenthide with 'Upper Longpuddle' and Piddle-hinton with 'Lower'. Moreover, a study of the itinerary of Burthen's van and Tony Kytes's waggon in *A Few Crusted Characters*, virtually eliminates Puddletown (see page 94). The only credible explanation is that on adopting his standard nomenclature Hardy changed the iden-tity of 'Lower Longpuddle', leaving Puddle-town solely as 'Weatherbury'.

Puddletown church—scene of the poem 'The Christening'—is the best example in Wessex of a mediaeval church that, eluding for once the hand of the Victorian restorers, has retained its high box-pews, musicians' gallery, seventeenth-century wooden altar and altar rails, pulpit, prayer-desk, and fine old timbered roof. Not only did the old 'quire' sing and play in this gallery, but the modern choir still sings there. The battered alabaster effigy in the poem 'The Children and Sir Nameless' commemorated one of the Martyns of Athelhampton ('Athelhall') who lie buried in the so-called Athelhampton chantry off the south aisle. Hardy probably had in mind Sir William, who is accoutred as described and has indeed lost his nose, as well as having initials scratched all over him. The effigy, now restored to its proper place on the tomb, measures nearly seven feet in length.

Outside the church, there is really nothing exceptional about the 'gurgoyles' on the tower; Beatty suggests that Hardy had in mind the gargoyle at the south-east corner of the south aisle of Stinsford church. As though consequent on the flooding of Fanny's flowers, one Puddle-town gargoyle is now prevented by a piece of piping from baptizing those passing beneath. Inside the north porch is a built-in bench old enough to be that on which Troy passed his uncomfortable night.

There have been some alterations to the fabric since the *Madding Crowd* period, mainly to roofs and ceilings. The present organ was installed in 1906, the chancel was restored and enlarged in 1911, and the pews were renovated in 1966 and later. Less happily, the remarkable triangular-faced clock with its rich chimes, made by a Puddletown blacksmith in 1710, was removed from the tower in about 1865 and disappeared: just why, no one seems to have recorded. This must have been the clock that 'moaned eleven' in the poem 'In Weatherbury Stocks', below the title of which appears the date 1850. The stocks themselves have vanished. Whether the clock was still in place at the time covered by the novel depends on one's estimate of when that time was. Weber assigns the action to the four years 1869–73. The Rev. O. D. Harvey's able booklet, on the other hand, which devotes a good deal of attention to Hardy, calls the novel 'a story of the

1840s and '50s'. Mr Harvey is supported by Hardy's preface and by the description of Water-ston Manor (page 92), which is depicted as it was before the serious fire of 1863.

Puddletown was extensively rebuilt from 1864 onward, but since the novel supplies no details of any building except the church and 'Warren's Malthouse' little light is shed on dates. The malthouse, which flourished until about 1875, stood some way north of Back Street; one or two lengths of its red-brick walls can still be seen. Much more complete is the old mill, which even retains the mill-wheel, now dry, down which the water dribbled in the poem 'At the Mill'. Just below the wheel the water entered a culvert, to emerge again as a shallow drinking-pool, before another culvert carried the stream under Mill Street. The pool was the Mill-tail Shallow of the poem 'The Country Wedding', and like the rest of the millstream it is now dry, though the culverts remain. Four cottages for-merly bordered this side of Mill Street, and their gardens, between the road and the mill—now a barn—continue to be tended. But the 'door by the shallow' was probably that of the nearer of two cottages (since replaced) north of the millstream—the birthplace of Tryphena Sparks. Near by, along Styles Lane and Fore Street, of which the former has retained its name but the latter is now (inexplicably) regarded as part of The Square, the wedding procession marched. Most of the 1864-period houses have survived.

The gate by which Bathsheba Everdene en-tered the churchyard is still there, surmounted now by a First World War memorial in the form of a wrought-iron arch and lantern. 'Behind church' referred to the opposite (south) side of the churchyard, but the position of the 'reprobates'' burial area is today unknown. Gabriel Oak met Fanny Robin beside the graveyard wall 'where several ancient yew trees grew' and there was a wide margin of grass. This must have been on either the south or east side, where the trees still include ancient yews.

Is the door by which Troy said he attended

The west end of 'Weatherbury' (Puddletown) Church, one of the very few throughout the land to have escaped the usually leaden hand of the Victorian restorer. Instead, much sensitive reconstruction was carried out in 1910. The gallery and much of the woodwork elsewhere date from 1695.

shortest route, but even if this arch had had a door to it such an internal feature would not have become sealed by ivy. Gabriel's version appears at first sight to be based even less on reality, since there is no official record of an outside stair or door, nor any trace of either unless we consider relevant the vestiges of two puzzling stone steps just inside the west window of the north aisle. However, this version receives unexpected support from Hardy's close friend and literary executor, the late Sir Sydney Cockerell, Curator of the Fitzwilliam Museum at Cambridge. Sir Sydney paid no fewer than forty-two visits to Max Gate, and on one of them, according to his biographer Wilfrid Blunt, he called at Puddletown church with his host, who pointed out the window in the south (*sic*) aisle which had formerly furnished the access to the gallery used by Hardy for the Troy incident. This is the word of a reliable witness (even if we concede that he has confused south with north), and taken in conjunction with the two unexplained steps it does furnish a case for believing in a reality of some kind behind the Troy anecdote. Lea also asserts that the 'little gallery door' used by Troy was factual, and still to be seen on the west side of the tower; but he confuses his readers by referring them to a photograph of a door (which exists today) at the back of the nave, underneath the gallery and communicating with the tower through the latter's *east* wall.

Just before the Wimborne road (A35) leaves Puddletown, a lane turns off on the right toward Beacon Corner and the Rhododendron Mile. Alongside this lane is the quarter where most of the new building has taken place, with a network of small new roads to serve it. Further west the lane passes through a deep cutting, beyond which a grassy hill on the right is the Kite Hill of 'The Sheep-Boy'. The poem 'In a Eweleaze near Weatherbury' probably refers to Coombe Eweleaze, south of the lane and now distantly threatened by the new houses. In former times it was a favourite area for outdoor revels. Coombe Eweleaze has also been suggested by some

services an invention? Many indications imply that it is. For one, Hardy is not consistent. Bathsheba tells Oak that Troy went in by the old tower door and thence up to the back of the gallery, yet to assess the truth of this Oak climbs some *external* steps and finds the door—evidently external also—overgrown with ivy. The 'old tower door' in Bathsheba's version is real and remains in use, and there is an archway, long boarded up, linking the tower with the back of the gallery. It is possible that a ladder was once set up in the ringing chamber to allow the bellringers to enter the gallery by the

Near 'Weatherbury' (Puddletown), 'Athelhall' (Athelhampton), prominent in two poems and one short story, is a Late Perpendicular mansion built in 1504 for a former Lord Mayor of London; a 'parlour wing' was added later in the same century.

(Deacon and Coleman; Bailey) as the scene of the poem 'A Spot'. Half a mile to the west, in the south-west angle of the Beacon Corner cross-roads there stood, in pre-Forestry Commission days, a small grove of conifers, Coombe Plantation—the 'Coombe-Firtrees' of 'Yell'ham-Wood's Story'. It is now merged in the general afforestation.

Tincleton, the 'Stickleford' where Car'line Aspent lived ('The Fiddler of the Reels') and where Venn acquired his dairy farm, remains a simple village scattered round a rectangle of lanes, and today, with the shrinking of the heath, belongs more to the Frome valley. In the parish,

replacing an older house demolished in 1842, is Clyffe House, the grounds of which include Pallington Clump, the 'Clyffe-hill Clump' mentioned in 'Yell'ham-Wood's Story' and the 'Clyffe-Clump' of 'The Paphian Ball'. Its pines still form a landmark, especially from the Frome meads and the hills south of them.

North-west of Clyffe lies Athelhampton. In addition to its role in 'The Children and Sir Nameless' and 'The Dame of Athelhall' it figures with some prominence in the prose tale 'The Waiting Supper'. The mansion lies north of the Puddletown–Wimborne road, in magnificent grounds that have changed a good deal since the period of the story, let alone the periods of the two poems, the layout of the gardens dating only from the late nineteenth century. Several branches of the Piddle pass through the flat vale north of Athelhampton—the 'Athel Coomb' through which the Dame made her return.

The house itself, mainly Tudor, has been shorn of the portion containing the original gatehouse and experienced various internal alterations. The Great Hall still has its fine timbered roof and musicians' gallery (the latter with a new parapet and sundry changes to the back partition). There is, as Hardy asserted, a spiral staircase in the thickness of one of the walls, but it does not and never did give access to the gallery. (For the link between Athelhampton and 'Endelstow House' in *A Pair of Blue Eyes*, see page 213.)

To the east is Tolpuddle ('Tolchurch'), which appears briefly in *Desperate Remedies*. Beatty thinks the description of the church and its restoration is drawn from Turnworth, where Hardy himself supervised the work and may even be the 'clerk of the works' sent from Budmouth. But the *site* of the church in the novel is exactly that of Tolpuddle church. The young Grayes lived in 'one half of an old farmhouse' that stood near the church and apart from the 'body of cottages'. This building is still easily recognizable in the Manor House, the long roof-slope of which, on the rear or north side, may indeed once have extended as far as the ground. The house commands a view of at least 100 yards up the main road, and a good deal more of the lane to Affpuddle ('East Egdon').

In other respects Tolpuddle has changed a good deal, but Affpuddle, by contrast, remains tiny, sleepy, and unspoilt. Although its mellow old church is really too far to the east, Hardy treated it as the parish church for 'Mistover Knap'. The parish includes part of the area in which that enlightened industrialist Sir Ernest Debenham tried (and failed) to relieve the agricultural depression between the two world wars with a scheme for modernized farming, better housing for farm labourers, and much else. Many of his cottages and other buildings remain. The Debenham scheme also embraced Briantspuddle (or Bryants Puddle), the unnamed hamlet to which Damon Wildeve went to look for a constable after he had been shot at. Sir Ernest restored much of the old village and doubled its extent with new-built thatched cottages.

Half a mile to the south of Briantspuddle, in a part of the heath displaying much afforestation, an oblong and solitary cottage lies in a dip so abrupt that its roof is on a level with the roadway near by. Rendering and recent retiling belie the age of Brickyard Cottage; but in fact it is of considerable antiquity, the rendering concealing

Oker's Pool, given its real name in *The Return of the Native* when Little Johnny Nonsuch fetched Mrs Yeobright a drink from it, is tiny, hard to find, but said never to dry up.

cob above a few lower courses of brick, and the upper windows being of a wooden, many-paned design long since discarded. Inside, the trim parlour shows further evidence of age, although the bread-oven has been filled in. The cottage is 'Alderworth', the marital home of Clym and Eustacia.

Many of the firs that clothe the high ground round the house are recognizably older than the Forestry Commission trees, and there is no mistaking the 'singularly battered, rude, and wild' Devil's Bellows. A few hundred yards away, today badly choked with vegetation, lies Rimsmoor Pond (in some editions 'Bottom Pond'), which young Jimmy Nonsuch said was dry when Clym's mother asked him for water. The other pond that he said was never dry, 'Oker's Pool', is a short distance west of Rimsmoor, on the other side of the broad track and to south of the open avenue between the trees. Lying in a deep hollow, at most times its surface is spectacularly green.

The Wood itself, a tract of mixed timber contiguous to, but much older than, the Commission's conifer plantations, is the 'fir and beech plantation' alluded to in the description of 'Alderworth', and is also the wood in Grandfather James's story, in *Under the Greenwood Tree*, about the bridegroom caught in the mantrap. Amid so many conifers the beeches now look especially handsome.

Throop ('Throope') Corner presents a problem, because it is given as the point to which Wildeve accompanied Eustacia after meeting her at the open-air dance; a 'short path branched off' to her house 'a few hundred yards' from the corner. The dance, however, was at Affpuddle, and 'Alderworth' lies *between* there and Throop Corner.

The first great change in this part of 'Egdon Heath' came with the establishment of Bovington Camp (1916), barely two and a half miles south of 'Alderworth'. The camp itself is a square mile of unsightliness (making a very poor comparison with, say, Larkhill), and as the headquarters of the Armoured Corps it has been responsible for the despoliation of the heath over a wide area to north and east. However, if we are to have tanks, this is probably unavoidable; the effect is no worse than that of the huge gravel pits strung along the nearby Piddle valley.

Unlike the shapeless and conspicuous camp, the Atomic Energy Research Establishment on Winfrith Heath manages to hide its large and growing spread to a degree one might regard as impossible except in some fold of the hills. If its buildings suggest H. G. Wells rather than Thomas Hardy, the layout at least has design; and at night the constellation of bright lights, suddenly come upon, is not without beauty. On the north-west, west and south sides of the research establishment the heath and its villages remain up to now surprisingly little affected; Winfrith Newburgh village might never have heard of atomic energy. Only toward Wareham is the amount of new housing conspicuous, and here it is still increasing. Hardy's poem 'The Slow Nature' tells us of a tragedy that occurred 'out by Moreford [Moreton] Rise'; in real life this hill is less than a mile north-west of the research station, yet even here the country is quite unspoilt. Change of a different sort from that associated with Bovington or Winfrith overtook the heath slightly farther west, when soon after the outbreak of the Second World War Mr Noel Paul of Woodsford Farm, one of the truly great agriculturalists of Wessex, reclaimed a vast tract of the supposedly unreclaimable gravel land toward Moreton station and turned it into a wheat prairie.

To revert to the northern side of the Frome: running diagonally across the western half of 'Egdon Heath' like a thread across a tapestry is the Roman road connecting Dorchester with Salisbury and eventually London; and like the tapestry thread, it is difficult to trace in its entirety, since long sections of it are hidden. Hardy knew it well from infancy, as his poem 'The Roman Road' testifies. He mentions it too at the outset of *The Return of the Native*, but misleadingly stating (and confirming on his map) that the Dorchester–Wareham road overlay much of it. In reality the Roman route runs farther north, passing close to the Rainbarrows.

One of the largest surviving wild heath parts of 'Egdon' lies within the area roughly bounded by Bere Regis ('Kingsbere'), Bovington Camp, Wareham ('Anglebury') and Lytchett Minster ('Flytchett'). This tract has escaped 'development' because it is part of the private estates of Charborough ('Welland') House; a large section is a nature reserve. Much is forested (conifers again), but some stretches, composed of heather and furze-clad heath seamed by narrow, sandy paths and pierced here and there by pools, are of great interest to students of Hardy because they closely resemble his descriptions of the Rainbar-rows end of the heath before the trees were planted—though here in the east the contours are much flatter. Somewhere in this area Hardy placed the hovel in which Henchard died; but although Lea professed to have found the site, no trace remains.

Readers of *The Hand of Ethelberta* will recall the early scene set in the tiny 'Weir House' with its neighbouring weir. From Hardy's statement that only two or three miles separated the 'Weir House' from Bournemouth ('Sandbourne'), and his account of the road-junction visible from the house, we must conclude that he was either evoking a scene that has since disappeared under the lava-flow of bricks and mortar, or, as I think more likely, depicting a genuine group of features, 'moved' to a different locality to suit the story; for a building much resembling the 'Weir House' does exist, and near it are a small stream, several pools, and 'some hatches and a weir' just as described. They all lie, today, within the strict privacy of the nature reserve, a short distance west of the Sandford–Sherford road (B3075).

The building is of brick, oblong (not square), with, until recently, a large fireplace across one corner, and a rudimentary window. Today it is deeply veiled in trees, though open moorland lies at a short distance on nearly all sides; it is in an advanced state of ruin, the roof having collapsed. If it is not Hardy's little house, it was built by similar people for an identical purpose.

The other pool, the 'whitely shining oval' that Ethelberta came upon when following the 'duckhawk', lies between here and the B3075, from which it is plainly visible.

The heath behind Bournemouth ('Sandbourne'), although this is now within Dorset, will be dealt with in Chapter 10. Here we may end with Lytchett Minster, the 'Flytchett' where Sol Chickerel and the Honourable Edgar Mountclere changed horses after their disagreeable journey along the wet and yielding sand roads of the heath. The cross-roads referred to is Upton Cross, now a large roundabout at a major intersection. 'Flytchett' is characterized as 'a trumpery small bit of a village' where a wheelwright kept a beerhouse, a mere cottage with a board on the wall advertising its function. Nowadays, thanks to the extreme nearness of Poole and several main roads, the Upton end of Lytchett Minster is slowly but surely becoming swallowed up in suburbia (1971 pop. already 5010; 1981, 6748); however, the original village to the west has changed remarkably little. It still has two inns, one a roadhouse of some pretensions—the true St Peter's Finger (see page 23)—the other more in the tradition of a village inn. But it is very doubtful whether either developed from the humble beer-house of *Ethelberta*.

4 SOUTH WESSEX
VALLEY OF THE GREAT DAIRIES
Dorset: the valley of the Frome

Ah! dairy where I lived so long,
        I lived so long;
Where I would rise up staunch and strong,
        And lie down hopefully.
'Twas there within the chimney-seat
He watched me to the clock's slow beat—
Loved me, and learned to call me Sweet,
        And whispered words to me.

TESS'S LAMENT

Among the best known of all Hardy's scenic portraits is the picture of the Frome valley that he sets before the eyes of Tess as she gazes down from the edge of 'Egdon Heath' after leaving her native Vale of Blackmoor (the 'Vale of Little Dairies'). At a first glance, the spectacle remains surprisingly little altered. Yet when one examines the details how much has changed! The 'tribes' of cattle are black-and-white instead of red or dun; there is hygienic, mechanized milking inside the long new sheds; the very pastures, with a few exceptions, are no longer the water-meadows known to Tess; the scores of weirs and sluices are now mainly derelict or dismantled to lessen flood risks. However, the waterways continue to make the landscape look like a gridiron, as it is expressed in *The Return*. One may still, like Angel and Tess, rove along the meads by the paths that creep alongside the brooks and periodically cross them by small wooden bridges. Floodwater is not as liable to cover the road bridges in these days as when Angel did his ferrying of the milkmaids, or when the widow in 'She Hears the Storm' listened on that wild night.

Inevitably, we arrive at the problem of 'Talbothays'. Just where, if anywhere, was the prototype of this, the most celebrated farm in all Hardy's prose or verse? Was it a real farm, or

was it, as Lea suggests, merely representative of a type? It is my belief that too much mystery is made of 'Talbothays'. This is partly due to the widespread impression that the place was modelled on Norris Mill Farm, and therefore lay north of the river. The legend seems to have been begun by Windle, and boosted nearly a quarter of a century later by 'Clive Holland's' assertion that during a cycle-ride past Norris Mill, Hardy admitted that he had had this farm in mind when creating 'Talbothays'.

Yet what are Norris Mill's claims? It is a valid assumption that during his early years at Higher Bockhampton Hardy got to know the farm, and that when he wanted to describe a typical Frome valley establishment, this nearby example sprang to his mind. But there is another dairy farm that he knew well as a boy, corresponding much more nearly with his portrait of 'Talbothays', and in a far more convincing situation. This is Lower Lewell Farm, between West Stafford and Woodsford. Notwithstanding his failure to say anything about Tess crossing the river during that celebrated first approach, the novel abounds in indications that Hardy pictured 'Talbothays' on the south bank.

The brief description of the parish church where Angel and Tess were married, with its louvred belfry and three bells, tallies only with

Lower Lewell Farm, the model for Talbothays. Beyond this splendid old barn the nearest first-floor window of the farmhouse lights what has always been known locally as Tess's Room – meaning, presumably, the room of her own that was allocated to her during the week preceding her wedding.

Was 'Shadwater Weir' in *The Return of the Native* this unnamed weir near Woodsford Castle, or was it the next downstream, Sturt's Weir? In *Tess*, Retty Priddle tried to drown herself in the 'Great Pool', which would seem to be the pool below one of these weirs. Opinion inclines to the unnamed weir as 'Shadwater'.

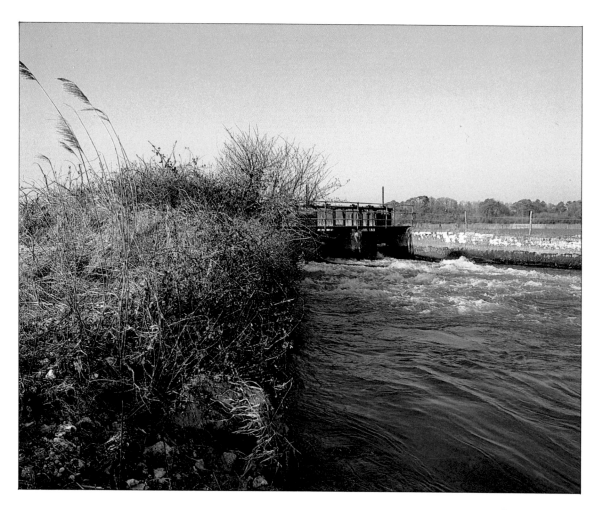

West Stafford church, whose parish does not extend north of the water. When the milkmaids in their Sunday finery were walking 'by the crooked lane winding from their own parish to Mellstock', they encountered the floods when the church was 'as yet nearly a mile off'. Not by any stretch of author's licence would Hardy have represented them as running into floodwater within a mile of Stinsford church along the Tincleton road, which would have set them somewhere near Bockhampton Cross! Nor is that road particularly crooked. A mile from the church by the Frome path and the decidedly crooked West Stafford road, however, brings us to an area highly susceptible to flooding.

Again, when Angel and Tess were driving the milk churns to the station the meads 'were backed *in the extreme edge of distance* [my italics] by the swarthy and abrupt slopes of Egdon Heath'—surely a description that makes sense only if the viewer is south of the river. Sometimes Mrs Crick sent the pair to 'the farmhouse on the slopes' where cows in calf were supervised, and one day, while returning, the lovers reached a 'great gravel-cliff immediately over the levels'. The farmhouse could be any one of many, but the only gravel-pits large enough to qualify are south of Lewell and Woodsford, although Hardy does seem to have brought them unrealistically close to the meads and river-channels. Finally, when Angel returned to 'Talbothays' from Beaminster ('Emminster') he paused and looked down into the Frome valley from a 'detached knoll a mile or two west' of the farm. This could perhaps have been some point in Stinsford Parish, but the most obvious detached knoll at the west end of the valley is the tumulus on Frome Hill, beside the road from Dorchester to West Stafford (see page 28).

There are one or two objections to this placing of 'Talbothays' in addition to Hardy's failure to say that Tess on arrival crossed the river. He states that the farm lay on the route from Wool ('Wellbridge') to Puddletown, which Lewell does not (nor, for that matter, does Norris Mill); and Lower Lewell Farm is not strictly speaking in West Stafford, but over the parish border in West Knighton. But against these points Hardy had good reason to feel associated with the neighbourhood. His father had owned a piece of farmland in West Stafford, not far from Lower Lewell, called Talbothays, to which the boy must often have been taken by Hardy senior and his men on their work expeditions. Later, the novelist designed a villa here for his brother Henry and their two sisters, the villa also bearing the name Talbothays. In it the elder sister, Mary, was to die, an event reflected in 'Logs on the Hearth' and 'In the Garden'. Today the villa is very little altered, and in the garden the sundial of the second poem continues to display the initials of the three Hardy residents.

Lower Lewell Farm bears a close resemblance to the 'Talbothays' of *Tess*, though not quite so close now as a very few years ago. On two sides of the barton the milking-sheds—long, thatched, and with wooden posts on the open side rubbed glossy by generations of cattle, all precisely as depicted in the novel—have been pulled down in favour of more modern structures, including a huge new steel-framed store filling most of the yard. The third side is still occupied by the old stables, the fourth by a wall dividing the barton from the garden. No longer 'derelict and weed-filled' as when Tess stole up on Angel so appropriately playing his harp, the garden is large enough for her to have kept hidden 'behind the hedge' while stealing up on him. On another occasion she took refuge in the 'thicket of pollard willows at the lower side of the barton'; such a thicket is still there. 'Talbothays' possessed a water-mill; so formerly did Lower Lewell—bereft now of its wheel, but still in occupation as a private house.

The farmhouse has less conspicuous affinities, although more than Norris Mill, the ruins of which show none at all. The former dairy-house at Lewell is of greater interest. The building is on two floors, the lower divided between the old cheese-room and a portion now converted into a residence for farm staff. The upper floor, if one mentally removes a single rough and clearly not original partition, exactly fulfils the description of Angel's room—'an immense attic which ran the whole length of the dairy-house', and could be reached only by a ladder from the cheese-loft. Hardy nevertheless evidently visualized a building of three storeys, for not only does he write cheese-*loft*, but assigns to the milkmaids 'a large room over the milk-house, some thirty feet long' from which Tess *ascended* to slip the note under Angel's door. At Lower Lewell the milk-house was a ground-floor extension (now demolished) of the dairy-house, *alongside* the only possible dormitory for the girls, which was that part of the ground floor now converted into the residence just mentioned.

Prior to the indirect hint contained in Pinion's reference, under 'Talbothays', to Hardy's familiarity with Lewell Mill, no writer as far as I can learn ever suggested Lewell for 'Talbothays'; yet at the farm itself the association has long been firmly accepted, and a window is pointed out as that of Tess's bedroom (if so, it must have been the separate room given her on the news of her betrothal). But with no published basis for the belief, how did it become established unless by Hardy himself during visits to his relatives' villa? *Tess* contains two further hints that this is the region of 'Talbothays'. A farmhand at the dairy is called Bill Lewell; and when Hetty and Marian go to seek some cheer after losing Angel, they walk to a public-house at 'Lew-Everard'. The Everard family, as Hutchins relates, formerly occupied [West] Stafford House ('Froom-Everard House' in Hardy's story 'The Waiting Supper'); and Hutchins appears to have regarded the Lewell area as *East* Stafford. 'Lew-Everard' would therefore seem to be some imaginary spot—or perhaps West Knighton—linking the two Staffords.

Stafford House, at West Stafford, was much altered by John Floyer in 1850. Since 'The Waiting Supper' opens in 1837, this tallies with Hardy's observation that 'at that time of the century Froom-Everard had not been altered and enlarged'. Elsewhere in the story he refers

with praise to the Elizabethan design with its mullioned and transomed five-light window facing the lawn. The splendid window continues to be a conspicuous and beautiful feature. The house went through the usual vicissitudes of a manor, becoming (as stated in the story) a farmhouse, and then being admirably rehabilitated in the present century as a private residence. Before the alterations of 1850, Hardy tells us, the public lane passed close under the walls, and a door opened directly into it from the old south parlour. An early picture in the possession of a recent owner corroborates this.

The church is still surrounded by a low stone wall and possesses three bells, but has otherwise undergone more changes than are apparent at first glance. The customary Victorian restoration took place late (1895-8), well after the period of the story, and included the extension of the east end to form a new chancel, with various internal rearrangements resulting. A new coloured east window was put in, and the glass in others was replaced, so that little is left of the 'bottle-green glass of the old lead quarries'. The churchyard is closely hemmed in by roads, but retains enough gravestones for Nicholas to have looked on the rows of his friends, side by side in death as in life. In West Stafford village, apart from a sprinkling of new houses, the principal change was the conversion of a large building, Barton Barn, into a general shop and crafts centre, but this is now closed.

The grounds of Stafford House continue to include extensive 'shrubberies and plantations along the banks of the Froom', and it is not difficult to identify the willow-grove called the 'Sallows'. The waterfall above which Nicholas used to wade the river during his arduous commutings, and where Bellston was drowned, can still be seen; the reconstruction of it at the end of the story was probably based on fact. Hardy told Hermann Lea that 'Elsenford', Nicholas Long's home on the other side of the valley, was either Bhompston or Duddle Farm. In view of his admission that Bhompston is at least partly identifiable with 'Blooms-End' (page

Sturt's Weir has fewer hatches than its neighbour, and nowadays they are heavily overgrown, as you may see here. Despite these handicaps, however, the force of the emerging water makes the pool seem both larger and more sinister than its neighbour.

45) I prefer to look on Duddle as 'Elsenford'; and it must also be the 'Duddle Hole' farmed by Festus Derriman's crony, Farmer Stubb, in *The Trumpet-Major*.

The Frome is not always placid and friendly; most sinister, in Hardy's estimation, was the reach between West Stafford and Woodsford. Here we have the drowning of Bellston in Stafford waterfall; the deaths of Eustacia Yeobright and Damon Wildeve at Shadwater Weir; the attempt of Retty Priddle to end her life at the same spot (called the Great Pool in *Tess*); and the finding of the body at Rocky Shallow in 'A Sound in the Night'. This eerie legend-poem is set in Woodsford Castle, a fascinating architec-tural jumble with windows of all periods from mediaeval to Victorian, a turret stair and postern as in the poem, and a vast thatched roof looking grossly out of place, yet not displeasing, above walls that should (and once did) terminate in crenellations. The 'farmstead once a castle' became a farmhouse earlier than most manors, and by the beginning of this century it was pretty down-at-heel according to Treves, though today everything about it is prosperous-looking.

'Shadwater Weir' is sometimes identified with the five- or six-hatch Sturt's Weir (its superstruc-ture now much overgrown) just behind Woodsford Farm, but more often it is equated with the next weir upstream—unmarked on the maps, and seemingly nameless. Here there are eight hatches, all operational. The mass of water above or below either weir would justify the name Great Pool, though in spate the pool below Sturt's Weir is the more awe-inspiring. Rocky Shallow lies between the two weirs.

The monastic vestiges at Bindon are fairly extensive, and include a number of tombs besides that in which Angel is supposed to have laid Tess. The Gothic-style house was built in the 1790s, originally as a House of Retreat.

Unfortunately the lonely and rather sinister atmosphere of the neighbourhood, which persisted well into the 1970s, has of late been considerably modified by extensive quarrying near the river, large cairns of stones peppering the meads over a wide area. This is forlorn territory; north of the river lies the lush Frome Mead, but south of it, between castle and farm, is a desolate strip of marshland.

Windle identifies the railway station to which Angel and Tess took the milk-churns as Wool; but in *Thomas Hardy and the Lady from Madison Square* Weber quotes Rebekah Owen as saying that Hardy himself had told her the station was Moreton, and that she had seen there the large holly tree under which Tess sheltered. In discussing which station Hardy had in mind it seems to have occurred to no-one to ask why Angel should have driven the milk all the way to Wool when Moreton Station, on the same line, lay at only half the distance (unless, of course, the train, like Ned and Car'line's in 'The Fiddler of the Reels', did not stop there). The advocates of Wool read into Hardy's description of the railway a pretence that at the time it terminated there; all point to his statement that the travellers passed 'an old manor house of Caroline date, formerly the property of the d'Urbervilles', which is always assumed to refer to Woolbridge. But the description of the route undoubtedly indicates the road *south* of the Frome, which, indeed, if 'Talbothays' is based on Lower Lewell, it would be; and this road reaches Wool Station *before* it gets to Woolbridge Manor. It is also to be noted that when Angel takes his bride to the Manor for their honeymoon, neither he nor she comments that this is the house he so lately pointed out from the road. My impression therefore is that, as an excuse to draw the d'Urbervilles into the conversation during the milk journey, Hardy adopted the stratagem of imagining that the travellers passed some other former d'Urberville mansion; he makes Angel remark (truthfully) that a number were to be found in the region. Moreover he says that the vehicle passed by the manor and 'left it behind'—an odd remark if referring to Wool, where manor and station are separated by less than a quarter of a mile. The station could nevertheless be either Moreton or Wool. Both are still operative today, Moreton as a modest halt, Wool with a smart new pre-fabricated booking hall and other amenities. Neither boasts a holly tree, though Wool is adorned with rose bushes and other flowers. Moreton too is the unnamed 'pretty roadside station' alluded to in 'The Fiddler of the Reels', and Moreton village, tiny and unspoilt, the 'Moreford' where his betrothed lived.

Woolbridge ('Wellbridge') Manor must be the most often-pictured building in all Hardy's works. Even today, when Wool village has enlarged itself along the main road in a dull amorphous straggle, the manor remains isolated in the riverside flats. Hardy accurately describes it as a dilapidated farmhouse in Tess's day; in our own it was for years a pleasant hotel, but is now once more a farmhouse. The renowned Turberville portraits, at either end of the small first-floor landing, have been so badly defaced by ham-fisted 'restoration' that one is virtually meaningless, the other just decipherable. Nevertheless, enough is left of the latter to make the original sinister effect credible, whereas the very indifferent replicas in the Dorset County Museum are little better than comic cartoons.

Near the old manor the Elizabethan stone bridge still stands, its parapet battered by First World War tanks from Bovington, but otherwise sound. A road continues to pass over it, but the main highway (A352) crosses the Frome by a modern bridge a short distance away. Also near, but less near than Hardy makes out, is Bindon Abbey, originally rescued from its post-Dissolution ruin by Thomas Weld two centuries ago, but in a fairly rough state until after the *Tess* period, for both Harper and Treves enlarge on its unkempt condition and the melancholy nature of the woods and waterways. Today all is vastly improved; the ruins are tidy, the grounds about them beautiful, and the woods and waterways well tended. The celebrated coffin of

One of the best-known buildings in all Hardy's works, seventeenth-century 'Wellbridge' (Woolbridge) Manor, had outwardly hardly changed when Angel and Tess entered it, nor has it since. The old bridge, recently spared from heavy traffic, is a century older.

Abbot Richard Maners, in which the sleepwalking Angel laid Tess, is in good condition. Angel's route on this journey is impossible to trace, perhaps not surprisingly in view of the falsified distance between manor and abbey. The abbey mill, where Angel intended to study, continues in operation, though in the mid-1960s electricity replaced water as the source of power. The mill-house is most graciously maintained.

Barely a mile farther down the river, close to the north bank, stand the ruins of the church of St Mary, East Stoke, the 'ancient little pile' to which Farmer Lodge and Gertrude repaired in 'The Withered Arm'. The action of this grim tale (based, Hardy maintained, on true events even grimmer) can be fairly accurately placed, from a date mentioned in the text, as between 1819 and 1826; and since the present church was not completed until 1828, there is no ambiguity here.

This is an area, extending west up the Frome from Wareham ('Anglebury'), in which much development is taking place, industrial as well as residential. The ruins of the church, creeper-clad and half-hidden by bushes, are on the fringe of an asphalt car-park belonging to the new red-brick offices of the Freshwater Biological Association River Laboratories. Close by is what looks like a covered swimming-bath, but is in fact a fluvarium, only the second such in the world, intended for the study of fish and other river life *in situ*, through a glass floor.

'Holmstoke', the 'white house of ample dimensions' where the Lodges lived, has been variously identified,* but the evidence points to its being Hethfelton House, between Bovington and Stokeford: not the present mansion, built only in 1930, but its predecessor, which was white, as the story states, and had farm buildings adjacent. On an estate map of 1828 the house is called 'Heffleton *Lodge*', a rare term in Dorset,

* Mr Martin Bond, of Holme Priory, sent me a detailed case for suggesting his own house as the prototype of 'Holmstoke'. Despite his well-reasoned arguments, however, I feel Hethfelton has stronger claims than either this or Lea's choice, Holme Farm.

Bindon Mill, originally worked by the monks of Bindon Abbey, is where Angel Clare intended to study. An interesting point overlooked by most students of *Tess*, and perhaps by Hardy, is that the Clares were rigidly Protestant, but since 1641 the Bindon property had been owned by a leading Roman Catholic family.

inviting speculation as to whether Hardy's choice of 'Lodge' for the surname of his chief characters was entirely coincidental.

Despite Windle and Lea, there are several good reasons why 'Holmstoke' should not be situated south of the Frome. The most conclusive is that when the Lodges are driving home from Wareham ('Anglebury') they come to a steep, short ascent where it was customary for travellers to walk their horses. There is only one such ascent, Worgret Hill, north of the river on the road to Dorchester (A352). True, Hardy remarks that the road was not a main one, but the absence of any other hill suggests that this statement was one of his red herrings. Nor is it any better justified if we suppose him to have been writing of the road to Dorchester via Tincleton, which forks off the A352 at the top of Worgret Hill, for this, too, was a main road in the first half of the nineteenth century, and furthermore is referred to as the direct route from 'Holmstoke' to Dorchester, which it would not have been if the Lodges had lived south of the Frome.

It is instructive, if not altogether easy, to study the itinerary of Gertrude's secret ride to 'Casterbridge'. She set forth 'in precisely the opposite direction', then 'as soon as she was out of sight' turned left 'by a road which led into

Egdon'. From a start on the south bank it is impossible to plot any route consistent with these data, and in plotting one from Hethfelton it has to be assumed that Hardy's description begins at the drive gates rather than the house. From here, on the Wareham road, Dorchester travellers would have turned west, so Gertrude headed east. Her left-turn would be up the track that skirted the eastern edge of the Great Plantation and on to South Heath. At some point she must have crossed the Tincleton road, because she arrived eventually at Rushy Pond, which lies north of it. The 'due westerly' wheel that she made must really have been north-west at first, across South, Higher Hyde, and Bere Heaths, probably as far as Gallows Hill. From that region more than one horseman alive today has made his way to Dorchester by Chamberlayne's and Throop Heaths, Clyffe, South Admiston, Castle Hill, and Rushy Pond; and even now, despite tank-proving grounds, gravel quarries, afforestation and cultivation, it remains true that 'a more private way down the county could not be imagined'.

The erection of the present Hethfelton House also saw the cutting-down of most of the Great Plantation. The 1828 map shows the estate extending well south of the Wareham road, almost to Bindon Abbey; and in the southern part lies Hethfelton Farm, or Hethfelton Old Farm, a subsidiary property corresponding with Lodge's 'outlying second farm' on which the story opens. In recent years the buildings have been taken over for industrial purposes and extensively altered.

On the river channel that formed the south-western boundary of the estate stands Stony or Bovington Weir. Control of the weir was some-what quarrelsomely shared between the Frampt-ons of Moreton and the Welds of Bindon, but it would be natural enough for a Hethfelton hand to speak of it as '*our* Great Weir', the phrase used by the old 'Holmstoke' dairyman. (Indeed,

at an earlier period Hethfelton had been a farm in the possession of Bindon Abbey.) The old man said the weir had been built forty years earlier, that is around 1779; Stony Weir, mediaeval in origin, was fully rebuilt by the Framptons in 1749, but in spite of this descrepancy the likeli-hood remains that this is the weir Hardy meant. Today the stone framework, which resembles a packhorse bridge, is intact, but the hatches were removed before the Second World War, and more recently sections of concrete piping have been fixed to the upstream side of the openings to ease the flow.

Rhoda Brook's cottage, 'up a by-lane some one and a half miles short [east] of the white farmstead', and the first house outside the

The territory of 'The Withered Arm'.

Looking westward up the Valley of the Great Dairies from the Isle of Purbeck. Though no longer worked as water-meadows – improved strains of grass have eliminated the need – the rich alluvial soil continues to produce fine dairy cattle pasture.

Lodges' parish (East Stoke), must be sought over the boundary of either Bere Regis or Wareham St Martin, probably up the lane between Stokeford and Stokeford Farm. Today, after a third or so of a mile, the lane peters out, but a heath footpath could have led into either parish. The cot would have been no more than one of those humble cob-and-thatch dwellings effaced as soon as their owners (if not always their occupants) had ceased to have a use for them. Just north of East Stoke a small level-crossing house where the lane from the village to the A352 crosses the Wareham–Dorchester railway-line is probably the 'gate-house' where Owen Springrove in *Desperate Remedies* stopped during his walk along the line after missing the train.

Wareham receives scant notice from Hardy. Unmentioned in the *Poems*, barely alluded to in 'The Withered Arm', and briefly cited as the market-town patronized by Old Mrs Chundle in the story that bears her name, it plays a small part only in *The Hand of Ethelberta*. Here the action centres on the Red Lion, 'an old and well-appointed inn' that had become popular with tourists 'because of the absence from its precincts of all that was fashionable and new'. This would be a somewhat unkind description of the hotel today, for if its exterior still looks old (it is the same building), the interior has been extensively and elegantly modernized. Although Wareham has grown, the fact that it is not on the Channel coast and not quite on the shore of Poole Harbour has spared it the hideous development of Swanage and, to a lesser extent, Studland. Built about its four wide streets, it remains Georgian, substantial, and dignified. If he could return now, after nearly two centuries, its illustrious historian-rector, John Hutchins, would not, I think, be distressed.

5 SOUTH WESSEX

BETWEEN EGDON HEATH AND UPPER WESSEX

Dorset: between the heath and Hampshire

How smartly the quarters of the hour march by
    That the jack-o'-clock never forgets;
·   ·   ·   ·   ·   ·   ·

    Just so did he clang here before I came,
      And so will he clang when I'm gone
  Through the Minster's cavernous hollows—the same
    Tale of hours never more to be will he deliver
      To the speechless midnight and dawn.

COPYING ARCHITECTURE IN AN OLD MINSTER (WIMBORNE)

After Crusted Character Mr George Crookhill had set out from Salisbury for Blandford and encountered his odd companion on Coombe Bissett Hill (page 185), the pair stopped for refreshment at the Woodyates Inn, just within Dorset on what is now the A354. This roadside hostelry, which in its latter days bore the name Shaftesbury Arms, ceased to be an inn shortly before Hardy, motoring past it in 1919, noted that it still retained its 'genial hostelry appearance'. Treves, on the other hand, earlier in the century, found it deplorably modernized and badly run. The empty buildings were finally razed in the late 1960s, the site, at the corner of the turning to Woodyates village, remaining a sad patch of weeds and rubble until sold for development in 1971. Today bungalows and their gardens occupy the scene.

The road has improved since 1904, when Harper described it as 'a glaring white road five inches deep in dust and powdered flint, the whole stirred up into a stifling halo of floating particles by the frequent passage of a flock of sheep'.

A very short distance south-west of Wood-yates, a cul-de-sac branches off to eastward and leads to Pentridge. This remote and sleepy place, more than a mile from the highway and without an inn, has always been accepted as the prototype of 'Trantridge' in *Tess*, the nearest village to Alec Stoke-d'Urberville's home 'The Slopes' (a fictitious house). It was left for Pinion to point out that 'Trantridge' is also the name of the spot where George Crookhill and his companion put up for the night—at an inn on the main road.

On Hardy's own sketch-map of 'Tess's Country' the position of 'Trantridge' unmistakably indicates Pentridge; yet in the first (magazine) version of *Crusted Characters* what later became 'Trantridge' appears as 'Tranton', surely derived from Tarrant Hinton, a village in the right situation for the story and boasting an inn. I think the explanation is that Hardy used the same name for two different places—as, for instance, he seems to have used 'Lower Long-puddle' for Puddletown and later Piddlehinton. It is conceivable that 'Tranton' was never meant to be changed, but that having appeared as 'Trantridge' the name stuck simply through failure to correct it. As for the *Tess* 'Trantridge', it ought to be possible to confirm it as Pentridge by following the girl on her two journeys to 'The Slopes' and back. Unfortunately, however, a comprehensive study of maps, guides, and directories of the period, supplemented by an exhaustive survey of the terrain, fails to reveal any itinerary that can be fitted more than approximately to the description of either of her expeditions. To dispose of the second journey first—that with Alec in the gig—the course is quite impossible to establish, for there neither is nor was a road answering to the story's requirements, and the two genuine place-names included, Melbury Down and Win Green ('Win-green'), are those of features whose positions only add to the difficulties. All we can say with certainty is that the 'crest' on which the vehicle from 'Trantridge' was to await Tess 'to save the horse the labour of the last slope' was the upper Shaftesbury–Blandford road, that the 'last slope' was probably the one-in-six ascent from Font-mell Magna, and that the description of the first of the hills down which Alec let the gig career exactly fits the western half of the lane to Ashmore from the 'crest' opposite Fontmell Magna. Here indeed is the 'long, straight descent of nearly a mile' between 'two banks dividing like a splitting stick'. They are hillsides rather than banks, today impressively clothed with forest. But once past this descent all close correlation between Alec's route and reality disappears.

On her first journey to 'The Slopes' Tess had travelled by carrier, alighting at 'Trantridge Cross' and walking uphill toward the house, which lay on the edge of Cranborne Chase ('The Chase'). On the obvious road to Pentridge, now the B3081, the crossroads would have to be where this route intersects the A354 at Handley Hill; but except for a stretch of a few dozen yards to the south-east, every direction from the intersection leads downhill, and the entire area is already deep inside Cranborne Chase.

The truth is, the topographical descriptions in *Tess* are in the main so faithful to reality that one is liable to forget that a few owe less to the landscape than to Hardy's fantasy.

As for the picture today, the whole stretch of country belongs to a quiet agricultural region in which change has been minimal in the villages, rather more in the countryside thanks largely to the efforts of one man, Rolf Gardiner. His work belongs properly to another section (see page 177): suffice it to note here that a considerable part of the reafforestation for which he has been responsible covers the heights between vale and chase.

Tarrant Hinton lies just outside Blandford's commercial expansion, and just clear of Blandford Camp. The Crown remains a small and unpretentious inn, probably little different in aspect from that which—if my identification is correct—greeted Mr Crookhill and his new friend. The by-road along which each in turn set out after their sojourn must have been either that leading to Tarrant Launceston and Tarrant Monkton, or some lane that has since disappeared, perhaps obliterated by the army camp.

Despite the nearness of this busy centre, Badbury Rings, an Iron Age fort four miles south-east of Blandford, has become a popular focus for summer Sunday outings, yet remains impressive beside a magnificently preserved length of the Salisbury–Dorchester Roman road. The grove of trees crowning Badbury has, of course, been planted since the time of the beacon fire mentioned in *The Trumpet-Major*.

Blandford ('Shottsford') Forum itself, never used as a direct setting but touched upon in 'The Three Strangers', 'My Cicely', *The Mayor of Casterbridge* and *The Woodlanders*, retains its attractive and homogeneous Georgian centre very much as in Hardy's day. A 'cup of genuine' can now be bought, and you can 'victual your carcase' without excessive expenditure, at quite a number of places, including the Crown Hotel mentioned in *The Woodlanders*.

Eight miles south lies Bere Regis ('Kingsbere'), a somnolent village in spite of a large watercress industry—its somnolence assisted by the diversion of the busy A35 on to a newly constructed bypass. The view from the church-

The meadow before this pair of 'Kingsbere' (Bere Regis) cottages is the site of the 'd'Urbervilles' ('Turbervilles') mansion, and the stones from which most of the right-hand cottage is built come from the mansion itself. In the background is part of 'Greenhill' (Woodbury Hill).

yard described in *Tess* now includes a small council-house estate, and inevitably there are a few new private houses, probably less than counterbalancing the cottages that have disappeared. But the place is habitable; in 1904, according to Harper, most of the dwellings were 'very ruinous' owing to the refusal of the estate owner to rebuild them.

The mansion of the Turbervilles stood where there is now a rough paddock—still called Court Green—east of the church. The house was demolished as recently as 1832, Wilkinson Sherren saying that one wall was retained and built into a farmhouse. A pair of cottages on the east side of the paddock does in fact incorporate an area of masonry probably consisting of stones from part of the house. The last acknowledged Turbervilles were twin ladies who died in 1780 at Putney.

Hardy's picture of the 'd'Urberville' aisle in the church is fully accurate, the inscription Tess read on the door of the sepulchre being com-

pleted by the date '24 June 1710'. The diminished legibility of the wording here is virtually the only change wrought by the years. In 1870, when the church was restored, the vault was opened and the skeletons were put into new coffins. It must have been at this time too that the musicians' gallery was removed, in which (in *The Return of the Native*) Yeobright senior had sometimes deputised on the clarinet. Outside, the churchyard is as little changed as a century's growth of trees and shrubs permits, and an outcast family could still (until the authorities learned about it) camp under the Turberville window. The wall against which the Durbeyfields' furniture was dumped also survives.

In *Far from the Madding Crowd* Hardy gives the full name of the town as 'Kingsbere-sub-Greenhill', 'Greenhill' being Woodbury Hill which, rising behind Court Green, was the scene of Woodbury Fair. Here Troy was discovered playing Dick Turpin in the circus. Hardy claimed that the hilltop, which is ringed by a double earthwork, enclosed twenty or thirty acres, the fair occupying the whole of it; in reality it embraces no more than ten acres, of which the fair proper covered no more than four. The sheep fair was held on the tableland outside the earthwork. For comparison, the permanent ground of the Bath & West Show at Shepton Mallet covers 130 acres, exclusive of car-parks. The fairground was not devoid of houses, nor is it now, although they are fewer than the 'sixteen or seventeen' reported by Harper. Near the centre stands the old-fashioned farmhouse. The approaches remain much as Hardy knew them.

We now come to his settings for the main action of *Two on a Tower*. That the mansion on which 'Welland House' was based is Charborough cannot be challenged, for when the

artist Macbeth Raeburn was commissioned, under Hardy's supervision, to devise a frontispiece for the novel embodying a real locality used in it, he sketched the house and tower at Charborough. Yet Windle and Harper both identified 'Welland House' with the remnant of the manor house (the greater part had been demolished in 1802) at Milborne St Andrew ('Millpond St Jude' in *The Madding Crowd*). The explanation lies with the tower of the title. Hardy wrote to Harper that this had 'two or three originals—Horton, Charborough, etc. The 'etc' is the column close to Milborne, standing on an anciently-fortified hill called Weatherby Castle or Ring's-Hill Speer; this is not open to doubt, because Hardy uses the latter name in the narrative. (As 'Weatherbury' Castle, the hill is also mentioned in 'My Cicely'.)

Just how much, in his amalgam of these prototypes, can be identified in the real aspects of Charborough and Ring's-Hill Speer? The *archi-*

This enormous obelisk erected in 1761 on 'Ring's-Hill Speer' (Weatherby Castle), within the ramparts of an Iron Age hill-fort, marks the *site* of the tower in *Two on a Tower*. Notwithstanding a village less than a mile away, and plentiful sounds of birds and cattle, the place seems wrapped in perpetual solitude, and when the trees spread their summer canopy the great monument looms eerily through the semi-darkness.

tecture of the Charborough tower, though certainly not Tuscan—it has been described as Strawberry-Hill Gothic—closely resembles the fictional portrait, except that the windows, which Hardy calls slits, are actually quatrefoil. The lichen-covered tablet is not on the door, but inside, and with the lichen now cleared away the 'letters or words' are revealed as a record of the heightening of the tower in 1839. It has recently been repaired.

The *setting* of the fictional tower follows equally closely that of the monument on Ring's-Hill Speer, except that hardwoods have succeeded most of the conifers clothing the hill and are now so tall that not even the copper ball crowning the column is visible from the surrounding meadows. Today this monument of brick, stone-dressed, square in cross-section and solid, is so dilapidated that only the creeper covering one side appears to be holding it up. The fields are grassed at present, and the

landscape in which they lie is indeed 'gently concave' (round Charborough it is flat). Sometimes Hardy refers, incorrectly, to a single enveloping field of fifty acres, but near the opening of the book Viviette halts her carriage on the 'old Melchester road' and asks to be driven to the tower across what her coachman calls Twenty-Five Acres, the true name of the field to the south-east of the Speer. The 'old Melchester road' is therefore probably a resuscitation of Hardy's favourite Roman thoroughfare that ran between Salisbury ('Melchester') and

The 'narrow lane' along which Viviette returned with her dog after visiting 'Little Welland'. The latter seems to have been imagined as occupying the site of Roger's Hill Farm, here out of sight at the far end of the track. The stream – further away than Hardy implies – flows alongside the low hedge seen to the right of the cottages that have replaced the 'half-buried' originals. The older hedge followed the line of isolated bushes and wooden posts in the middle distance.

Dorchester, since this passes just south of Twenty-Five Acres.

The status of the church as the lone survivor of a demolished village is taken from Charborough. Its surroundings, however, although corresponding superficially with Charborough, have been shown by Beatty to contain several features, such as the wall separating graveyard and house lawn, clearly borrowed from Stinsford. The fabric itself, including the tower, is probably modelled on that of Milborne St Andrew, the *only* church in the area that is 'many-chevroned' (rich in dog-tooth ornament). How many other features Hardy took from here is unascertainable, for the building was drastically restored by Street in 1878—midway through the story—and no account exists of its previous design or furnishings.

Except to remark on its 'long, low front'—Charborough again, before the addition of a later wing—Hardy does not describe 'Welland House', and apart from the position of its church his details of the grounds are wholly imaginary. This is not surprising, seeing that he never entered the gates until the last months of his life. Today Charborough Park and house are immaculate, a stately home in the truest sense.

'Little Welland', the village in which Swithin lived with his grandmother, Mrs Martin, is generally regarded as fictitious, in spite of identification by Lea with Winterborne Zelstone, west of Charborough. There are, however, grounds for believing that Hardy had a real situation in mind, though not a real house (unless it was one he had seen elsewhere). The scattered epithets add up to a picture of a 'little dell', a green and 'bosky' basin, 'Welland Bottom' by name, at the end of the parish remote from the church. Walking to it from Ring's-Hill Speer, Swithin comes upon his home 'quite

unexpectedly on the other side of the field-fence'; and on another occasion Viviette after visiting him returns to her mansion 'along a narrow lane divided from the river by a hedge', a lane later referred to as 'flanked by half-buried cottages'.

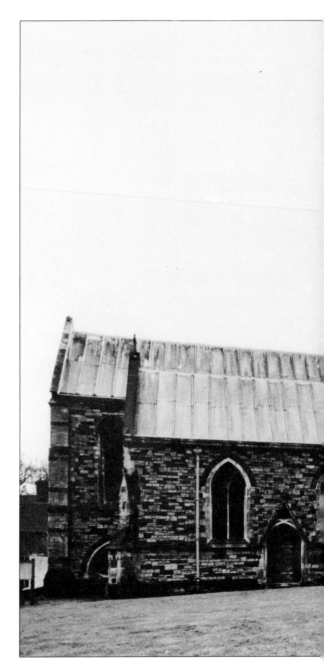

Hardy strongly objected to the practice, unfortunately by no means obsolete today, of uprooting churchyard tombstones and arranging them round the walls or, worse, turning them into flagstones. He expressed his feelings, with considerable humour, in the poem 'The Levelled Churchyard', which refers specifically, if not by name, to the graveyard of Wimborne Minster, seen here.

74

Perhaps all these details are invented, but it is striking how many of them fit Roger's Hill Farm, one mile south-east of the Speer. It stands at the extreme edge of the parish. The lane leading to it from the north is narrow, and separated from the Milborne or Mill Bourne (a true 'rippling stream') by a hedge that is now close to the road, but used to be equidistant between road and river. As the farm is approached, the river basin, called Ashley Bottom, drops lower, so that when one reaches two pairs of cottages midway down the slope from the lane they do appear half-buried, and by the end of the route the farmhouse is low enough to present itself 'quite unexpectedly' and to give the impression of being in a dell, although really on a hillside.

Roger's Hill farmhouse itself bears no resemblance to Mrs Martin's abode, but it is noticeable that although Hardy's normal epithet for this is a cottage, he once (as if by mistake) calls it 'the farmhouse'. The present 'half-buried' cottages were erected by Sir Ernest Debenham between the two world wars, but they replace a cob-and-thatch pair set still lower on the slope. It is true that the lane leads from Roger's Hill in the opposite direction to Charborough, but at more than one point in his novel Hardy appears to treat 'Welland House' as if it stood in the position of the Milborne manor, as when Swithin and Viviette leave the Speer for their homes 'in opposite directions'. This accords with her use of the lane after calling on him. The 'old turnpike road' linking 'Welland' with the station at Wimborne Minster ('Warborne') mostly followed the line of the present A31, but east of Charborough's Stag Gate it coincided with the now unclassified lane through Sturminster Marshall and Pamphill. Hardy rightly depicts the public highway as at one time running through the park, though it never passed close to the house. It was re-routed outside the park in 1844.

Roger's Hill lies in the heart of the area taken in hand by Sir Ernest Debenham. Dairy and other buildings erected under his aegis are distributed on either side of Milborne St Andrew—a dreary and graceless village, unhelped by lines of dull new cottages in sad contrast to the Debenham designs.

East of Charborough one quickly comes to the fringe of the Bournemouth–Poole subtopia. On the border is Corfe Mullen, 'Elm-Cranlynch' in 'The First Countess of Wessex'. Here in the manor, now Court House, lived Stephen Reynard's rival Charles Phelipson. In real life he was Charles Phelips, the manor being held by a branch of the Phelips family of Montacute

('Montislope', see page 200). Some third of the Elizabethan mansion is now standing: stone-built, mellow, with very tall chimneys.

Almost adjoining Corfe Mullen to the south-east, on the now defunct railway link between Hamworthy and Wimborne, stand the remains of Broadstone station, originally called Poole Junction. This was the junction, twice alluded to in *The Hand of Ethelberta* when Sol Chickerel and the Honourable Edgar Mountclere were trying to get back to Swanage, at which the Bourne-mouth spur left the main line. When the novel was published (1876) the spur was barely two

Still dignified and relatively secluded amid the vast extension of Poole's suburbia round Corfe Mullen is this surviving fragment of early seventeenth-century 'Elm-Cranlynch' Manor, now Court House, home of Charles Phelipson in 'The First Countess of Wessex'.

years old. Today the crumbling station is un-officially used as a dump for heavy rubbish.

North-east of Corfe Mullen, across the Stour, stands Farrs House, the original of 'Yewsholt Lodge' in 'Barbara of the House of Grebe'. At first sight the house in its trim whiteness looks later than eighteenth-century; but inside there is no mistaking the 'central hall with a wooden gallery running round it'. After a grim occupation by the military during the Second World War, and by squatters afterwards, Farrs has been fully and imaginatively restored, and is now a small mansion of great and unusual beauty. Hardy nevertheless exaggerated the smallness: the rooms are much larger than 'closets'. In the wooded grounds outside there are still many song-birds.

Wimborne Minster retains a nucleus of old-world lanes and houses, but has undergone much expansion. Hardy and Emma lived here for a short time, and there is a note of his that he wandered into the minster one evening in 1875 and sat down to listen, an audience of one, to the organist practising. The organ as it then was remained unaltered until 1965, when the pipes were modified by adding to each a brass tube, like a trumpet, projecting at right angles near the top. Recitals are occasionally broadcast. The building has changed little. Hardy brought it into the poems 'Copying Architecture in an Old Minster' and 'The Levelled Churchyard', which does not identify Wimborne but is known to be

West of 'Warborne' (Wimborne Minster), 'Yewsholt Lodge' (Farrs House) has been fully restored to a condition in which Edmond and Barbara would have recognized it in 'Barbara of the House of Grebe'.

about it. The 'jack-o'-clock' of the former poem continues very much in evidence.

In Hardy's prose works the town is alluded to here and there, but the only specific features named, the railway station and Grammar School, appear in *Two on a Tower* (which was written here). Today Wimborne has joined the long list of abandoned stations, and passengers must use Poole, six miles away. The Grammar School, where Swithin was educated, was until 1849 a stone building with mullioned windows and a dormered shingle roof. It was then poorly reconstructed in red brick, and enlarged in the 1930s and again in 1954. If we take the eclipse of 1881 as dating the action, Swithin attended the old school after its reconstruction. (The railway situation rules out Weber's earlier dates.)

'The Pedestrian' was said by Hardy himself to have been composed with Colehill in mind, now an elegant but dismayingly huge north-eastern suburb of Wimborne in which the sufferer in the poem could now undertake his nightly ten-mile walk entirely under street-lamps.

Canford Park, containing Canford ('Chene') Manor, parental home of Barbara Grebe (really Webb), is so far still in rural surroundings. But only a little is left of the mansion of those days; demolitions were followed by new building in three different decades of the nineteenth century, until in 1923 the pile became a public school. The so-called John o' Gaunt's Kitchen, mentioned in 'Barbara', with its two tremendous hearths and tower-like chimneys, has become a library classroom; beside it is a further fragment of the house that Barbara would have known. An engraving of 1786 shows the old kitchen looking very much as it does today.

'Barbara' also mentions Horton ('Lornton') Inn, where the modern B3078 from Wimborne to Cranborne and beyond intersects the road from Woodley Down to Ringwood ('Ooze-wood'). The 'solitary wayside tavern' is solitary still, but a far cry from the 'rendezvous of many a daring poacher', having been smartened up as a luxury port of call for the motorist. The building has been doubled in size by the addition of a wing at right angles to the eighteenth-century original, which has virtually disappeared from view beneath elegant modern embellishments.

A few miles to the north-east stands Wimborne St Giles House, the prototype (again in 'Barbara') of 'Knollingwood Hall'. Inside, the seventeenth-century building has hardly been altered since it was refurnished in 1750—shortly before the period of the story. The gallery to which Barbara took Edmond's statue extends round a lofty but smallish oak-panelled room hung with portraits, and is bounded by a decorative white iron balustrade. Unhappily the whole mansion is currently in a state of extreme disrepair.

Between Horton village and Horton Heath is Horton Wood, presumably the 'Lornton Copse' mentioned in *Two on a Tower*. On Horton Heath the Ordnance Survey map marks Monmouth's Ash, supposedly the spot where, after the battle of Sedgemoor, the miserable Duke of Monmouth was found hiding in a ditch beside a young ash tree. Betrayed, according to one story, by an old hag, in another version he owed his capture to a young housewife, as in Hardy's poem 'At Shag's Heath'—a local name for the part of Horton Heath where Monmouth was found.

Pace the map, there is now no ash tree at the site marked. The original lived its allotted span and died, its bark, Treves tells us, scored with many initials. Harper says it was finally blown down, and that a new tree grew from the same root. Certainly a new tree did grow, which Treves in 1906 estimated to be between fifty and sixty years old. It should therefore still be in its prime, but according to Harper it was already propped up in 1904, and although it still existed in 1965, today only a plaque marks the spot. The 'Justice Ettricke' of the Monmouth poem was quartered at Holt Lodge (now Holt Lodge Farm) near God's Blessing Green. Perhaps the Duke would have fared better had he hidden at this last.

Close to Holt is West Moors, site of the unnamed 'next station' to Wimborne on the way

'Chaseborough' (Cranborne) was the little town in which the young Tess and her friends used to atone for the monotony of the working week by living it up on Saturday nights. Today the 'Flower-de-Luce' (Fleur de Lys) Inn is quiet enough, and indeed the whole town wears a perpetual air of Sunday afternoon.

to 'the junction' in *Two on a Tower*. West Moors station (itself a junction for nearly a century) and both the lines it served have been lost to passengers since 1964, although the one-time hamlet is now part of the string of horticultural and dormitory centres that have spread north from Bournemouth. A freight line still connects with Poole.

The last few places I have mentioned have all been in the borderlands between Cranborne Chase and the New Forest ('The Great Forest'). The finest Hardy picture of Cranborne Chase occurs towards the end of *Two on a Tower*, when Viviette's brother Louis takes the train from Wimborne to Salisbury. It is also a very fair description of the Chase today, although the balance is gradually shifting from woods— forest fragments—to more profitable agricultural land. Wholly vanished during the past few decades are the cider orchards that used to be attached to many Chase farms. Yet this remains a quiet and empty area: in the surviving woodlands huge, aged yews and mistletoe-bearing oaks continue to grow, their numbers diminishing, but their tough resistance promising many years of life yet.

At Cranborne ('Chaseborough') the Fleur de Lys tavern ('Flower-de-Luce' in *Tess*) carries on, the décor of its single bar so little altered that one could fancy the Trantridge folk had left it the previous evening. No one could call it smart, but it would be surprising if any 'maids' today failed to find it respectable.

The road between Salisbury and Poole via Wimborne, 'one of the finest examples of a macadamised turnpike-track that can be found in England' ('Barbara of the House of Grebe'), ran from the Salisbury–Blandford turnpike (A354) at the top of Coombe Bissett Hill along the present unclassified road to Rockbourne as far as the bend at the Hampshire border, then straight along what is today a superior farm track over Toyd Down to the Martin– Cranborne lane at Tidpit. It followed this lane to Cranborne, then the modern B3078 to Wimborne, and finally entered Poole down the line of today's A349 via Fleet Corner. Constructed in 1755, the road cannot have been macadamized from the outset, because Macadam's essay setting forth his system was not published until 1819. But it was among the first macadamized roads in Wessex.

6 SOUTH WESSEX
EGDON HEATH TO MID-WESSEX
Dorset: the heath to Wiltshire

I had slowed along
After the torrid hours were done,
Though still the posts and walls and road
Flung back their sense of the hot-faced sun,
And had walked by Stourside Mill, where broad
Stream-lilies throng.

THE MUSICAL BOX

Not far north of Milborne St Andrew stands Milton Abbas, the 'Middleton Abbey' of *The Woodlanders* and the home of Joseph Damer, 1st Earl of Dorchester, whose evil conduct is recorded in 'The Doctor's Legend'. He built the celebrated model village and the mansion, planted the woods that grace the surrounding hills, and calmly destroyed the entire market-town of Milton Abbas because he found it an eyesore. This type of conduct was by no means unique, but more than two centuries later resentment at it still lingers, as it does against similar high-handedness on other estates. The new cottages, moreover, were grossly over-crowded, and remained so until long after the period when Mrs Charmond must have seen them. Like the village, the mansion, grounds, and abbey church have undergone very little change since her day, and almost the only additions have been the open-air swimming-bath and playing-field appurtenances incidental to their current function as a boys' school (scene of the TV serial *To Serve Them All My Days*).

The woods are the 'Milton Woods' of 'The Revisitation'. They are quite unspoilt, and north of them the chalky uplands extend similarly undisturbed to Turnworth, the original of Mrs Charmond's seat, 'Hintock House'. Although Windle had already made this identification,

complete with full-page sketch by New, Lea for some reason was mystified by 'Hintock House'; but many years later Hardy corroborated Windle's identification by accompanying Donald Maxwell, the artist, over to Turnworth to make a watercolour of the Charmond residence.

In *The Woodlanders* the position of the house is 'moved' many miles further west, but its setting 'in a hole' is the setting of Turnworth. The description of the building, to judge from New's drawing, which is clearer than Maxwell's watercolour, is also strictly accurate. The illustrations and Hardy's description suggest a fine Elizabethan manor, but in reality Turnworth House was a nineteenth-century pastiche, and jerry-built at that. It was erected by William Parry-Okeden, who became High Sheriff of Dorset in 1849. Between the two world wars it was acquired by a young and energetic owner who spent £10,000 on trying to make it sound, only to be killed in the Second World War before he could learn that all his money and enthusiasm had been wasted; for experts called in by his successor pronounced the building beyond salvation. Behind a thin stone facing the construction was of brick, held together by steel ties most of which had rusted through. Pieces of masonry kept falling off like autumn leaves. The only sound wood in the place was the oak staircase and panelling put in by the late restorer.

So the mansion was pulled down, and on the site was built a low, rambling house of timber, more Alpine than English, yet not inappropriate to its environment. Some stables survive from the former establishment, also a walled garden, a lawn, and the original drive. The 'dense plantation' still grows on the steep slope at the back, and in front the equally steep slope on which Grace Melbury stood remains 'richly grassed, with only an old tree here and there'. One younger tree is also there, planted by the would-be saviour of the mansion in memory of a favourite horse. It may be thought of today as a memorial to himself and his high hopes.

Three miles away across the Stour rises Hambledon Hill, which entered Tess's thoughts during her journey home from 'Flintcomb-Ash', and where Hardy, according to *The Life*, was once lost in a fog. The high triple ramparts of the twenty-five acre Iron Age fortress surmounting the hill are undamaged, and to stand amid them on a misty day makes Hardy's experience indeed credible. In clear weather there are extensive views to north and west over the Vale of Blackmoor or Blackmore (the 'Vale of Little Dairies') also called more rarely the Vale of the White Hart. The same panorama, but looking southward, is to be had from the 'level terrace where the Abbey gardens once had spread' at Shaftesbury ('Shaston'). The terrace, asphalted since Jude walked there while waiting for Sue, remains a deservedly popular resort. Behind it the few remnants of the abbey in their mellow garden enjoyed a moment of late glory in 1931, when the bones of the tenth-century king, Edward the Martyr, which had 'vanished into oblivion' at the Dissolution, were re-discovered.

The 'extensive stone-built schools' operated until a few years ago, but now the largest building has become an auction room, and beside it stands a big, very new and very alien-looking residential block, south of which are various other fragments of the schools. Across the street (Bimport) from the auction room one of the 'two enormous beech trees' continues to flourish, its feet in a small car-park. A little farther along Bimport is 'Old-Grove's Place' where Sue and her husband, Phillotson, lived. Curiously built with its floors lower than the outside ground on all sides, it has been modernized in a manner that must, to say the least, surprise Hardy addicts. The 'wainscotting of panelled oak reaching from floor to ceiling' of the front parlour has been painted white, the 'dismalness' of the room in which the Phillotsons breakfasted and were nodded to by passers-by has been alleviated by covering the whole of

Often photographed and often sketched, 'Old Grove's Place' (the Ox House), 'Shaston', in which Sue and Richard Phillotson lived, appears unaltered, yet has lost the big dormer formerly to the left of the projecting section, and this itself has acquired a gable-end where its roof was originally hipped.

A bird's-eye view of Milton Abbas, the (unnamed) 'model' village in 'The Doctor's Legend' built in 1780 by the 1st Earl of Dorchester (also unnamed) to replace the small market town he had ordered to be demolished because it lay too near his home.

one wall with mirror, and the staircase, which originally rose from the front of the house towards the back, has now been reversed, causing the disappearance of the cupboard in which Sue slept on one occasion. I should add that none of this is the work of the present incumbent!

Upstairs, the bedroom with the forty-mile view across the vale 'even into Outer Wessex' (Somerset) is the principal room at the back of the house. From its window, according to Hardy, Sue took her panic leap. Yet it is 'on the gravel' at the *front* of the house that he makes her land, close to the 'heavy door' specifically named as the 'front door'. To compound the confusion, the mullions of the back-room window are too close-set for even Sue's slender form to have passed between them.

Hardy's odd name for the house stems from its occupancy, long ago, by one Grove; the owner responsible for the alterations also restored the proper name, The Ox House. He had the upper storey of the projecting porch rendered and painted white; his successor has changed it to grey-green. The rest of the exterior remains in its natural stone. The porch roof is now gabled, not hipped, and the large dormer seen in early photographs was removed many years ago.

Farther along Bimport there is a sharp turn to the left and the name changes to St John's Street, very steep and narrow. Here, above the high bank to the right, is the burial-ground of the church of St John, Hardy's 'chief graveyard [that] slopes up as steeply as a roof' (*Jude*). The graveyard is itself level, but the ground on either side fulfils his description. Today it is a place of weeds, nettles and unkempt trees, with a few headstones here and there, some with still-legible inscriptions. Two modern benches, however, invite the public to enter and tarry.

Toward the centre of the town, the other 'venerable graveyard'—that of Trinity church—where Jude walked after he had missed the bus to the station, remains trim enough, its paths still bordered by 'avenues of limes'. But the church itself, secularized a decade or so ago, now accommodates the WRVS, a health organization, and various other bodies. Close by, the tiny former market-place (the new market is on the edge of the town) affords space for one to appreciate the handsome eighteenth-century façade of the Grosvenor Arms, the 'Duke's Arms' of *Jude*. The station referred to in the novel is Semley, two miles to the north: closed now, leaving Shaftesbury travellers with a choice between Tisbury and Gillingham. Ironically, it is toward Semley that Shaftesbury

'Shaston' (Shaftesbury), spectacularly perched on its high ridge, plays a large role in *Jude the Obscure*. This is a view from Park Walk, the terrace along the southern edge of the promontory, showing the lower town round St James's Church. Beyond lie 'Marlott' (Marnhull) and the southern half of the 'Vale of Little Dairies' (Blackmoor or Blackmore Vale, or the Vale of the White Hart).

(having no more building-room at the top of the hill) has mostly spread. Except for some new shop fronts, there is not much recent construction in the rather dull streets at the summit.

When Phillotson felt the need to consult his friend Gillingham he walked from Shaftesbury to the town of Gillingham ('Leddenton'), 'leaving Duncliffe Hill on his left'. This is a solitary conical hill in the Stour plain, partly encircled by woods and faintly forbidding. Gillingham is described as 'a little town of three or four thousand inhabitants'. In the intervening century it has grown, but not dramatically: its 1981 population was 5440. The boys' school of the novel (red-brick Victorian) is now a primary school.

Five miles south lies Tess's home at Marnhull ('Marlott'), a 'long and broken village' widely scattered about a network of lanes. Among the inevitable crop of claimants to be the Durbey-field cottage (which Lea declared 'swept away') all but one can be dismissed out of hand. This building stands at the head of a narrow, bent cul-de-sac ('a crooked lane or street') off the west side of the B3092, a little north of Walton Elm Cross. During the 1920s Barton Cottage, as it was then called, was owned by a Major Campbell-Johnston, who lived one field away by the old Marnhull Brewery in Carraway Lane. A path still connects Carraway Lane with the head of the cottage lane, thus justifying Hardy's references to people *passing* the cottage (although in including Alec on horseback he appears to have ignored the stiles).

Though unnamed by Hardy, the 'chief graveyard' in 'Shaston' alluded to in *Jude the Obscure* is easily identified with St John's churchyard seen here. The church itself vanished long ago, but its graveyard, lately adorned with one or two public benches, has become a kind of small, unkempt park.

The major employed a factotum named Blake, who on a day in 1924 was tending the garden of Barton Cottage with his assistant when they saw an elderly figure scrutinizing the house. On Blake asking if he could be of service the stranger replied, 'No, thank you, I was only seeing where I put my Tess'. It has been said that Hardy was much too reticent to have been so forthcoming. But he had been caught in a situation that he may well have felt demanded an explanation. Whether this answer meant anything to Blake is not known, but evidently Hardy amplified it, for Blake ended by asking if he would care to meet Major Campbell-Johnston. The major was away at the time, as he often was, but according to Blake's account the meeting did take place—one imagines, in view of Hardy's age, at Max Gate. Shortly afterwards the deeds of the property were altered, and the name was changed to Tess Cottage.

Such is the version of the story given to me by the Blakes' nephew and virtually adopted son, Mr Ernest Allen, who heard it several times from Blake himself. The account differs only slightly from that given to the present occupants of the cottage by Mrs Blake shortly before her death in 1965 (Blake died in the 1930s). But corroboration is elusive. Neither Hardy nor Campbell-Johnston left any known letter or diary entry referring to a meeting between them. The major's son and daughter, though adults at the time, heard nothing of the matter then or later, but admit they spent long periods away from Marnhull; that their abnormally reticent father was fully capable of considering an encounter with Hardy none of their business; and that their infrequent appearances at home might explain their not hearing of the incident from the Blakes. Professor Geoffrey Cheshire, who with his wife and two sons lived in Tess Cottage for some years, during which he became the major's friend, never heard from him that he had met Hardy, but did hear repeatedly that the cottage was where Hardy had placed Tess. The professor adds that Campbell-Johnston was by no means a literary man, and would have been most unlikely to have linked his property with anything in a book unless he had strong reason. All these informants, together with Group-Captain

Tess Cottage, 'Marlott'. Was this or was it not where Hardy imagined the Durbeyfields' home? Strong opinions flourish both for and against. See the full account in Chapter Six.

Leonard Cheshire and his brother, testify that the Blakes were an honest, conscientious, and solid couple incapable of inventing or even embroidering their story. It is worth noting that, if Hardy left no record of the episode, *Tess* was certainly in his mind in 1924, for his notes witness that he attended several rehearsals of a new dramatic production of the story that year at Dorchester.

The cottage itself neither invalidates the claims made for it nor tallies with Hardy's snippets of description closely enough to clinch the matter. At the period of the novel it was divided into two, a fact—if our identification is correct—discarded by Hardy. No one recalls a stable, such as Durbeyfield had for Prince, but where the garage has been built there were outbuildings and pigsties. Apart from the conversion into a single dwelling and the necessary practical improvements, Tess Cottage is substantially as it was in the late nineteenth century, and the great amount of recent building that has changed much of Marnhull has not yet affected the immediate neighbourhood. Just beyond the garage stands an agreeable single-storey wooden structure with large windows, built as a place of recreation for the two Cheshire boys.

How does the position of the cottage and its lane, in relation to the rest of 'Marlott' fit the novel? Ever since Windle gave a lead it has been assumed that Hardy visualized the 'club-walk' dance in the meadow between the Crown Inn ('The Pure Drop') and the crossroads. The walkers 'came round by the Pure Drop Inn, and were turning out of the high road to pass

church
The Crown
To Shaftesbury
via Todber
rectory
Church Farm

------- footpaths
------- field boundaries
(approx)

malthouse

Marnhull
Brewery
brewery

home (later)
of Major
Campbell-
Johnston

LARRAWAY LANE

Barton (Tess)
Cottage

WALTON ELM HILL

"Furlong" Field (suggested
as site of club walking dance)

WHITEWAY HILL

EASTWELL LANE

To Shaftsbury
via Margaret Marsh

The Lamb
Walton Elm House

To Sturminster Newton

through a wicket-gate into the meadows' when old Durbeyfield was observed driving past in a carriage from the direction of Shaftesbury. However, the dance meadow must have been still a fair distance off, for when the girls teased Tess about her father she 'threatened to walk no further with them', but later 'moved on with the whole body to the enclosure where there was to be dancing on the green', and 'by the time the spot was reached' had recovered her equanimity. All this hardly suggests that they were going to

Central and southern Marnhull ('Marlott') in the Durbeyfields' time.

dance in the meadow they had already reached when she became upset.

Let us suppose that 'coming round by the inn' means that they came *down* to the crossroads by the 'Pure Drop', turned *toward* Shaftesbury, and entered the meadows of Church Farm, where until recently a gate gave admittance to a network of public footpaths extending to East-

87

If the Durbeyfields' cottage was in the south of 'Marlott', Hardy probably took the site of the Lamb Inn, now handsome Old Lamb House, for that of the off-licence 'Rolliver's'. True, the Lamb had a full licence, but it fitted Hardy's description of 'Rolliver's' as the only liquor-purveyor at its end of the village.

well Lane, the eastern arm of the Walton Elm crossroads. Under this re-routing the procession would still have met old Durbeyfield.

But the Clare brothers, walking from Shaftesbury to 'Stourcastle' (Sturminster Newton), also passed through 'Marlott' while the dancing was in progress. After the elder pair had gone on, Angel ran down the lane *westward*, 'passed the hollow and mounted the next rise', and looked back for a final glimpse of the dancers. If the brothers had come into Marnhull by the road John Durbeyfield had just driven along and the dancers had been in Crown Meadow, the Clares' route to Sturminster would have lain south at

the crossroads; and if despite this Angel had run west, the church would have cut off his view of the revels almost at once. But suppose the Clares had approached Marnhull through Margaret Marsh and Eastwell Lane, and the clubwalkers had been dancing in one of the meadows beside the lane, Angel would have had to continue westward as far as Walton Elm Cross before turning south. True, the intervening hollow now becomes a piece of author's licence, but a more probable one than a false compass-direction. Again, if Tess's home was in Tess Cottage, the placing of the dance-meadow by Eastwell Lane eliminates the problem of how she could have passed within sight of it during her subsequent return from 'Flintcomb-Ash' through Hazelbury Bryan ('Nuttlebury').

Like Durbeyfield's home, the cottage is at one end of the village, and at the right end for Tess's backward glance 'at Marlott *and her father's house*' [my italics] when setting out for Sturminster on her way to 'Talbothays'. At the same end stood 'Rolliver's'. There is no inn or alehouse near by today, but just west of Walton Elm Cross stands Old Lamb House, formerly the Lamb Inn. Despite its full licence, Windle clearly indicates this inn (without naming it) as 'Rolliver's'. Timothy O'Sullivan displays an old photograph of an unidentified alehouse bearing a notice-board that precisely describes the role of 'Rolliver's'. On the other hand the picture shows no palings (though they could be out of sight), whereas the front garden of Old Lamb House is bounded by black iron railings that have only recently replaced just such palings. 'Rolliver's' is described as 'the only alehouse at this end of the long and broken village', and the 'Pure Drop' a little later as being at 'the further part of the dispersed village' from 'Rolliver's'. The Crown is in fact pretty well in the centre of Tess's Marnhull. Lea's and Harper's claimant to be the original of 'Rolliver's', the Blackmoor Vale Inn (now completely and unattractively rebuilt), stands about as far north-west of the Crown as the Lamb stood to the south, and not quite so near its end of the village as the Lamb to the south end; moreover between the Blackmoor Vale and the Crown is a small inn, the Retreat, also dating from before Tess's time. Finally, even if the site of the unknown alehouse in O'Sullivan's book should be traced, it does not follow that Hardy, after his fashion, did not 'lift' the provisions of its notice-board and transfer them to where he wanted them.

In appearance the Crown has not altered much since the 1890s. A gravelled car-park now occupies all Crown Meadow. The church too has altered little, but its neat graveyard shows no trace of the nettle-filled corner once reserved, with true Christian charity, for burying the unbaptized and the ungodly.

South of Marnhull, alongside the old turnpike road to Sturminster, lies Yewstock Farm; a small red-brick cottage flush with the road here used to be the turnpike house in which Tess left her baggage when returning home after the parting with Angel. The 'back lane' by which

she then reached home was probably the track from Hinton St Mary past Cut Mill and Yard-grove Farm.

Sturminster Newton is chiefly associated with the group of poems inspired by the short period, early in their marriage, during which Hardy and Emma enjoyed what he long thought of as 'our happiest time', until he realized too late that his self-absorption had made it far from 'A Two-Years' Idyll' for her. 'Stur', as the locals call it, has had its old-world somnolence considerably jolted in recent years by heavy lorries, though the centre of it still nestles under plenty of the 'thick thatch' mentioned in *Tess*. Thomas and Emma Hardy rented a grey Victorian semi-detached villa, 'Riverside', on the edge of the high town, overlooking the Stour valley. This is the 'dusky house that stood apart', with Emma the lady 'waiting there', in 'The Musical Box'. The house is still rendered in dusky grey, the porch unchanged, the interior modernized with restraint. It is reasonably certain that the Hardys occupied the northern half of the building, and here Thomas wrote *The Return of the Native*. The monkey-puzzle tree he planted in the small garden was removed when it grew too large.

From the windows of this little house one may gaze yet upon the view he delineated in one of his loveliest peoms, 'Overlooking the River Stour'; happily, man has not so far driven away the swallows, the moorhens and the honeybees, nor ripped out the kingcups. In the wide ravine beneath can be seen the iron bridge of 'On Sturminster Foot-Bridge'; and farther down the curving river the 'Stourside Mill' of 'The Musical Box' remains in operation, though with electricity now supplementing water-power. In a little-altered quarter of the high town stands the church, and beside it, also little altered, the churchyard that is the scene of 'The To-be-Forgotten'.

Some two miles south-east of 'Stur' lies Okeford Fitzpaine, the 'Oakford Fitzpiers' pointed out to Grace by her father in *The Woodlanders* as the place where the Fitzpiers family had been lords of the manor for so many

Landscape north of 'Weatherbury'. Hardy, who in his fiction always saw to it that his scenery contributed to the mood of events, would have made the most of these dead trees.

'Little Weatherbury Farm' (Druce Farm), the home of William Boldwood in *Far From the Madding Crowd*.

Bathsheba Everdene's 'Weatherbury Upper Farm' (Waterston Manor), the south front. Hardy's idea of a lady farmer (as distinct from the actual character) was based on a real-life example in Waddon Chase, near Weymouth.

centuries. The village remains handsome and almost unspoilt.

In many ways the great tract of lush clay that is the Vale of Blackmoor has changed less than any region in Dorset except the other great clay vale to the south-west, Marshwood. The fields are small and hedged, and with patience one may still find a building on stone staddles, as one will never do on the coastal downs where the staddle-built granary stood in *The Trumpet-Major*. But alas, no patience will now discover the cider-apple orchards so important in *The Woodlanders*.

Some of the vale lanes once constituted through-routes of some importance. Among them that which runs between Sturminster Newton and Dorchester through Hazelbury Bryan ('Nuttlebury') and Hartfoot ('Stagfoot') Lane—a hamlet, this, not a road, and recently renamed Melcombe Bingham, presumably in order to cause confusion with Bingham's Melcombe nearby—figures more than once in *Tess*. Bingham's Melcombe suggested the name of Parson Tringham in *Tess*, who is said to have been indeed founded on a real vicar of the parish. On her walk home from 'Flintcomb-Ash' Tess 'passed the village inn' at Hazelbury and was greeted by its creaking sign. Lea thinks this was the Antelope, as it may have been; but there were at least three other Hazelbury inns at the time. How, if 'Flintcomb-Ash' is situated in even the most easterly of its possible positions (see page 96 and map on pages 20–21), Tess can have included both Bulbarrow and Hazelbury in what Hardy calls 'the nearest course' to Marnhull, he does not explain.

To the south the long route eventually divides, one branch entering Puddletown, the other joining the Puddletown–Piddlehinton road (B3142) at Druce Farm, William Boldwood's 'Little Weatherbury Farm' in *Far from the Madding Crowd*. The farmhouse is a mellow, antique building, creeper-faced; and the whole farm contrives to look exceptionally prosperous, although its modern additions are almost invisible from the road.

Running NNW from the farm, and forming a cross with the Hartfoot Lane road and the two arms of the B3142, which here makes a turn of ninety degrees, is a track leading up to Druce Higher Barn. The small vale through which it lies, though difficult to reconcile with the account of the pursuit of Bathsheba by Oak and Coggan, is Puddletown or Druce Bottom, the 'Weatherbury Bottom' in which Hardy set the gipsy camp. There are one or two cottages, remnants of a larger number, beside the lane. Halfway up its length the valley forks, and the tree-crowned promontory at the top of the western arm is Dole's Hill Plantation, 'Dole Hill' in the poem 'The Revisitation'.

The true position of Waterston Manor ('Weatherbury [Upper] Farm') is a mile west of where Hardy placed it, which was within half a mile of Puddletown. After being (as in the novel) a rented farm for longer than most lapsed manors, the house and some of the land have reverted to independent ownership; but the long period of subjection explains Hardy's true references to mould, rot, and the ravages of worm. The place was first rebuilt, somewhat inartistically, by the 5th Earl of Ilchester following a severe fire in 1863. Hardy's detailed picture describes the house before the fire. The extent of the damage caused by this fire is the subject of conflicting views. A brochure issued at the manor during the late 1960s (and eventually superseded) describes the house as having been 'almost completely gutted', yet a subsequent owner was emphatic that the degree of damage had been grossly exaggerated. In part the ambiguity arises because shortly before the First World War the gifted architect Morley Horder was commissioned to undo the clumsy handiwork of the 5th Earl, and today the building, more especially the interior, presents so harmonious a synthesis between old and new that it is not everywhere easy to tell which is which.

Certainly the south front, with its tower-like central bow, survived the fire. At the time of the novel the main entrance was still on this side (it is now on the west), and the public road ran close to the house. Hardy's 'fluted pilasters' adorn the

Great Gable, a projecting feature of the east front with a most elaborate design. This too is a seventeenth-century survival and little changed; but the rest of the east front was probably rebuilt, and the house has been extended to the north.

Inside the house (no longer open to the public) the lay-out is unorthodox and extremely attractive; no less so since the alterations made by the present owners. The uneven, worm-eaten boards have gone from the upper floors—destroyed in the fire, no doubt. But although Lea says that *all* the old woodwork was lost, part of the panelling is pre-fire, and, despite some assertions to the contrary, it seems likely that Hardy's great oak staircase, so minutely described, is the one we see today. Its position was shifted slightly during the rebuilding, but the existence of various pieces let in by way of repair, and of replaced balusters, in addition to the general appearance of age, do not suggest a nineteenth-century substitution.

The odd arrangement for the shearing supper, whereby Bathsheba sat in her parlour at one end of a long table, the rest of which extended through an open window so that her staff were outside on the 'grass-plot', must refer to either the south or west front to have caught the rays of the setting sun, but it is difficult to tell which window Hardy had in mind since all are obstructed by stone mullions. The beautiful gardens laid out by Morley Horder are entirely different from their predecessors.

The fern-brake with oaks and beeches in a swamp beside the road, to which Bathsheba wandered after the opening of the coffin, is probably imaginary. The sheep-washing pool however, was not only still in existence, but still in use, until less than a decade ago, but has now been completely demolished. Its meadow had long ceased to be a water-meadow. A similar sheep-wash—technically these are not 'dips'—does still exist, nearer to Druce Farm, but much smothered by vegetation.

The prototype of the great barn in which Sergeant Troy led the alcoholic revels was never at Waterston but at Cerne Abbas, and is dealt with in Chapter 7 (page 99). 'Nest Cottage', to which Gabriel Oak retired, stood on Chine Hill, between Puddletown and Druce Farm; a row of somewhat later cottages (1869) now stands near the site.

7 **SOUTH WESSEX**
CASTERBRIDGE TO OUTER WESSEX
Dorset: Dorchester to Somerset

And are ye one of Hermitage—
Of Hermitage, by Ivel Road,
And do ye know, in Hermitage
A thatch-roofed house where sengreens grow?
And does John Waywood live there still—
He of that name that there abode
When father hurdled on the hill
    Some fifteen years ago?

THE INQUIRY
(from *A Set of Country Songs: At Casterbridge Fair*)

According to Lea, whom on this occasion there is no reason to doubt, the farm in 'The Revisitation' where Agnette lived was Muston Manor Farm, once a Turberville property, about a mile south-east of Piddlehinton. In general the surrounding land is little altered; a bare quarter-mile to the north Piddlehinton Camp, opened in 1938, but vacated by the army after the war, is at present used by the Local Authority to accommodate homeless families. The road that passes between Muston and the camp, B3143, has always been assumed to be that taken by Burthen's van in *A Few Crusted Characters* and by Tony Kytes in the first of the stories. But on attempting to follow these travellers, we find that Tony's experiences do not fit in with this route at all. There is no 'corner where we *drop down* [my italics] to Lower Longpuddle', whether the latter be taken as Puddletown or Piddlehinton. It is impossible to reconcile the three points at which Tony saw the three girls. In another of the stories the coffin bearing Jack Winter is heard approaching along the turnpike road, which the B3143 was not.

There is, however, another route from Dorchester to Piddlehinton, somewhat unlikely though not much longer, which deserves notice because it unexpectedly solves nearly all the problems raised by the B3143. We know that Burthen set out from the White Hart and crossed Grey's Bridge. Since he certainly did not go to 'Upper Longpuddle' through Puddletown he must have turned into the B3143. But suppose about a quarter of a mile along it he again turned left, into the lane leading back west to Charminster. From here he could have proceeded along the upper Sherborne road and turned right beyond Charlton Higher Down towards Piddlehinton. This route would have furnished (1) a turnpike road, (2) a climb (mentioned by one of the storytellers), (3) the corner and 'drop down' to 'Lower Longpuddle'. Tony's horse overset the waggon by taking the corner too fast, causing the *offside* wheels to mount the bank. This suggests a right turn, which the corner here is, whereas the corner in the B3143 is to the left.

In the *Crusted Characters* tales Puddletown is referred to unmistakably only once, and then as 'Weatherbury'. All the odds therefore seem against its still being 'Lower Longpuddle' when these stories were written. Hardy gives a list of the names in the fictional churchyard, but they are not names in the registers of any of the real churches.

If Plush is the model for 'Flintcomb-Ash' village, then this can hardly fail to be the cottage 'whose gable jutted into the road' where Tess leaned against the wall to protect herself from the rain and felt the warmth from the hearth just inside – as it is here.

The most likely prototype of 'Flintcomb-Ash' village, in *Tess*, is Plush, seen here. In the background the slopes of Church Hill are similarly the most likely situation of the purely imaginary 'Flintcomb-Ash' Farm.

'The inn' (where the carrier's journey ended) is used as if there were no other, although there were several inns in each of the three villages. The 'Tinkers' Arms' named in 'Absentmindedness in a Parish Choir' is fictitious, but we do know that the church in which Hardy set his richly comic episode is that of Piddletrenthide (gallery removed about 1850), for its identity is made unequivocally clear in the passages linking the three Satchel stories. Furthermore, Piddlehinton church had no gallery, and at Puddletown the 'quire', unlike its absent-minded counterpart, contained no violins. 'Longpuddle Spring' is identifiable as the spring that feeds Morning Well, a natural beauty-spot north-west of Piddletrenthide church (now a new residential area). The manor house at which old Andrey Satchel tried to make believe he was a fiddler is that of Piddletrenthide, a comely eighteenth-century house flanked by beeches. There are some new houses in the twin villages, but even the coming of the camp produced no major expansion.

The short poem 'The Sexton at Longpuddle' refers to Piddletrenthide or Piddlehinton, and the Piddle ('Pydel') valley, somewhere along its length (Piddlehinton, according to Lea), is the setting of another poem, 'A Sunday Morning Tragedy'.

Within the parish of Alton Pancras lies the most likely site of another much-disputed place, 'Flintcomb-Ash'—in the earliest version of *Tess* significantly called 'Alton Ash'. The poem 'We Fieldwomen' is also set there. Lea considers 'Flintcomb-Ash' to be unidentifiable; Windle and Harper equate it with Dole's Ash Farm, ENE of Piddletrenthide; 'Holland' says it is near Nettlecomb Tout, two miles NNE of Dole's Ash; Pinion positions it north-east of Alton Pancras and south of Church Hill; J. Stevens Cox, who normally echoes Lea, places it very precisely on the site of the Iron Age village 'on Barcombe Down'. The village site is in fact on the south slope of Church Hill—thus tallying with Pinion's version—Barcombe being the next down to westward.

The conduct of affairs at 'Flintcomb-Ash' was unpleasant enough to bring it under Hardy's rule of avoiding real (or at least identifiable) houses for such events. On this ground alone it therefore seems unlikely that Dole's Ash Farm is the prototype; and a further objection is that Dole's Ash is too far south for the route Tess took to walk to Beaminster. But from Church Hill—on which there is no real farmstead—a bridleway runs almost directly westward to Little Minterne Hill, then along this to Dogbury Gate where one picks up the Beaminster route as given by Hardy.

In their endeavour to locate the farm, most writers have forgotten that 'Flintcomb-Ash' is also a village. Only Harper mentions Plush—somewhat oddly he says that Dole's Ash Farm is there—yet Plush, less than a mile from the Church Hill camp, conforms with all Hardy's few clues. It lies in a depression; during the nineteenth century it was small and poor enough for the novelist, bent on giving the worst impression, to call it the 'remains' of a village; at the period of the novel it was mainly owned by one absentee family; and on the south-western perimeter of the *older* houses the lane has to turn at a sharp angle because the gabled end of a cottage juts into it, exactly as Hardy writes of Tess's lodging.

Modern Plush is still tiny, but no longer poor, having begun to attract the well-to-do retired. It also accommodates an unusual industry—an orchid nursery. Nor is there anything 'starve-acre' today about Church Hill, or for that matter Dole's Ash. Gone are the great fields of swede turnips, and new strains of grass have hidden the 'stony lanchets or lynchets'. Much of Church Hill is now wooded, as are most of the slopes enfolding Plush.

Just off the B3145 lies quiet, unspoilt Buckland Newton ('Newland Buckton'), whose clock Dr Fitzpiers heard strike twelve while he watered his horse at 'Lydden Spring'. There is no 'Lydden Spring' as such, but the small river Lydden, a tributary of the Stour, is fed by several headstreams that cross what would have been

The former 'Revellers' (Revels) Inn, now for many years just a farmhouse but still containing reminders of its former function. It was here, in *The Woodlanders*, that Winterborne and Fitzpiers met as they travelled in opposite directions.

the doctor's route. The hamlet called King's Stag or Kingstag, up the B3143 north of Alton Pancras, takes its name from one of Dorset's more famous bygone inns to which, as to many another in the county and in Somerset, came the four friends in that most wide-ranging of Hardy's narrative poems, 'A Trampwoman's Tragedy'. The inn appears too in 'A Last Journey'. It was burnt down in about 1910 and the site filled with the cottages seen there today. The magnificent sign alluded to by Lea escaped the fire but was shortly afterwards blown down and re-erected in a field called the Brickyard, where it remained until moved in 1921 to yet another position north of the crossroads. In 1959 it was collected by a Bournemouth firm to be repainted; and that was the last that was heard of it, for the firm went into liquidation and the sign was inadvertently sold with the assets. The purchaser has never been traced.

Five miles north is the small town of Stalbridge, and beside it Stalbridge Park, the 'Stapleford Park' of 'Squire Petrick's Lady'. The 'splendid old mansion now pulled down' in which the squire (in real life Peter Walter) lived was demolished in 1822, but the remarkably tall gate-pillars noted by Lea are still in place.

Between Dorchester and Sherborne ('Sherton Abbas') there are two routes for more than half the way, the upper or old road and the lower or A352, with the river Cerne flowing beteeen; the two unite at Middlemarsh ('Marshwood', 'Marshcombe'). Although by the period of *The Woodlanders* the upper road was already little used except by drovers, the 'forsaken coach road' on which Mrs Dollery's carrier-van plied between Sherborne and Cerne Abbas was in fact the lower road, 'forsaken' because its traffic had been taken by the railways; the failure of the railway-builders to include Cerne, however, left a small opening for the carrier service.

The Tithe Barn, 'Abbot's Cernel', showing the south end converted into a house in the late eighteenth century. Believed to date from the mid-fourteenth century, the barn was originally several bays longer at the north end. Hardy specifically stated, in writing, that this was the barn 'typified' in *Far From the Madding Crowd*.

One point on the upper road does figure in the novel—Revels ('Revellers') Inn, where Giles Winterbourne met Fitzpiers on their respective journeys to and from Milton Abbey. Now Revels Inn Farm, the building retains a few relics of its hostelry days, notably the door mentioned by Lea (but not the bench), today stored in a lumber room, and some exceptionally fine carved panelling on the walls of what was presumably the best parlour. Near the southern end of the upper road stands Charminster, now expanding so rapidly that it already fills the half-mile to the converging lower road. The old part of the village, however, preserves an attractive appearance. In the centre stands the church

where, according to Hardy in *A Group of Noble Dames*, the Lady Penelope lies, with her third husband, Sir William Hervey ('Hervy'), beside her, 'under the tomb which is still visible'. Lea infers that he saw it, but in truth there is no trace of it nor record of its existence.

The Lady Penelope lived at Wolfeton House, built by the Trenchard ('Drenghard', 'Drenkhard') family, one of whom was her first husband. The 'ivied manor-house', now divided into flats, is ivied no longer, to the benefit of its stonework and great mullioned windows. The two round French-looking towers flanking the gateway are still intact, with the Trenchard arms over the gate between them. The bowling-green near which Penelope walked was probably the upper of the two lawns. The descendants of the nearby willows where basket-makers were cutting osiers, are still to be seen, but not the work associated with them.

Cerne Abbas's fortunes are marked by a long period of prosperity, a shorter one, lasting into the present century, of penury and almost unbelievable dilapidation, then a rise to renewed and still increasing ease. Observing its quiet comfort today, and noting the evidence of bygone riches, it is hard to believe the descriptions given by Treves, Harper and others within the memory of people still alive. The decline set in with the transfer of traffic from road to rail—for the lines stayed remote from Cerne on either side—and the revival came only with the reversal of the trend and, coupled with it, the development of the town for commuters and people in retirement. The lowest population figure, 448, was registered as late as 1931. Today after rising to double that, it has again dropped to 572, notwithstanding a sizeable acreage of new buildings behind the old houses of the main streets. In view of the condition of the older structures in the depressed days, it is a cause for wonder as well as pleasure that so many could be saved.

Impressed by its roof—for it had little else to commend it above many rivals—Hardy chose the tithe barn at Cerne Abbas as his model for the 'great barn' in *Far from the Madding Crowd*. Despite the widespread impression that the latter is based on the huge barn at Abbotsbury, the claim of Cerne is indisputable. It was first attested in print by Viola Meynell, editor of the correspondence of Sir Sidney Cockerell (see page 53), and confirmed by Wilfrid Blunt in his Cockerell biography. In 1915 Hardy took Cockerell to Cerne, and followed up the visit by sending him a copy of the novel in which he had written the note: 'After a visit to a mediaeval barn typified in the description at pages 164–165'.

With such a wealth of fine barns in the county it is not surprising that so many people mistook Hardy's prototype. Long before his birth the northern end of the Cerne barn had been truncated, and the southern end converted into a residence with sadly alien windows. The roof, however, was as splendid as his description, and it is sad for us that in the 1880s it collapsed. Orders were given for it to be rebuilt to the same

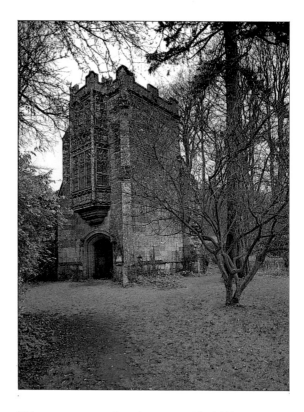

This sumptuous porch to the now vanished Abbot's Lodging at 'Abbot's Cernel' (Cerne Abbas) is where the secretly married heroine of 'The First Countess of Wessex' had one of her clandestine rendezvous with her husband. The Abbey is also associated with the delightful poem 'The Lost Pyx'.

design but in a cheaper wood—deal. The deal was certainly used, but the builder preferred a 'modern' design, the ugly and unimaginative results of which are there today. The non-residential part of the building is now a garage Both house and grounds are strictly private.

To Cerne Abbey belonged the priest of 'The Lost Pyx'. The poem tells us that he later became sub-prior and that his '... bones are now bare / In the field that was Cernel choir'. Probably they are, but there is no telling where, for although various fragments of the abbey have survived, not even the exact site of its church is known. The most striking survival is the so-called gatehouse, in reality the entrance porch to the abbot's hall. It contains a turret stair and a porter's lodge in which Betty Reynard, *née* Dornell, and her husband had one of their secret meetings (*A Group of Noble Dames*). In appearance it has changed very little in its now beautiful setting—at one time it was surrounded by a farmyard!

On Trendle Hill to the north sprawls the great chalk figure of the Cerne Giant, alluded to in *Tess* and in *The Dynasts*. Miraculously allowed to survive in all its pagan sensuality by monks, Puritans, and finally Victorians, this naughty figure is now assured of preservation by the National Trust. When Hardy knew Cerne, the maypole still flourished in the earth-camp above the Giant's head; and it is said that even today childless couples go in all seriousness to see what the great chalk likeness may do for them. Barely a mile to the north-east runs the highest stretch of the old Sherborne–Dorchester road, the 'Fairmile-Hilltop' that is one of the two possible settings for 'The Dear' (see page 207).

Just over two miles north of Cerne Abbas is Minterne Magna, a tiny village that Hardy allowed to be identified in his copy of Heath's *Dorchester and its Surroundings* with 'Great Hintock'. This is the threshold of the country of *The Woodlanders*, the most elusive of the regions in which the Wessex novels are set, particularly when it is realized that Hardy changed many of the locations between editions. A lengthy and careful analysis by Pinion in the *Thomas Hardy Year Book* no 2 (1971) takes the reader effectively through the maze. There is no space here to examine the changes in detail, but they may be summarized by saying that originally, beyond question, Hardy imagined his 'Little Hintock' between Melbury Osmond and Bubb Down, but later shifted it several miles eastward, close to High Stoy; other places were shifted east as well to preserve their relative positions. Pinion gives as the reason for the transfer Hardy's anxiety that the dubious Mrs Charmond should not be identified with any member of the Ilchester family, whose possibly disapproving attention he was about to risk with the publication of the

'First Countess of Wessex'; for in the original landscape of *The Woodlanders* 'Hintock House' occupied the site of Melbury House. But in the stories 'Interlopers at the Knap' and 'The Duke's Reappearance' Melbury House is unmistakably 'King's Hintock Court', as Melbury Osmond is 'King's Hintock'. In *The Woodlanders* this village was also the original 'Great Hintock', which may have altered its position but never lost its Melbury features. To quote Pinion again, 'Hardy had imagined [the Hintocks] in the Melbury Osmund district, and . . . despite the changes in place-names and in occasional topographical detail . . . the essentials and features of the whole setting were never altered'.

Several names appear not only in *The Woodlanders* but elsewhere. High Stoy and Dogbury (with the dell between them called the Devil's Kitchen) were passed by Tess on her journey from 'Flintcomb-Ash' to Beaminster, the trees on High Stoy and Bubb Down 'twanged' at one another in the storm that beset the priest of 'The Lost Pyx', High Stoy was climbed by the four friends in the poem 'Under High-Stoy Hill', and the neighbourhood of Dogbury Gate is the setting for another, 'Life and Death at Sunrise'. So little has the region been modified that even the mediaeval priest would still find it familiar.

Lyons-Gate is a group of cottages on the main road a mile north of Minterne Magna; Middlemarsh, already mentioned, is equally tiny but boasts an inn, the White Horse, which is '"The Horse" on Hintock Green' of 'A Tramp-woman's Tragedy'. In spite of its situation on a main road it continues outwardly unpretentious, though some modernization has recently been effected inside. It is still without a near neighbour. The extensive woods west of Middlemarsh are the largest remaining in the scattered *Woodlanders* landscape. Just clear of their farther flank lies Hermitage, still small, diffuse, very quiet—'This tiny Rip Van Winkle village', Treves called it—but with signs of beginning to be favoured by the well-to-do retired and the Yeovil commuter. No 'sengreens'—houseleeks—grow today out of the thatch.

One of the scenes in *The Woodlanders* that has not been moved east is the last, the brilliant and poignant ending which sees Marty in the moonlight beside Giles's grave in 'Great Hintock' churchyard. We bear in mind that before Hardy transposed it 'Great Hintock' was Melbury Osmond; and the reference to the views from the churchyard rules out any substitution of Minterne Magna.

Where the A352, on approaching Sherborne, is joined by the A3030 from Sturminster Newton, there stands in the fork a small dark stone house called West Hill Cottage. This is the former 'Sherton turnpike on the Bath road' where Bathsheba Everdene's faithful employees caught up with her on her flight.

The 'Earl of Wessex', the impressive mullioned coaching inn at Sherborne ('Sherton Abbas') with the central courtyard, which, as correctly stated towards the end of *The Woodlanders*, was destroyed to make way for the

Even before Hardy complicated the topography of *The Woodlanders* by shifting most of the locations several miles further east for later editions, 'Little Hintock' was never more than a fanciful amalgam of several villages. One of them is Hermitage, where even the church, seen here, carries a note of equivocation, having a pronounced seventeenth-century appearance though dating in fact from 1800.

railway, stood where the station now stands. Its real name was the New Inn. To replace it a new hotel, the Digby, heavy and ugly, was built nearby; but now this in turn has been taken over by Sherborne School, a fact advertised by the construction of a large, pallid new scholastic building at the back. Weber, taking as his premise the change in the divorce laws that came about in 1878 and is prominent in *The Woodlanders*, places the action between 1876 and 1879. But the railway had reached Sherborne in 1860, and the Digby had therefore long replaced the New Inn; indeed, after the final reconciliation of

Grace and Fitzpiers it is specifically stated that they visited the hotel 'rebuilt contemporaneously with the construction of the railway'. Yet the description in the account of Grace's earlier visit, which would have been in 1877, is unquestionably a portrait of the New Inn. Today there is again a hotel beside the station.

'Sheep Street', through which she drove looking for Giles, is Sherborne's smart main shopping thoroughfare, Cheap Street. Midway along it, a structure that looks like a chapel is the Monks' Conduit, which Grace's father was passing when he was hailed by Lawyer Beaucock, and behind which the eloping lovers of the poem 'In Sherborne Abbey' hid their horse. Appropriately, the conduit has been adapted to house a public drinking-fountain. Less appropriately, the pleasant effect of its fifteenth-

Dogbury Hill, seen here, is one of a chain of mid-Dorset heights much admired by Hardy, who brought them into several novels and poems. For the most part they remain unviolated by building or other disfigurement.

'Emminster' (Beaminster) Rectory, Tess's destination when she undertook her marathon walk to call on Angel's parents. Like so many others, the Rectory is today just a private house.

The church and churchyard at Melbury Osmond, the original model for 'Great Hintock' before Hardy shifted most of *The Woodlanders* settings further east. In real life his own parents had been married in this building.

century grace has been ruined by the nearby erection of a large traffic sign. The market-place in which Giles Winterborne stood holding his ten-foot apple-tree is either the former market site now occupied by the main car-park, or the area round the Monks' Conduit in which a small market is still regularly held: certain references in the novel seem to imply the latter.

Looming over the houses west of the Conduit is Sherborne Abbey, the 'Abbey north of Blackmore Vale' in 'The Lost Pyx' as Cerne is 'the Abbey south thereof'. Its glory is the fan-tracery of its roof, yet all Grace does when Giles takes her in there is to regard the tomb of John Digby, 3rd Earl of Bristol, and his two wives. This tomb was doubtless among those noticed by the lovers of 'In Sherborne Abbey' as they waited in the moonlight, and they may have also noticed the resting place of the Horseys, father and son, of whom the son was Hardy's 'Master John Horseleigh, Knight'.

Sherborne Castle appears in *The Woodlanders*, but is more prominent as the scene of the tale of 'Anna, Lady Baxby'. When Anna's husband (in life Lord Digby) was defending it against the Parliamentary troops led by her brother, the Earl of Bedford, it was still intact; but when Grace Melbury went there it lay in the ruined state to

The monument to John Digby, Earl of Bristol (d. 1698) in the South Transept of 'Sherton Abbas' Abbey; on either side of the Earl are his first and second wives. The sculptor was John Nost. This is the memorial that, in *The Woodlanders*, so engrossed Grace Melbury.

which Cromwell had ordered it to be reduced. In 'Anna' the features mentioned owe much to Hardy's imagination. The 'little gate to the south' through which she stole to meet her brother probably did not exist; the 'west terrace' on which she later met her husband's lover may have existed, but if so is now under the turf; and no circular stair is apparent hereabouts, although the remnant of one can be seen elsewhere.

During Bedford's siege Lady Digby was really in occupation of the newer castle, the Lodge, built by Sir Walter Raleigh on the other side of the lake, and still the seat of the Digbys today. It was from here that she rode out, of her own accord, to tell Bedford that if he destroyed the Lodge, not the older castle, he would find her dead body under the ruins.

A photograph of 1857 shows the old castle heavily creepered and overshadowed by trees. Grace must have seen it in this state, but today the only plants in the grass-clad bailey are a few ornamental shrubs; for the old castle has undergone protracted strengthening by the Department of the Environment. Crumbling edges, dangerous cracks, have been made good by a kind of invisible mending, using 'secret' formulas and techniques to match the effects of time. The work has taken many years.

The next radial road out of Dorchester is that route so familiar to Hardy readers, Long Ash Lane ('Holloway Lane' in a few early editions), otherwise the road to Yeovil ('Ivell'), the A37. In both 'Interlopers at the Knap' and 'The Grave by the Handpost' Hardy dilates on the lonely and ill-kept state of Long Ash Lane, and it was not until the 1930s that it was rehabilitated throughout its length. It is lonely even now.

High on the downs in the broad fork by Charminster, where the 'lane' parts company with the A352, is a likely site of 'Higher Crowstairs' in 'The Three Strangers'. It is doubtful whether this cottage ever existed, but the 'hog's-back elevation which dominated this part of the down' can be pinpointed as Hog Hill, south-east of Grimstone Down. On the crest a splendid thatched barn of brick, magnificently solitary, can without much effort be imagined as the cottage. The lynchets over which the search-party stumbled are on the eastern or Stratton Bottom side; the Bottom itself is the 'grassy, briery, moist defile' where they searched; and there are still several small areas of woodland. Another school of thought places 'Higher Crowstairs' farther east, on Waterston Ridge, where all Hardy's 'requirements'—except the cottage itself—are also to be found.

It must have been across Hog Hill or very close to it that (in *A Few Crusted Characters*) Parson Toogood and his clerk set out after the hounds, leaving Andrey Satchel and his bride-to-be locked in Frampton ('Scrimpton') church tower—the same tower that we see today. The hunt proceeded by 'Lippet Wood', 'Green's Copse', and 'Higher Jirton' toward Yellowham Wood; of these only 'Higher Jirton' can be given a possible real identity as Higher Forston. 'Lippet' may derive from Skippet, three miles to the south.

From Long Ash Lane a narrow way, once a turnpike, leads under the railway to Sydling St Nicholas, site of 'Sydling Mill' in the poem 'Old Excursions'—in fact there were two mills, both gone now but recalled by older villagers—and the 'Broad Sidlinch' of 'The Grave by the Handpost'. The post stood where the Maiden Newton ('Chalk Newton')–Sydling road crosses Long Ash Lane, and where a newer signpost stands today. The 'North Eweleaze' of the story is North Field Hill, the bare down in the north-east angle of the cross. Long Ash Lane is here at its straightest and loftiest. Where a few houses flank it at Holywell it is crossed by the road from Dogbury Gate to Evershot ('Evershead') and Beaminster, Tess's route. East of Long Ash Lane this road crosses Batcombe Down, and in

On lonely Hog Hill a magnificent barn
occupies one possible site of 'Higher
Crowstairs', the imaginary cottage that
is the principal scene of action in the
finest of all Hardy's short stories, 'The
Three Strangers'.

Part of the extensive ruins of 'Sherton
Abbas' (Sherborne) Old Castle, built in
the early twelfth century by Roger,
Bishop of Salisbury and accomplished
military architect. Hardy made this the
setting for his Civil War story 'Anna,
Lady Baxby', whose real counterpart,
Lady Digby, was one of a number of
titled chatelaines in Dorset and
Wiltshire who skilfully defended their
husbands' properties.

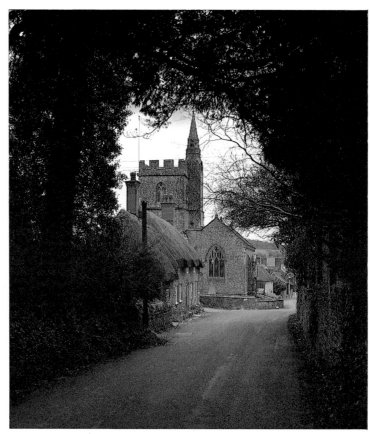

Above right:
'Evershead' (Evershot), including the
cottage (this side of the church) in
which Tess breakfasted on her way to
'Emminster'. The remains of the barn in
which Alec preached are to be found
down a turning on the left.

'Owlscombe' (Batcombe), huddled
under its hill. In the churchyard you
may still see the curious tomb of
'Conjuror' Mynterne. Beside the road
on the hill above stands the enigmatic
little pillar, the Cross-in-Hand,
prominent in *Tess* and in 'The Lost
Pyx'.

the roadside grass at nearly the highest point (around 800ft) stands the mysterious stone pillar, the Cross-in-Hand ('Crossy-Hand' locally).

Several guesses have been made at the nature of the now worn-away carving that once decorated it: one is that the shaft showed the figure of a woman with crossed arms, another that the moulding on the south (road-facing) side of the bowl-shaped capital originally represented a hand. Of the many conjectured purposes of the little monument—more even than cited by Hardy—the most charming, and I fear least likely, is that it was a memorial to mark the site of the miracle related in 'The Lost Pyx'. But one authority does postulate a connection with Cerne Abbey, suggesting that the concave capital was designed to receive offerings.

At all events, there the pillar stands, the grass round its base occasionally cut by the authorities, and all around it the country remains as desolate as ever. Batcombe ('Owlscombe') church is a little to the west, close under the hill; here, reputedly, in a very odd tomb still to be seen, lies buried 'Conjurer' Mynterne, one of the curious company of soothsayer-witchdoctors common in Hardy's pages, and collectively discussed by Dairyman Crick in *Tess*.

Evershot is mainly associated with *Tess*, but here too, in 'The First Countess of Wessex', Squire Dornell's man, Tupcombe, sat in the inglenook at the 'Sow and Acorn' (the Acorn) in the hope of hearing news of Betty, and Philip Hall collected Sally's dress from the carrier in 'Interlopers at the Knap'. The small inn has been very little altered outside, but completely redesigned within. Tess breakfasted and supped at 'the cottage by the church ... almost the first at that end of the village'. This is popularly taken to mean the stone cottage immediately west of the church; even today there is only one other before the open country. The barn in which she discovered Alec ranting stood not far off the road 'near the central part' of the village. Looking much out of place, such a barn did exist until a few years ago, down the lane called

Tanyard beside the Bakery. Built of brick, thatched, and with very dilapidated woodwork, it had been extended at one end to form a garage, and other garages had been built facing it. Its double doors looked north, not west toward the winter sunset as in *Tess*; but Hardy also said that they were on the side away from her as she approached from the main street, which would be correct. Today the old barn has been finally demolished to provide a turning-space in front of the new garages, but the lower parts of its west and south walls have been left to contain the area, and are recognizable from the age of the brickwork.

North-east of Holywell Cross stands Woolcombe, touched on in 'The Rash Bride': 'I knew him—one from Woolcomb way—Giles Swetman ...'—a reminder that Hardy's maternal forebears once owned considerable property out here, including Woolcombe House, of which all that remained even when he was born was the stables incorporated into Woolcombe Farm, as may be seen to this day.

Because of its close links with the Minterne Magna–High Stoy region the Melbury Osmond area, which properly belongs here, has already been discussed. However, a few points remain. The 'obscure gate to the east' of Melbury ('King's Hintock') Park by which Charles Phelipson made off with Betty Dornell continues to stand, nearly opposite Bubb Down Hill—the 'Rubdon Hill' of *The Woodlanders* first edition. The only parts of Melbury House that would not have been known to Betty are the west wing and tower, both nineteenth-century; since Hardy's day much creeper has been removed. The 'little flowered frock' in which Betty was married is still preserved at the house, just as Hardy says.

Melbury Sampford church, to all intents the private chapel, was heavily restored during the nineteenth century, but its monuments were kept, including Stephen Fox's, from the rhymed inscription on which Hardy applies two lines to Stephen Reynard. Melbury Park is finely timbered, a setting still appropriate to the poem

'Autumn in King's Hintock Park'. One may yet cross the park on foot, as did the enigmatic stranger in 'The Duke's Reappearance', by a private road from Clammers Gate (the real name) in the north to the 'Evershead' gate in the south. A short distance south of Clammers Gate, to the west of the road, is a shallow valley called Stutcombe Bottom—the 'Tutcombe Bottom' where Melbury came by one of his aches.

To the west of the park lie the small villages of East and West Chelborough. It was 'in King's Hintock Wood, by Delborough' that Grace found Giles Winterborne's modest (and fictitious) home 'One-Chimney Hut'. Certainly 'Delborough' suggests Chelborough, but Grace's journeys to the Hut, and afterwards back in search of Fitzpiers, do not fit in with either of the Chelboroughs, and Pinion suggests a site nearer Woolcombe. All this is a region remote and unspoilt even by Dorset standards.

The extremity of Melbury Osmond nearest to

The principal street of Melbury Osmond from just above Town's End. The house with the curious access over the roots of a sycamore in 'Interlopers at the Knap' and the poem 'One Who Married Above Him' has been tentatively identified with the second cottage on the left here. An ancient tree root – in fact a yew – does indeed border the road opposite an obsolete entrance.

Clammers Gate is called Town's End. Hardy uses the name, spelt 'Townsend', and also the real names of his maternal ancestors, in 'The Duke's Reappearance'. In *The Life* he notes the loss of the stone chimneys and an oak staircase from the house involved, which is the one facing Clammers Gate. The old house with the 'sycamore'-root steps to the door featured in 'Interlopers at the Knap' and the poem 'One who Married Above Him', though stated by Lea to have been pulled down, is nevertheless identified by some with Manor Cottage—formerly, as so often, two cottages. In the road under the elevated terrace on which the house is

High Stoy, one of the chain of verdant hills in the revised
'Hintock' country of *The Woodlanders*, mentioned too in
more than one poem. The range forms the southern
boundary of the 'Vale of Little Dairies' (Blackmoor).

built is the massive stump of a yew (not a
sycamore), its projecting roots now cut away to
facilitate the passage of traffic. The stump is not
opposite the present front door, but did face one
now blocked. The position has some affinities
with Hardy's indications. The cottage is near, if
not at, the top of a slope beside 'King's Hintock'
village street, a mile or two from 'King's
Hintock Court', and three miles from where the
travellers succeeded in getting to along the
wrong road. There was a brook forty yards off—
there is; it crosses the road. The details of the
house were visible far up the road as one entered
the village—it can be seen from some distance
below it.

There is a second brook reached by a path that
leaves the road beside the house of 'The Duke's
Reappearance'. This is the Buttock's Spring
mentioned in that story. The name is still in local
use.

Melbury Osmond churchyard, though vigorous tree growth has now restricted the former
fine views, is crossed today as formerly by a path
that would have permitted George Melbury to
avoid going round by the road on his way to
'Great Hintock', thus providing further
evidence that when Hardy shifted his scenes
eastward he retained his original church. The
churchyard is the scene of the 'strange inter-
ment' that inspired the poem 'Her Late Husband'; neither inscriptions nor registers reveal
the real protagonists, but Bailey suggests the
two Swaffields and John Swetman (1822).

Chetnole ('Catknoll') lies east of Long Ash
Lane, on the railway into near-by Yeovil. It still
looks less suburban than one might expect. This
is the scene of the poem 'The War-Wife of

Catknoll', although it is an entry in the register of baptisms at Melbury Osmond that provides the basis for the anecdote. The Wriggle, the stream in which the 'Catknoll' wife drowned herself, looks too tiny for the purpose, except perhaps after a storm. Even closer to Yeovil and much more suburban despite some fine older houses, is Yetminster, the 'Estminster' of 'The Inscription'. In the church the inscription is now seen to better advantage since in 1890 a Major Harvey caused the brasses to be set in a concrete tablet on the north wall of the nave. The John Horsey commemorated was the grandfather of 'Master John Horseleigh' who built Clifton Maybank ('Clyfton Horseleigh') hard by. Why Hardy should have written that 'hardly a trace now remains' of this mansion is a mystery, for although only the east wing survives, the rest having been demolished in 1786, the fragment, in spite of its now disproportionate height, continues to be 'seductive and picturesque',

Eggardon Hill, the 'Haggardon Hill' of *The Trumpet-Major* and 'hill-fortress of Eggar' of 'My Cicely'. The hill is in fact crowned by an Iron Age hill-fort, large but yielding little of interest when excavated some years ago.

thanks to careful maintenance and some judicious nineteenth-century restoration. No longer a farmhouse, it is once more surrounded by spacious lawns and gardens. One or two features from the main part of the house were incorporated in it after the demolition, and others were taken away for incorporation in neighbouring Montacute (see page 200). There is still, as in Hardy's time, good timber in Clifton Wood.

Reverting south, at the White Horse in Maiden Newton Darton's bailiff in 'Interlopers at the Knap' took over Helena's orphaned boy, and at the same inn in 'Destiny and a Blue Cloak', Agatha boarded the carrier's van on her way back from Weymouth. The town was also familiar to Tess, but figures most prominently in 'The Grave by the Handpost', which brings in the church, churchyard, 'riverside rectory' and old Ezra's (unidentifiable) cottage. The church, having escaped major Victorian restoration, retains much of its early and late mediaeval appearance. The former rectory, through the garden of which runs the Frome, is a Tudor mansion fit for an archbishop. Largely rebuilt with the original stones in 1844—later than the date of the story—it ceased to be a rectory in 1938.

Alas that similar regard was denied the White Horse! The gracious Elizabethan stone inn, with central archway, diamond-paned mullioned windows and dormered thatch, was pulled down early in this century—not many years after Emma Hardy sketched it—and replaced by a dreary structure in red brick. In the roadway before it the 'stone stump of the cross' remains, dwarfed by the towering proximity of an electricity-supply pole bearing a number of enamelled route signs. Aesthetic considerations have not predominated in twentieth-century Maiden Newton.

The small town is quiet, despite its railway station—no longer a junction for Bridport—and lacks much evidence of development. The old mill now makes equipment for silk-screen printing. Just outside the town is Whitesheet Hill, namesake of a hill on the edge of Beaminster. Pinion suggests that the former is referred to in 'Molly Gone', the latter in 'The Homecoming'. About the second there can be little doubt, but in 'Molly Gone' it seems to me either hill may be intended. Both remain open meadowland.

South-west of Maiden Newton, above the rolling downs, rises Eggardon Hill—'Haggardon Hill' in *The Trumpet-Major* and the 'hill-fortress of Eggar' in the poem 'My Cicely', but *not*, as sometimes stated, the site of Gabriel Oak's 'Norcombe' farm—a lonely height, at times strangely unprepossessing notwithstanding its vast views.

The real 'Norcombe' lies three or four miles farther north, 'near lonely Toller Down' and the stretch of the A356 formerly called—as in 'A Trampwoman's Tragedy' and 'The Dark-Eyed Gentleman'—Crimmercrock Lane. The features of 'Norcombe' are generally dismissed as drawn from the imagination, but in fact almost every one of them is to be found in the area; all that Hardy has done is to edit them, as it were, into the arrangement he required.

The road from 'Norcombe' to Dorchester, 'sunk in a deep cutting', is the route from Hooke to Lower Kingcombe. Today this is an unfrequented (and exceedingly narrow) lane with banks that are nearly vertical; at one time it was part of the coach road between Beaminster and Maiden Newton. The route, however, was never turnpiked, and to provide the 'turnpike gate at the bottom of the hill' Hardy has 'moved' the turnpike from the crossroads on Toller Down; the true site is still marked on the map as Toller Down Gate. Originally it was known as Catsley Down Gate, and on Catsley Down itself there used to be a sheep fair, now commemorated in the name Fair Field.

The 'featureless convexity of chalk and soil' that was 'Norcombe Hill' would fit most of the hills in the area. The beech plantation on the northern side was 'ancient and decaying' and may well have vanished, but there are at least three woodlands today that answer to the topographical requirements, according to which hill is picked as 'Norcombe': these are Ridge Coppice, Westcombe Coppice, and the plantation near Higher Kingcombe. One may note the simple change of compass-point needed to make 'Norcombe' out of Westcombe.

'Norcombe' is also the name of a village with a church. The likeliest original is Hooke. On its outskirts, at the foot of Westcombe Hill, there used to be a mill that we may take for the 'Tewnell Mill' of the novel. By the middle of the present century it had degenerated into a seedy cottage, but in 1969 it was acquired for restoration as a better-class residence. A little north of it, on the hill, are the remains of a chalk-pit that once employed twenty or thirty panniered donkeys to carry away its product; there are several other pits of various sizes near by, and a very large pit north of Higher Kingcombe, in the shadow of the BBC's Rampisham radio masts. No pit is surmounted by the converging hedges that guided Oak's sheep to their doom, but close to the Kingcombe pit a gate set diagonally across the corner of a hedge-girt field produces a suggestively similar effect. As for the pond, on the east slope of Westcombe Hill there is a pond called Park Pool, and another lies at Toller Whelme. Only Gabriel's rented farmhouse and Mrs Hurst's cottage and cow-byre cannot be related to precise features in a district of less than two square miles. Today this is a sequestered part of the world, and Hooke is a dying village, though the agricultural land in the area is well maintained.

In an article in the 1980 *Thomas Hardy Review* Geoffrey Thompson makes the interesting point that about the time when Gabriel Oak would have gone from 'Norcombe' to Upper Weatherbury Farm as bailiff, in real life one Robert Walden left Toller Whelme to become the bailiff at Waterston Manor. Toller Whelme, however, though much larger in the mid-nineteenth century than now (population in the 1981 census, 10), is less likely than Hooke to be 'Norcombe' village, having, apart from its pond, none of the features I have just noted. It may nevertheless have provided Hardy with the prototype of Bathsheba's aunt's cowshed built in 'a cutting into the slope of the hill, so that at its back part the roof was almost level with the ground', for just such a shed can still be found.

Kingcombe Hill is another name with two claimants. In addition to the one near Hooke, there is another near Dole's Ash Farm; but the former is the more probable 'Kingcomb Hill' of the poem 'The Pat of Butter'. Toller Down, which features prominently in 'The Homecom-

To illustrate the opening scenes of *Far From the Madding Crowd*.

ing', continues lonely and windswept, dominated by the near-by Rampisham masts. The minor road leading east from Toller Down Gate crossroads is Benvill Lane, twice mentioned in *Tess*. To the west is Beaminster ('Emminster'). This pleasant but dull small town appears in 'Destiny and a Blue Cloak', but is mainly known to Hardy readers for containing, in its vicarage, the home of the Clares. Despite a fairly extensive programme of new housing nearby, church and

Opposite above:
Now fully rescued from a somewhat dingy retirement 'Tewnell Mill' (Hooke Mill) appears only in the early pages of *Far From the Madding Crowd*. The road in the foreground is the old coach route – but not the narrowest part!

Opposite below:
Looking towards 'Norcombe' village (Hooke) from the downs on which Gabriel Oak had his sheep-farm before he entered Bathsheba's service. In the middle distance, not far from a disused chalk-pit, a pool glitters just as it glittered when Oak discovered the loss of his animals.

vicarage show no departure whatever from Hardy's picture, including the lawn with its shrubs. Even the sole innovation, a garage, has now been removed. The road in from Evershot is still hedge-girt as when Tess lost her boots there.

A mile or so south of Beaminster is the pretty village of Netherbury, suggested by Pinion as the 'Cloton' of 'Destiny and a Blue Cloak'. Certainly the mill—now a private house—where Agatha lived, conforms to the description of 'Cloton' mill. The stream does form the boundary of a garden, orchard, and paddock, and does separate the property from the 'village highroad'. 'Heavy-headed' trees still grow near. Only the 'little wooden bridge' in its swampy surroundings cannot be found; but there is a stone bridge beside the house. The other house in the tale, Farmer Lovill's, is not identifiable.

The Netherbury–Broadwindsor area has superseded that of the 'Hintocks' as the region of

The Mill (no longer operative) in which Agatha lived at 'Cloton' (Netherbury) in 'Destiny and a Blue Cloak', one of the few short stories not included in the four collections made by Hardy himself.

Today just a farm track, this rough trail is typical of even main roads until well into the last century. Much of Tess's long traipse to 'Emminster' and back would have been along ways like this, and the fact gives added significance to the loss of her boots before she began the return journey.

called the Wynyard's Gap Inn, formerly the King's Arms, it has, to judge from an old photograph, undergone only very slight external changes. Internally, the principal bar has been enlarged and discreetly modernized, and the cellar, with the old hooks still in the beams, has been turned into a cellar bar. The Gap is also mentioned in 'Molly Gone', and gives its name to the long dialogue poem 'At Wynyard's Gap'. The view of 'half South Wessex' (and much more) is as splendid and unspoilt now as when 'He' and 'She' gazed upon it.

Among the places that 'He' pointed out from Wynyard's Gap are Lewesdon Hill ('Lewsdon' in 'Molly Gone') and Pilsdon Pen—Dorset's highest point. The two heights lie between Broadwindsor and the point where Dorset, Somerset, and Devon meet. In appearance they are quite dissimilar. Lewesdon Hill (893ft) is roughly conical and has a thickly wooded summit, but is accessible by public pathways, since from 1943 it has belonged to the National Trust. Pilsdon Pen (908ft) which is much longer than it is wide, was acquired by the Trust only in 1979. Most of it is covered with hedged fields, and a fence now surrounds the thirty-six acres owned by the Trust. The western end is covered with heather and scrub and is crowned by a prehistoric hill fort, the scene of excavations during the 1960s, as the outcome of which it was described as 'the scene of intense activity over 2,000 years ago'. In 1982 the Trust carefully restored the site to its pre-excavation appearance. The views from Lewesdon are limited to what can be seen from any one point on the periphery of the trees; but from the open sausage-back of Pilsdon there are tremendous panoramas over the three counties and the sea. Conversely the hill itself is a landmark, as Hardy was fond of remarking, for miles around. He may have called it 'little Pilsdon Crest' in his poem 'Wessex Heights', but all the evidence is that he did not think of it as little; and he would certainly have agreed with the archaeologists on 'the feeling of mystery and antiquity that is the essence of Pilsdon Pen'.

farm-made cider, but Broadwindsor is primarily in dairying country; and one of the places mentioned in 'A Pat of Butter', Netherhay, is a tiny, hoary hamlet three miles north-west of the town.

North of the point where the A356 begins to drop down towards Crewkerne it passes 'the cosy house at Wynyard's Gap', another haunt of the Trampwoman and her friends. The licensee is well aware of the epithet in the poem, and the inn remains cosy. It is also completely solitary and likely to remain so, for the country all about it belongs either to Chedington Court (the manor house) or to the National Trust. Properly

8 **SOUTH WESSEX**
THE COAST FROM LOWER WESSEX TO BUDMOUTH
Dorset: the coast from Devon to Weymouth

> . . . The boats, the sands, the esplanade,
>   The laughing crowd;
>   Light-hearted, loud
> Greetings from some not ill-endowed;
>
> The evening sunlit cliffs, the talk,
>   Hailings and halts,
>   The keen sea-salts,
> The band, the Morgenblätter Waltz . . .
>
> AT A SEASIDE TOWN IN 1869

In the 1820s and earlier the flat lands about the multiple headstreams of the Char and Simene were a good deal less well drained than now; Hutchins describes Marshwood Vale as 'hardly passable by travellers but in dry summers'. When the Trampwoman and her 'fancy-man' were 'stung by every Marshwood midge', they were probably being plagued by mosquitoes, some still malaria-carrying. The peril of malaria has passed, but the dual legacy of unhealthiness and inaccessibility (the latter not vastly improved) accounts for the absence of development in this lush but sparsely-occupied and secretive quarter.

Also in the tramps' itinerary was '"The Hut" renowned on Bredy Knap', an inn that stood north of the Dorchester–Bridport road (A35) in the angle formed by the lane leading down to North Barn. When Lea wrote, the building was no longer an inn, but in the old lane (traceable just east of the new one) Mary Ann Bull, the last reddle-seller, used to park her cart and dispense her wares. Finally, the ex-inn was demolished, but only a few years ago archaeologists came across its foundations and a number of old-fashioned bottles, unfortunately empty.

Farther east, where the A35 starts to curve toward Winterbourne Abbas, stand the Nine Stones, the 'Nine-Pillared Cromlech' passed by the rider in 'My Cicely'. This tiny prehistoric circle is now heavily shaded by trees, one of which has even imprisoned one stone in its roots. The site has been railed in by the Department of the Environment.

The rider next went along the valley of 'the Bride-streams', the River Bride and its tributaries. There is now a minor road along the five miles of this old-world vale, west of the mouth of which lies West Bay, prominent in the story 'Fellow-Townsmen'. This is the little harbour so well fashioned by nature that it 'appealed to the passer-by as only requiring a little industry to finish it and make it famous'. But the apparently perfect harbour suffers from constant silting. West Bay has had a modest success as a holiday resort of a kind, but it has failed to grow. An enormous building, erected in 1885 as a boarding-house and residences, is now (since a

Marshwood Vale, Dorset's most westerly and secretive area, criss-crossed by a maze of lanes each seeming narrower and more sinuous than the last; yet for those who do penetrate it rich in charm. This view is from the top of Pilsdon Pen.

fire in 1925) residences and flats; and in the season there is a large municipal holiday-camp.

As far as possible the harbour is still kept open; its main patrons are pleasure-craft, the last of its Scandinavian timber trade long gone. Hardy's 'Harbour Inn' is in real life the little-altered Bridport Arms; but Barnet would not have had to take a boat to reach it from the east beach, nor would he to get to the other inn of the period, the George. The third inn, the West Bay Hotel, is more recent. There are some nondescript cafés, a church built in the 1930s, and even a sort of promenade. In 1887 the railway was extended from Bridport ('Port-Bredy'), only to vanish again less than a century later, in 1964.

On the whole West Bay still justifies Treves's description as 'probably the queerest seaport in any part of the British Isles'.

Inland, new villas and bungalows have all but closed the gap between West Bay and Bridport, and have so interspersed themselves among the surviving Victorian villas that it is no longer possible to pick out Lucy Savile's home, if indeed it existed outside the imaginations of Hardy and Lea. 'Château Ringdale' certainly never existed, but its site is real, and on it there was once a mansion of comparable importance. This was Wanderwell, and it stood on a rise just as did Château Ringdale; even the elm-trees really existed, and the only discrepancy is that the Bridport road passes to the west of the rise, not the east. Wanderwell has been demolished and the elms cut down, but the name lives on in one of the streets of the bungalow estate now occupying the ground.

The strange cliffs flanking West Bay, close to 'Port Bredy' (Bridport), and the scene of important events in 'Fellow-Townsmen'. The oolite sands forming these impressive strata are exceptionally rich in fossils.

As West Bay Road merges into Bridport's South Street—Hardy's 'long street ... at right angles to the broad main street'—new buildings become fewer, and South Street itself can have changed only here and there. St Mary's church, where Downe and Lucy were married, remains as when Hardy wrote. The architect whose restoration work in 1860 drew his acid comment was Talbot Bury; and it must be admitted that he left precious little of the original fabric except the 'ancient font'. Near by, the Five Bells (its sign shows ringers on one side, bells on the other) is most probably the 'Ring of Bells' in the poem 'The Whaler's Wife'.

According to Lea, Barnet lived nearly opposite the church. But Lea for some reason was totally defeated by Bridport. Barnet's house, sold in the closing phase of the story to the 'Congregational Baptist' trustees, 'who pulled down the time-honoured dwelling and built a new chapel on its site', was not in South Street at all, but where the Congregational church, built in 1860, stands today, in East Street. Hutchins says the church authorities bought a site that had not previously been built on; but an eighteenth-century map shows an unbroken line of houses on East Street's southern side, so Hardy is probably correct.

Nor is Lea much happier with Downe's house, which he places in Downe Street. Hardy, however, states that when Barnet was driving Downe home 'their route took them past the little town-hall, the 'Black Bull Hotel', and onward to the junction of a small street on the right'. This means they were travelling eastward

In one of these modest houses in King Street, 'Port Bredy', Hardy placed the home of Charles Downe and his family. The street is not named in the story, but is easily identifiable. Such was the town's rope-making fame that in the days of widespread capital punishment, to be 'killed with a Bridport dagger' meant to be hanged.

along the main street; not only is Downe Street then on the left, but it is *between* the town hall and the Bull Hotel ('the Black Bull'). In fact, after passing the hotel the small street on the right to which the friends would have come is King Street. Many of its small houses have been pulled down, but enough remain to show the applicability of Hardy's picture. The reference at the end of the tale to the Downes having lived in East Street is clearly a slip.

The eighteenth-century town hall has acquired some public conveniences at its back, but is otherwise externally unchanged, and still dominates the town. The Savings Bank to which Barnet had recourse was at 36 East Street, near the Bull, in an eighteenth-century mansion that now has a cleaned exterior and solicitors within. The Bull itself has preserved its frontage but modernized its interior. A glass door still divides the porch from the hall.

The rope-making and net-making for which the town has so long been famous continue to flourish—the nets at Wimbledon are Bridport-made. The industry even lingers on to a limited extent in private houses, where special orders involving uncommon sizes or mesh are carried out. But the banks of the little River Brit (not to be confused with the Bride) are no longer devoted to the flax-growing that made Barnet's father rich, for the raw material used now is a synthetic fibre. In 1857 the railway 'invaded the town, tying it on to a main line at a junction a dozen miles off' (Maiden Newton). The branch no longer operates, and the track is torn up, though enthusiasts may still discover one of the level-crossing gates in a local yard.

Close to West Bay is the western end of the Chesil Bank or Beach ('pebble beach' in *The*

Well-Beloved, Chesil Bank in *The Woodlanders*). Hardy, however, bestows nearly all his attention on the Portland ('Isle of Slingers') end, where bank and so-called isle form between them the 'Deadman's Bay' of *The Well-Beloved* and *The Dynasts*. Here, close under Portland, lies the hamlet of Chesil or Chesilton, today joined up with Fortuneswell ('the Street of Wells'). On the beachward side of the group of stone cottages there are still some roofless shells and broken walls, remnants of the houses destroyed, as recounted in *The Well-Beloved*, 'by the November gale of 1824' which swept the sea right over Chesil Bank and drowned some two dozen sleeping people. During the 1960s a similar gale, playing on a spring tide, caused waves to break over two rows of buildings into the roadway behind, and still more recently a repeat performance briefly made an island once again of Portland. Luckily an advance warning system is now in operation, and there was no loss of life.

Under an upturned boat on the beach here-

'Port Bredy' (Bridport) is the setting for the long short story 'Fellow-Townsmen': old-fashioned to look at, perhaps, but maintaining its reputation as a world-famous source of ropes and nets, dating back at least to the rigging for Henry VIII's navy, and in modern times including nets for Wembley Stadium, the Wimbledon Championships courts, and more than one Olympic Games stadium.

abouts Jocelyn Pierston and Marcia Bencomb sheltered from the rain on their way to the mainland. In those days, before the making of the modern road, they had to walk along two miles of pebbles until they came to the 'precarious wooden bridge', now long replaced, that had itself supplanted the ferry. From here they continued round the 'Inner Bay or Roadstead'— Portland Harbour—past King Henry VIII's or Sandsfoot Castle. In 1906 (Treves) this Tudor fortress was still backed by a broad stretch of open downland; today Weymouth's suburbia has engulfed it, though the shore remains

Though this is a smaller boat than the one under which Jocelyn and Marcia in *The Well-Beloved* sheltered from the rain, the 'pebble beach' remains as inhospitable as ever on a stormy day.

Chesil Bank or Beach ('pebble beach' in *The Well-Beloved*, Chesil Bank, correctly, in *The Woodlanders*) from the 'Isle of Slingers' end, showing Chesilton in the foreground and, to the right, the Fleet, the irregular seawater lagoon that separates nine of the Beach's sixteen miles from the mainland. Well might Hardy call the sea here 'Deadman's Bay'. The nearby church and churchyard of Wyke Regis abound in memorials to the victims of wrecks.

undeveloped and the ruin itself barely changed. Its rocky base, recently in danger of erosion, has been strengthened.

The railway to Portland has been closed to passengers, and the little station which stood as a 'strange exotic' close to Chesilton was demolished in 1969. Beside the line is a row of round, silver-shining fuel storage tanks, and beside that again a sizeable area of the vast harbour has been reclaimed and made into an extension of the Royal Navy's helicopter base.

The appearance of the peninsula has changed less than have many of its functions. What goes on in the rock-cut labyrinths belonging to the Ministry of Defence only those who work there know, but the set-up is very different from that of the old infantry garrison, for Portland is today a top-secret underwater-weapons centre. The Royal Naval Hospital is now civilian. The once-military Verne Citadel has become a civilian prison, the Victorian prison a Borstal. Improved techniques have invaded the quarries, but except for the large modern sheds the buildings where the stones are prepared look pure Victorian. The action of *The Well-Beloved*, 1852–92, begins a few years before and ends a few years after the immense harbour walls were built, yet this extremely conspicuous feature is not mentioned in the novel.

The Martinmas Fair lives on at Fortuneswell. So does the glare on the now tarred roads, for although the trees in the grounds of Pennsylvania ('Sylvania') Castle are no longer the only ones on Portland, others are still few. Hardy describes the old Roman road ascending 'in the stiffest of inclines' to the summit, while a modern road farther left led to the forts. Today a still newer route has been cut to the right of the Roman road, which, however, remains unimpaired, except by a covering of grass in the upper reaches. The handrail by which Pierston eased his climb has survived. Near the new luxury hotel close to the summit of the roads is Top-o'-Hill where the returned Pierston stood gazing down at the quarries.

The Caros' cottage is the last on the east side of the wide thoroughfare that leads southward from Easton ('East Quarriers') before one reaches the Pennsylvania Castle grounds. The cot is of stone, with a tiny stone-walled court or garden at the back; but the stone stile, pigsty and stable mentioned by Hardy were probably imaginary. During his lifetime the building fell into serious disrepair, but was purchased, rehabilitated and presented to the local authority to serve as a museum, by the late Dr Marie Stopes, who lived for many years in the older of the two Portland lighthouses. The cottage and its immediate neighbour, which was included in the purchase, now communicate internally. To make the museum loftier, the upper floor of the second cottage has been taken away, but the old bedroom fireplace remains. Somewhere close at hand stood Jocelyn's father's home, the garden whereof 'ran out into a corner which adjoined the garden of the Caros'. However, later in the novel the parental home is said to be 'the furthest house out there on the cliff', *west* of Pennsylvania Castle. Did Hardy intend to imply that the Pierstons had moved, or was he simply careless? In neither site can any building today be satisfactorily identified.

Between the museum and the castle grounds is the mouth of Church Ope (*not* Hope) Lane, no longer the 'dark little lane' of *The Well-Beloved* but with its small houses brightened and made fashionable. The church of St Andrew, or Old Ope church, was, as Hardy reminds us, first ruined and then obliterated by successive landslips. Recently, however, a good part of the ruin has been 'rescued' and cleared of undergrowth. The churchyard too collapsed into what has since been a ravine, thickly covered with grass, shrubs, and a self-seeded extension of the Castle trees; but here also there has been a recent clearance. One solitary arch of the church remains upright in its new site, and in the undergrowth it is still possible to read bits of the inscriptions on some of the tumbled gravestones.

Pennsylvania Castle itself—a pastiche built in 1880—is today an elegant hotel, with an agreeable circular bar in the principal tower. Beeches and chestnuts now add variety to the original elms, and a new entrance on the west side of the grounds has supplanted the earlier one close to the Caros' cottage. A few yards from this older gateway a curious little building built into and above the wall is probably the 'Elizabethan-style garden house' of the novel. Elsewhere along the wall a small door gives access by a rough path to the shore, and below the door a cavernous, water-filled opening at the base of Rufus Castle ('Red-King Castle') must be what Hardy referred to as the 'dip-well'; certainly it supplied water to the fortress.

Immediately outside the south wall of the grounds there is a small holiday-chalet camp, which might well be an eyesore but in fact looks very pleasant. Far beneath it is a gracious little bay, Church Ope Cove, from which Avice Caro III and Leverre embarked on their flight, and where, some decades earlier, Anne Garland had boarded the Weymouth ferry (*The Trumpet-Major*). Two or three beach huts and a startling public convenience are the only modern intrusions into this nook, which is still reached by a long staircase-cum-footpath alongside the older path noted by Hardy. At the top of the paths, rising sheer from the rock, is Rufus Castle, or what is left of it, for much of this building too has fallen from its perch. The great blocks of masonry observed in *The Well-Beloved* continue to litter the lower slopes.

Easton, where Jocelyn's father had his quarrying business, is hardly a 'little' village, being after Fortuneswell the largest settlement on Portland; but whatever growth it may have seen in the twentieth century has not altered the appearance of its remarkably wide main street. South of Easton the scenery becomes open, although there is still one more village before the land descends toward the Beal or Bill. This famous headland, from which Anne Garland

watched HMS *Victory* sail past, must have been more radically transformed since 1902, let alone 1805, than any other part of Portland. New's sketch almost agrees with the engraving in the first edition of Hutchins and the description in *The Trumpet-Major* of the 'wild, herbless, weather-worn promontory [where] saving the one old lighthouse about fifty yards up the slope, scarce a mark was visible to show that humanity had ever been near the spot'. In reality the second lighthouse was there as well, having been erected in 1789; but that Hardy had the older one in mind he made clear many years afterwards,

Not until a landslip brought down most of St Andrew's Church – Portland's original parish church – was it realized that a much older building, probably contemporary with King William II's Rufus (or Bow-and-Arrow) Castle, seen here on the skyline, had preceded the fifteenth-century edifice. The surviving arch probably led into the chancel of the later church. The ruins have recently been cleared of much undergrowth.

Ope Cove, the small, snug bay on the east coast of the 'Isle of Slingers' used in both *The Well-Beloved* and *The Trumpet-Major*. From primitive loading-points still to be traced along this coast of Portland was shipped the stone for facing the Banqueting Hall in London's Whitehall and St Paul's Cathedral.

when at the age of eighty-three he and Florence visited Dr Stopes, and for the first time he entered the edifice and climbed to the top. This lighthouse too is probably the one on whose 'turreted ledge' the sprites alighted in 'The Souls of the Slain'. The building is now a bird observatory.

The marks of humanity today include a large wired-off Ministry of Defence area, a car-park with its signs and ticket booths, a yellow-brick inn (in this nearly all-stone world!), two wooden café-and-curio shacks, and an extraordinary row of black huts that from the back look like hutches on a turkey-farm, but prove on frontal inspection to be beach-chalets set on the cliff-

top. Amid all this a small obelisk inscribed 'T.H. 1844' is a product of Trinity House, to which the initials refer.

And yet the Bill has not entirely lost its magic. On a sweltering summer day it is as cool as the deck of a ship at sea, and on a wild day in winter one can forget the twentieth-century clutter and recapture the atmosphere prevailing in the days of the three Avices or even of Anne. Out to sea, the patch of water called the Race, into which plunged many of the spirits in 'The Souls of the Slain', is a turmoil of frothing white crests. A view of the Race and the coast from the sea is to be found in *A Pair of Blue Eyes*. The Shambles lightship, also mentioned there, was replaced in 1971 by a new type of automatic lightbuoy and foghorn.

The Well-beloved mentions the 'treacherous cavern known as Cave Hole'. This is on the east coast, a short distance north of the turkey hutches; part of the roof at some remote time fell in, leaving a bowl-shaped depression in the flat

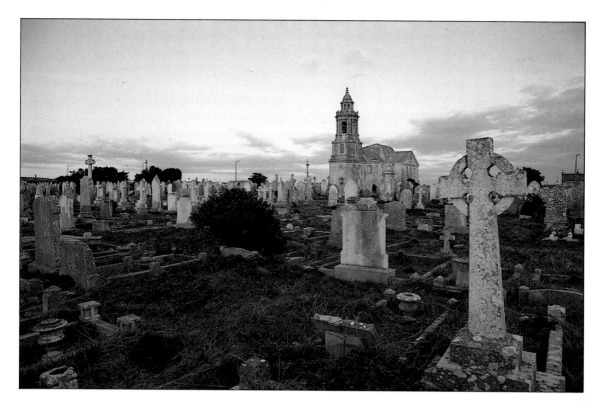

The bizarre cemetery of St George Reforne, the principal piece of ecclesiastical architecture in the 'Isle of Slingers' (Portland). Here lie buried, in their legions, what Hardy termed 'the island fathers'.

turf (as it now is) above, and in the bottom of the depression a hole through which the sea used to spout like a salt-water geyser, until spectacle was sacrificed to safety and stout iron bars were set across the hole. Prior to this, according to Wilkinson Sherren, notches cut in the rock made it possible to descend to a ledge in the cave.

On the west side of Portland the principal building is a large church surrounded by a most extensive churchyard, 'the bleakest churchyard in Wessex' according to Hardy. The church, St George Reforne, is where we are told in *The Well-Beloved* that 'the island fathers lay' and where Pierston watched the burial of the first Avice. Hardy refers to its tower, and indeed it has a small one at the west end, but its main feature is the central dome. The long grass that almost hid the masses of gravestones has been cut down since responsibility for the upkeep of the church was taken over by a voluntary body under the aegis of the Redundant Churches Fund. The church is no longer in regular use,

and is locked most of the time. From this side of Portland one can look along the Chesil Bank to Abbotsbury ('Abbotsea', 'Abbot's Beach') and its two sinuous terraces of warm-tinted stone and thatch, seemingly immutable despite the ever-denser traffic threading between them.

The massive stone pillar erected in 1846 on Blackdown ('Blackon') Hill, a National Trust property some three miles to the north-east of Abbotsbury, honours Admiral Hardy, but since it bears only an inconspicuous inscription, it is not surprising that many visitors who drive up to it for the magnificent views believe it commemorates Thomas Hardy the writer. In 1980 the column was repaired by a steeplejack. This Blackdown, one of several in west Dorset, tallies closely with Hardy's description in *The Trumpet-*

Major and is also the 'Blackon' of 'After the Club-Dance', the third section of the poem 'At Casterbridge Fair'.

Captain Hardy's house stands at the foot of Blackdown Hill in the village of Portisham ('Po'sham'). This little doll's-house of a manor faces one of the angles of what has become a bustling road-junction, but is unaltered except for windows modernized in Victorian times and the removal of creeper. Treves writes of a stuccoed front, but today we see it as it must have looked originally.

About three miles east of Portisham, and less than a mile west of Maiden Castle, stands Winterborne St Martin, more often known as Martinstown, scene of the great horse mart commemorated in the poem 'A Last Look round St Martin's Fair'. This fair is yet another that was already dwindling by 1914, although it lingered on until 1939, when the army took over the fairground. The site was a large paddock south of the church and divided by the village street. Today the smaller portion nearer the church has been retained as a green; the larger supports a housing estate.

South of Martinstown and east of Portisham, extending nearly to the Weymouth–Dorchester road, is Waddon Vale. Under the title of the poem 'The Lacking Sense' is the note: 'SCENE—A sad-coloured landscape, Waddon Vale'. But on a bright day it is cheerful enough with the Pucksey Brook threading its centre beside the embankment of the long-vanished Upwey–Abbotsbury branch railway. Most of it is lush pasture; there are farms and a plantation or two, but no villages at all. Amid the hills at its north-east corner, where the Wey has its source, stands Upwey, which has an interest for Hardy readers because of its mill. This, a splendid specimen of a watermill still in full commercial activity, has by some means become identified with 'Overcombe Mill' in *The Trumpet-Major*, although 'Overcombe' is admitted to be Sutton Poyntz. The evidence for believing that at best the assumption contains only a very small grain of truth will be found on pages 134–5.

Broadway and Upwey station is the scene of the poem 'At the Railway Station, Upwey'. Once the junction for the Waddon Vale line, the station is still open for main-line traffic. Although Upwey is some $3\frac{1}{2}$ miles from Weymouth ('Budmouth', 'Budmouth Regis'), the houses of the resort have been extended along the A354 to form an unbroken link. Still nearer to Weymouth, but off the main road and therefore retaining much more of a village appearance, lies Nottington, the original of the anonymous spot where Anne Garland met King George III beside the 'sulphorous spring, good for various ailments'. Nottington is a spa that died. By the late eighteenth century treatises about its waters were already being published, yet it was not until 1830 that Thomas Shore built the so-called Round House—actually octagonal—for the comfort of patrons. By the turn of the next century it had become a laundry, and today it is a private house. The little spa's best time was when the spring was enclosed, as Anne saw it, only by a simple 'stone margin ... to prevent the cattle treading in the sides'. The sole relic of that era, a short flight of steps, with Georgian handrail, where visitors bathed in the near-by stream, disappeared within the last decade.

The references to Weymouth in Hardy's prose and verse are many. George III and his family, whose visits are so prominent in *The Trumpet-Major*, stayed at Gloucester Lodge, the 'homely house of red brick' now somewhat expanded to form the Gloucester Hotel, but still Georgian in appearance. Next door stands the Royal Hotel. The present building is late Victorian, but its predecessor with the 'circular bays' passed by Dick Dewy and Fancy Day was Stacie's Hotel, in which there were 'rattling good dinners' (*The Trumpet-Major*) while King George and his entourage danced in the Assembly Rooms below.

Except for the Gloucester and the Royal, almost the whole of this part of the seafront is unaltered Georgian, William IV, or early Victorian. The Victorian terraces consist entirely of small private hotels, among them the Belvidere at 3 Belvidere, Esplanade. Early in *Desperate Remedies* Miss Aldclyffe interviews Cytherea 'at the Belvedere Hotel, Esplanade'. The modern hotel of this name has been in existence only since the Second World War, but in 1867 number 13 Belvidere was listed as a lodging-house, which Hardy, who knew Weymouth well in the 1860s, evidently upgraded for his chatelaine. The spelling used by him is found in various contemporary documents. These terraces carried the new resort a fair distance eastward, but for three-quarters of a century the development had no depth. There are people still alive who recall when behind the terraces there were stables, and behind these the open fields bordering Lodmoor Marsh. In later Victorian times, when Weymouth experienced something of a renaissance, the area was rapidly built over. An early structure was the town station, near which stood the 'little Temperance inn' where in *The Well-Beloved* Marcia Bencomb put up. The inn's prototype, if there was one, is not identifiable.

Weymouth had two sets of assembly rooms. Those featured in 'The Ballad of Love's Skeleton' were probably in Stacie's Hotel. The other set, no less fashionable, were at the Old Rooms Inn across the harbour, where in *The Dynasts* burghers and boatmen discuss Trafalgar. The inn is situated in the oldest, most picturesque and least changed part of Weymouth beside the quays. Here old buildings remain on both sides of the water, their charm not diminished either by the modern cranes or by the sight, more familiar in Continental ports than in British, of passenger and goods trains making their way along the street with the motor traffic. Many of the 'heavy wooden bow-windows which appeared as if about to drop into the harbour by their own weight' (*The Trumpet-Major*) have not yet dropped, nor have they been eliminated by other means, except in the old High Street which was largely destroyed by bombs in the Second World War and is now the site of new municipal offices. There is even an illusion that green

shutters still abound, until one perceives that the green belongs mostly to the window-paint and fascias of Messrs Devenish's many taverns.

The harbour-side is also the territory of the tale 'A Committee-Man of "The Terror"'. He put up at the Old Rooms Inn (now open in summer only), the frontage of which has been modernized, with distinction lent to it by baskets of flowers hanging above the ground-floor windows. The harbour bridge (more often called the Town Bridge) that he approached from 'Thomas Street' was modified in 1880 by the substitution of a flat swing section for the central arch, and finally replaced in 1930. In its original form this bridge was the subject of the poem 'The Harbour Bridge'. St Thomas Street is now a major shopping thoroughfare, but above the modern shop-fronts many of the houses still exhibit their bow-windows.

The 'office of the town "Guide"' to which the Committee-Man went may have been any one of several establishments; since by 1804 there were already a number of guides. But if we assume the reference to be to the latest, then the office was Harvey's, probably in the same building as the library owned by him at 4 Charlotte Row on the sea-front, where the Dorothy Café now stands. The Committee-Man also called at the newspaper office, about which all that can be said is that the only local news-sheet circulating in Weymouth at the time was the *Sherborne Mercury*.

On the sea-front too was the theatre attended by Anne Garland and Bob Loveday in the King's presence, and in which the Committee-Man and Mlle V— watched Kemble in *The Rivals*. The theatre was very tiny. Fanny Kemble called it 'a doll's playhouse', Hardy 'a little building'; its capacity was probably less than 500 seats. It occupied the site of the present Weymouth Hotel and Malibu Club, near the western end of the Esplanade. Sketches show its principal entrance facing the sea, but it appears to have had access for carriages from Bond Street, where the jeweller's window is now. The last performance was given in 1859, ten years before Hardy worked in Weymouth for Crickmay. Today the

Above:
Some of the many pleasant bow-fronted houses still surviving on the western side of 'Budmouth' Harbour. The trees in the background are on the Nothe or Look-Out. Weymouth is prominent in Hardy's work.

Opposite:
'Budmouth' Harbour, looking toward the Backwater. The boat on the quay is awaiting repair at a Cove Row yard just out of sight. This is almost exactly where the boat-builder in *The Trumpet-Major* worked nearly 200 years ago.

Left:
The Old Rooms Inn, facing 'Budmouth' Harbour, is closed nowadays during the winter.

only vestiges of the theatre are in the basement: a small room with a fireplace, probably a dressing-room; a staircase near it ascending to the former stage area (today service stairs behind a bar counter); and a large cellar extending under the street, where perhaps scenery was stored.

Behind the theatre, parallel with St Thomas Street, runs St Mary Street, the 'Mary Street' of *Desperate Remedies* down which Manston's pursuers saw him making for the quay. At the end of this street too, near George III's statue, where 'the white angle of the last house in the row cut perpendicularly' into the seascape, Fancy Day met Dick Dewy for the drive home.

In the 130-odd years since the *Greenwood Tree* period the appearance of this corner has scarcely varied. The King's statue, brightly painted as a ship's figure-head and of about the same artistic standard, continues to gaze at the traffic on the Esplanade; the end house is now half white, half buff. St Mary Street, like St Thomas, has become an important shopping centre, but many old upper bow-windows survive.

Along the Esplanade the boatmen still offer skiffs for hire, as they did to those Crusted

Characters the Hardcomes. The date of the Hardcome story can probably be set some time during the second quarter of the nineteenth century. The allusion to 'the pier', therefore, even if we have to concede a possible measure of anachronism, is likely to be to the first true pier, built about 1840. Further west, between the

harbour and the new streets towards Sandsfoot, is the promontory called the Nothe, or in earlier times the Look-Out. Its dominant feature is still the great semi-underground fortress alluded to in *The Dynasts*; but the top is now laid out as pleasure-gardens, with lanes, rockeries and serpentine paths. When the Committee-Man walked there with Mlle V— it must have been like any other wild cliff-top. A year or two later Festus Derriman and Matilda, in *The Trumpet-Major*, also strolled there, and from its shelter the Melancholy Hussar and his companion rowed forth on their disastrous enterprise. Finally, the Hardcomes are seen upon the Look-Out with their fiancées.

Mlle V— and the Committee-Man had met by Cove Row, the terrace in which dwelt the boat-builder of whom Matilda had hopes. Cove Row nowadays is another of the unspoilt groups of little, mostly bow-windowed, houses unexpectedly surviving round the port; and there is a boat repairer, if not builder, there today.

Although so much nearer the sea, these old terraces are safer in bad weather than some of the buildings near the inner reaches of the harbour, at the back of the town. A song in *The Dynasts* treats of a wild night when the wind raved 'and the Back-Sea met the Front-Sea'. A footnote explains that the 'hind' part of the harbour was formerly called the Back-Sea. Today it is the Backwater; and when the wind whips up a spring tide the behaviour of the sea is sometimes no less alarming than in the old ballad.

At the northern (Radipole) end of Weymouth—in the period of *The Trumpet-Major* well outside the town—is the site of the cavalry barracks erected between 1795 and 1804. The barrack square, now built over, occupied the area bounded by Dorchester Road, Alexandra Road (on two sides), and Westbourne Road. The houses of Alexandra Terrace are thought to have been the officers' quarters, and the curious house facing into the elbow of Alexandra Road is also a barrack relic, as are one or two of the older villas in Dorchester Road.

9 **SOUTH WESSEX**
THE COAST EAST OF BUDMOUTH
Dorset: the coast east of Weymouth

Had I but lived a hundred years ago
I might have gone, as I have gone this year,
By Warmwell Cross on to a Cove I know,
And Time have placed his finger on me there:

AT LULWORTH COVE A CENTURY BACK

The route from Weymouth to Dorchester follows the ancient Ridgeway until, just north of the Upwey turning, it swings east and then sharply west again as it climbs to the crest of the downs. The old road, still present, ran nearly straight over the brow, along which a track also sometimes called the Ridgeway forms a white seam. While Laura Maumbry was living at Preston ('Creston') during the Fordington cholera outbreak, her husband used to meet her near where the road and this track cross; and dry-stone walls of the type that he kept between them still 'form the field-fences here'. When Lieutenant Vannicock turned up at the same spot Laura made him go down to the milestone 'on the north slope of the ridge, where the old and new roads diverge'. In fact the milestone stands at least a third of a mile north of the point of divergence; buried in 1940, it has now been disinterred and re-erected.

A few yards up from the southern end of the old road stands the Ship Inn, 'with a mast and cross-trees in front', where Dick Dewy installed Fancy Day in 'a little tea-room', probably a private parlour. The inn continues to flourish, with minimal alteration, and the pole outside was still a ship's mast, complete with fittings, until the 1970s, when decay caused its replacement by a dull concrete post.

A stage-coach passenger in *The Dynasts* remarks that there seems to be a deal of traffic over Ridgeway. On a modern summer day there is an even greater deal of it, but it is also well peopled with Hardy ghosts, crowding forth from *The Dynasts*, *The Trumpet-Major* and the poem 'The Alarm'. Hardy's own visits are recalled in 'Old Excursions' (with Emma) and perhaps in 'Where the Picnic Was'; this poem has been generally assumed to belong to Cornwall, but on his copy Lea pencilled a note, '"The hill to the sea"—?Ridgeway'; and Bailey suggests a picnic in June of the last year of Emma's life, while the poets Yeats and Newbolt were both visiting Max Gate. He could also have drawn attention to the lines 'I am here / Just as last year'; for Hardy did not visit Cornwall in two consecutive years after Emma's death. Today the ridge track is a favourite resort of holidaymakers from Weymouth and the many caravan camps.

Just at the point of the V where the motor-road is joined by one end of the loop-lane through Bincombe, is the scene, with Bincombe Down, of the tale 'The Melancholy Hussar of the German Legion'. Near the junction, by Bincombe Farm, Phyllis met Corporal Tina before changing her mind. In the village a mood appropriate to the small sad story (mainly a true one) is not hard to come by, for Bincombe is a tiny forgotten place with a population half what it was a century ago, and still declining. Some bright new barns are conspicuous, but there are few new houses. The small parish contains nearly fifty barrows, one of which is believed by Pinion to have yielded 'The Clasped Skeletons' of the poem thus called (see page 28).

The country about is very hilly, and Phyllis's parental home indeed stood almost level with the top of the church-tower. In its latter years divided into two cottages, the house has now been pulled down, but fragments of the floors and stones from the walls can still just be discerned in the long grass, together with vestiges of the cottage gardens. On the other side of the tiny lane an ancient stone wall, probably dating from the time of the story, must look very like the wall on which Phyllis sat. The church was restored in the 1860s. In the south-east corner of its little churchyard lies the site of the two Hussars' graves, and in the parish registers the record of the burial may still be read.

The troops who loom so large in Hardy's Napoleonic stories were encamped all along the downs above Bincombe and Sutton Poyntz ('Overcombe'). But 'The Ballad of Love's Skeleton', although set in the 1790s, has no martial associations. In its opening lines the speaker invites his girl to Culliford Wood on Culliford Hill to 'watch the squirrels climb, / And look in sunny places there / For shepherds' thyme'. The wood is now merged in Came Wood (the 'Damer's Wood' where Miller Loveday bought his weather-vane mast); shepherds' thyme still grows there, but the red squirrel has long been ousted by the grey. On the eastern edge a round barrow, crowned by tall beeches and named Culliford Tree, is perhaps the 'hill-top tree' of 'The Walk'. Some of the unmodernized old chalk roads are still 'gated'.

Along one of the chalk tracks stands lonely Northdown Barn. Beside it are the ruins of a stone cottage that seems likely to have been the one with the bricked-up windows used by the troops in *The Trumpet-Major* as their powder-magazine. Some of the windows are still filled in (with stone, not brick). The large barn intended for a hospital is no longer traceable, for if the identification of the powder-magazine is correct, Northdown Barn is surely too dangerously close. The granary 'on tall stone staddles' into which John Loveday saw his brother enter with Anne has almost certainly perished.

'Overcombe Mill' has been the subject of an

High on the downs behind Sutton Poyntz stands Culliford Tree, a 12-foot-high 'bowl' barrow tree-crowned and tree-girt. The site is very probably that of the 'hill-top tree' of the poignant little poem 'The Walk', composed after Emma Hardy's death.

Above:
The monstrously chalky downs behind 'Budmouth' make for difficult working. On this prairie-like expanse near Came Wood (seen in the background) some of George III's troops would have been stationed as part of the long defensive line against the expected Napoleonic invasion.

Opposite above:
Close to the busy 'Casterbridge–Budmouth' road, indeed close to 'Budmouth' itself, Bincombe remains isolated and tiny, even dwindling. In the foreground here are the slowly disappearing vestiges of the house occupied by Phyllis and her parents in the largely true story 'The Melancholy Hussar'.

Opposite below:
On Bincombe Hill, site of the barrow thought by some to have inspired, on being opened, the poem 'The Clasped Skeletons'.

unnecessary amount of confusion, the commonest belief being, as already mentioned (see page 128), that it was modelled on the mill at Upwey. Certainly Hardy was familiar with Upwey Mill; he made several trips to it, including one in 1879, the year in which *The Trumpet-Major* was written. But it is very unlikely that he had any purpose other than to refresh himself on the technicalities of the machinery, for neither the buildings nor the environment are reflected in 'Overcombe'. The mill in the novel is a largely imaginary creation, utilizing, however, easily recognizable features of the two mills then at Sutton Poyntz; and with a little industry it is not difficult to distinguish which features are taken from which.

The situation at the extreme end of the village, close under the downs, the description of the mill and millhouse as forming a single edifice, the details of the house and many features of the garden, are drawn from the Upper Mill; the relative positions of mill, millpond and cross, the statement that Anne ran out and looked 'up and down the road', the reference to a bridge at the

The dwelling-house of the Upper Mill at 'Overcombe', later the residence of the Superintendent of the Waterworks. The mill itself, demolished to make way for the Waterworks, was on the left.

mill-*head*, and the short distance Anne and Matilda had to carry Bob to reach the 'little stream', are based on the situation of the Lower Mill (see plan opposite).

There is still a Lower Mill, long abandoned but now being restored, though it is not the one in existence in Napoleonic times. The Upper Mill was pulled down in 1856 to make way for the Weymouth Waterworks pump-house. Hardy is therefore unlikely to have seen it, but twenty-three years later, during his researches in the neighbourhood, he must have found plenty of people to supply him with an authentic picture; and his description of the millhouse is none other than a portrait of the building that later became the home of the waterworks sup-

erintendent. The house looks far too new, but its appearance is deceptive. Its walls are much thicker than is to be expected of a residence put up in the mid-nineteenth century, and contain recesses and other features inexplicable in terms of that time. The hipped roof, though covered with modern slates, exactly fits Hardy's picture. When certain modernizations were carried out in Edwardian times several antique structural features were found, indicating that the house had been part of the mill. Hardy writes of four chimneys; today there are two, but a pair were removed during the work just mentioned. Plans drawn up for the pump-house show the mill residence in precisely the position of the present dwelling. The cover design, executed by Hardy himself, for the first edition of *The Trumpet-Major* shows a building so similar to the house there today as to compel belief that it was based on an imaginary reconstruction of the missing mill half.

The real millhouse, like Hardy's, had a large garden, which is still for the most part cultivated, although the house is now unoccupied. By local tradition the millpond occupied the north-east corner of the garden, above the point where one may still see the site of the sluice that controlled the backwater. Hardy, however, has clearly transferred the *Lower* Mill's great pool to the garden site, together with the road junction, the Cross, at its upper end.

There is no sign of the thorn-hedge so dense that the mill-boy could have walked along the top of it, but the 1856 plan shows the garden and forecourt bounded by a 'fence' of prodigious width. Two millstones recently dug up may have been the pair Hardy said were used for courtyard paving. (There is also a *path* of millstones at the Lower Mill, but Hardy specifies two stones, in a courtyard.) The tree into which Bob leaped to make his escape belonged to the Lower Mill, and was only recently felled.

The 'eastern road' by which the press gang returned to resume their search for Bob still exists in the form of a track that after leading east from outside the waterworks gate, turns north through some industrial premises and meanders up to the crest of the downs. Unless the traces of the zig-zag path cut by the cavalry have vanished only since Lea's day, it is probable that in claiming to have seen the path he was really looking at this route. The 'spring or riverhead' at the back of the mill is in fact some distance up the escarpment. The water authorities have built a brick surround, converting it into a miniature reservoir, and enclosed the neighbouring area with an iron fence.

The novel's many references to bridges are, with one exception, all but impossible to follow on the ground, and Hardy probably put bridges where he wanted them. The exception is the bridge under which the girls hid Bob, 'where a little stream passed under the road' about 200 yards from the mill. This has been variously identified with the footbridge at the southern

Sutton Poyntz before the building of the waterworks.

Here, toward the southern end of 'Overcombe', is the modernized version of the bridge to which Anne and Matilda carried the unconscious Bob Loveday before hiding him under the arch from the press-gang. The stream is a western tributary of the Jordon.

Opposite left:
Part of the large pond at 'Overcombe' (Sutton Poyntz) which was in reality the millpool for the Lower Mill, but which Hardy transposes in *The Trumpet-Major* to serve the Upper Mill – a source of much confusion to students of the novel's topography.

'entering the opening by which the cattle descended to drink' on the down-stream side, and carrying their burden into the tunnel.

Modern Sutton Poyntz clings desperately to its former status as a pretty, old-world village, but it is losing the battle. At one end the best group of cottages looks across the pond at a very plain inn, at present unoccupied, just north of which is the monstrous excrescence of the waterworks. At the other end the fight is against the encroaching villas and bungalows of Weymouth's outer suburbs. Even the centre had its aesthetic handicap—a light-engineering factory, but this has now been converted into housing.

Preston, astride the A353, forms virtually one village with Sutton Poyntz, sharing the church to which the miller's household were going when they noticed the proclamation on the elm-tree. Here suburbia vies with groves of holiday caravans (making 'Creston Shore' very different from when Edward and Cytherea directed their boat thither in *Desperate Remedies*), and apart from the church, only a dozen cottages and the pleasant old Ship Inn (mentioned in *The Trumpet-Major*) remain from Laura Maumbry's day and even the inn is now closed.

Between Preston and the real-life Overcombe is Jordon Hill, on which are the remains of a Roman temple first excavated during 1843 and the years following. Lea states that this is the 'Pagan temple' of the poem 'The Well-Beloved', without, however, explaining why Hardy should have transferred the site to Bere Regis. In any case, later research has shown that the temple was not dedicated to Venus, but (probably) to Aesculapius. The original discoveries were covered in, re-exhumed in 1932, and are now in the care of the Department of the Environment.

end of the present Lower Mill pond, and the so-called Roman bridge a long way to the south-west, mistakenly sketched by New. The correct bridge is situated slightly south of the union of Sutton's two main lanes, and carries the road over the stream from Poxwell ('Oxwell') that joins the Jordon close by. The modern bridge is of brick, with parapets, but its predecessor may well have been unparapeted, and its arch, to judge from today's, would have been suitable for the concealment. Houses now flank either side of the road, but a little meadow surviving on the upstream side makes it easy to visualize the girls

Above:
A photograph taken in the garden (part of which is still cultivated) of the millhouse once attached to the demolished Upper Mill at 'Overcombe'. The real pool serving this mill has been filled in, but traces of the sluice controlling the backwater (overflow channel) and other workings are still identifiable.

Below:
'Oxwell Hall' (Poxwell Manor House), dilapidated home of the dilapidated Derrimans in *The Trumpet-Major*, has long since been restored. In this view of the former entrance front, the little gate-lodge usually shown is behind the camera, to allow an uninterrupted sight of the seventeenth-century façade.

The White Horse on the downs continues to be a landmark, as intended, though it would be more of one if the chalk were weeded and perhaps whitewashed; most of the white horses in Wiltshire put King George and his mount to shame. Not far away the Derriman home, Poxwell Manor, pictured in *The Trumpet-Major* in the last stages of dilapidation, has been fully restored, and is undoubtedly better kept and more beautifully furnished than at any time since the Hennings (Hardy uses the correct name) built it over 300 years ago. The 'great parlour' in which the cavalrymen roystered is now the dining-room. The main entrance is now at the back, where the fleeing Anne, after going through a door in the kitchen-garden wall, found herself on 'a rutted cart-track, which had been a pleasant gravelled drive'. This, like the last part of her approach from Sutton, bears little relation to fact, being largely a carry-over from Hardy's original placing of 'Overcombe' nearly north of Weymouth, close to Radipole.

The short carriage-drive leading to the gateway at the front is yet in evidence, although no longer used. There are still fine trees nearby. The arched gateway with the porter's lodge over it has also been unobtrusively renovated; its outside stone stair is straight, not spiral. The house used to be subject to flooding, but today land-drainage has been much helped by the creation of a beautifully designed ornamental pond in the area between the lodge and the road. Within the walled 'quadrangle' where Old Derriman kept his livestock, beautiful flower-borders surround a smooth, rich lawn. In the façade of the mansion modern metal casements have replaced those stanchions worn away to 'mere wires'. Puzzlingly, there is no trace at all of the vertical sundial in the middle of the porch, nor were there ever any battlements.

Inside, the dining-room 'traditionally called the great parlour' has been superbly restored. The stone fireplace is separately scheduled for preservation, and the plaster ceiling and furniture are exquisite. Mellow farm buildings adjoin the manor.

It was over the Pokeswell Hills (Hutchins's spelling) that the sea mists came which sent the bees fleeing in the poem 'The Sheep-Boy'. These coastal downs give an impression of utter changelessness, and it is surprising to discover that 'Clive Holland's' photograph of 1899 (the New York *Bookman*) shows them, above Sutton Poyntz, criss-crossed with many hedges. All these have disappeared, although the downs are still scored by the old chalk roads, in contrast to which the only modern route is the A353.

Where this meets the A352 and continues beyond it as the B3390 is Warmwell ('Warm'ell') Cross, mainly of interest for the ambushing of the Revenue men in the tale of 'The Distracted Preacher'. Nowadays the cross has become a large roundabout, and in place of the 'plantation which surrounded' the crossroads we have a group of tall conifers growing out of the central island itself. The old cross was not exactly in the position of the roundabout, but a little to the east. Several fragments of the former approaches survive; one even shows traces of a central white line—an indication of how recently it was superseded. Warmwell village is the 'Springham' of *The Trumpet-Major*.

The action of 'The Distracted Preacher' takes place mainly in Owermoigne ('Nether Moynton', 'Nether Mynton'), a quiet village just north of the A352. Though quiet, it has not been overlooked by the modern developer, and has many new houses of the smaller type, most of them lining a completely new street. The church was rebuilt in 1883, but the old tower remains; access to the platform at the top is still obtained just as in Hardy's account, except for the first stage, the 'singing gallery' having disappeared. Entry to the bell-loft is now gained by an enclosed spiral staircase attached to the tower.

The churchyard is, as described, higher than the road outside, but to the east a comparatively new wall now divides it from a farm-building enclosure. If Lizzie Newberry's garden was genuine, it has become separated from the churchyard by this agricultural intrusion; for her house, again assuming that it existed, must have been east of the church, and was probably one of the two attractive cottages still extant. Both accord with Lea's description, 'nearly opposite the Rectory'. On the opposite side of the churchyard there is an old, high-walled garden locally believed to be the prototype of Owlett's orchard, although it contains no trace of the famous hide-out, which was modelled on genuine examples. More or less facing this, at the corner of Holland's Mead Avenue, the new street already mentioned, stands the old forge; much altered and modernized, but still containing the smith's bellows.

There was never a Methodist chapel in Owermoigne, but up a narrow gravel track on the other side of Holland's Mead Avenue stands an ancient stone thatched house, Chilbury Cottage, where Methodist services were held during the last century. The cottage later fell on hard times, but has been excellently restored; the large parlour used for the meetings is now subdivided into kitchen and living-room. In 1983 the house was put up for sale. The old main 'street or lane' of Owermoigne is very long, and since it is not the principal theatre of modern development, it continues to display 'more hedge than houses'. At the far end stands the former mill, now a private house; even the stream has been diverted. The mill had previously been rebuilt in about 1850.

The other places in 'The Distracted Preacher' can easily be identified, Hardy having used many real names. Immediately across the A352 a lane leads over Gallows Hill to the tiny hamlet of Holworth, once a sizeable village but now consisting of two farms and a pillar-box. Lizzie Newberry took this route on her nocturnal expedition to Ringstead Bay ('Ringsworth Shore'). Beyond Holworth a chalk track leads directly over the magnificent empty downs to the bay. The latter too is magnificent—nearly a mile of golden curving beach backed by tumbled grassy hills rising to 500 feet, and in all of it scarcely a house or even a caravan visible. But just round the western horn a nascent holiday-villa and chalet colony stands ominously poised.

With the White Nothe and the Chaldons we come to territory associated more often with other writers, T. F. Powys, Llewellyn Powys and David Garnett, than with Hardy. Chaldon Herring ('Chaldon') appears in 'The Distracted Preacher' when Lizzie makes her second night journey. This time, after crossing the main road, she turns east along the hillside and then south over Lord's Barrow, which is at the intersection of two chalk lanes. Apart from the fact that the north–south lane, which leads to the Chaldons, has been given a modern surface, this landscape can hardly have changed in a single detail. Hardy says that the travellers reached Chaldon Down, and then a ravine on the outskirts of 'Chaldon'. In fact, both Chaldons and the ravine linking them lie between Lord's Barrow and the down, so that Lizzie and the preacher must have come to them in the reverse order. The next landmark was the earthwork called Round Pound, a low circular enclosure on a hill-crest. There is a measure of shrub vegetation that obviously changes with time, otherwise yet again an unaltered scene.

From Round Pound Lizzie led the way to Dagger's Gate ('Dagger's Grave'), stated by Hardy to be 'not many hundred yards' from Lulworth ('Lullstead', 'Lulwind') Cove, but in fact about a mile off. Here was her rendezvous with the smugglers, who went on to the edge of the cliff and descended by rope. Dagger's Gate is simply a point in a shallow valley where the road from Winfrith Newburgh to the cove is crossed by a chalk track, the old chalk road along the hills; some farm outbuildings of various dates stand a short distance away. At the foot of a coomb between White Nothe and Durdle Door there is still to be seen an old wire rope, put in place by fishermen or smugglers, no one knows when, to give access to the beach.

Durdle Door, a much-pictured natural arch extending from the cliffs, is referred to by Hardy in the last stanza of 'The Bird-Catcher's Boy'. A rough stairway, blending with the rock, has been made over the neck of the arch to link the two small bays on either side of it; there are paths

The coastal downs near 'Chaldon' (Chaldon Herring) crossed by the smugglers in 'The Distracted Preacher' and by many a real smuggler: the story is far from entirely fictional. The region is still exceptionally bare.

An unusual view of 'Lullwind' (Lulworth) Cove from 'Dagger's Grave' (Dagger's Gate). The familiar nearly circular inlet is here hidden by the dark hill on the right. The Cove suffers today from a garish response to over-popularity.

along and up the steep grass slopes above the cliffs; and on the level summit, partly masked by a grove of pine-trees, there is a caravan camp. In summer the area is crowded enough, but out of season it must be allowed that the scene has escaped serious disfigurement.

In *Desperate Remedies* the picture of Lulworth Cove, to which Owen took Cytherea, is preceded by a description of the excursion paddle-steamers that used to ply from Weymouth. The practice lasted well into the twentieth century, but nowadays the only visitors by sea come in motor-boats. There is, however, one link with the paddle-steamers: landing and embarkation were effected 'by the primitive plan of a narrow plank on two wheels—the women being assisted by a rope'. A contraption of this sort is still drawn up on the beach, and another, only slightly modified, stands beside it for use with the small launches that take excursionists for short round trips. The visiting vessels no longer land their passengers.

In Lulworth Cove the drowned bodies of Stephen Hardcome and his cousin's wife (*A Few Crusted Characters*) were cast ashore, and here Sergeant Troy set out for the swim that gave rise to the belief that he had been drowned. It is also the scene of the poem 'At Lulworth Cove a Century Back' and appears in *The Dynasts*. The Cove today is the victim of its own popularity. Old buildings include a terrace of fishermen's cottages, and some other cottages of charm, thatched and otherwise; but a large car- and coach-park right in the centre, a raw red-brick restaurant in the midst of this, various pieces of uninspiring construction in the lane leading down to the sea, and a general atmosphere of lollies and Cola bottles, squawking children and fat grannies with bad feet, do not make for picturesqueness or dignity, whatever their other virtues.

There are several hotels, but the inn mentioned in *Desperate Remedies* is none of these; it is somewhat toward the back of the village, north of the church, and is now a pleasant private residence, long and low, with two porches and colour-washed walls. The 'perfectly straight' road 'more than a mile in length' by which Troy approached the coast cannot be identified, because none of the approaches is straight.

The army camp at Lulworth is as hideous as the worst features of the Cove village, with none of the latter's redeeming aspects. Adjoining it is the large zone closed to the public 'temporarily' in 1940 as a firing-range. The area, including Tyneham and several smaller settlements, is still prohibited, but in 1974 the military at last relaxed their hold to the extent of allowing access to certain roads, paths, and sections of coast at designated times, before each of which these regions have to be re-cleared of explosives. It is even possible now to explore the ruins of Tyneham. As it chances, only one of Hardy's settings is affected. This is Steeple, the 'Kingscreech' of 'Old Mrs Chundle', which at firing times may be approached only from the east. Pinion identifies 'Kingscreech' with Kingston ('Little Enkworth'), three miles to the east. But 'Kingscreech' was in the charge of a curate, which Kingston was not and Steeple was, under the rector of Tyneham (a rector is also mentioned in the story). Steeple church, unlike either church at Kingston, used to have a gallery like 'Kingscreech' and still has an octagonal wooden pulpit, albeit not at the top of eight steps. The old lady's cottage, near the parish boundary where a lane branched off to Encombe ('Enkworth' or 'Enckworth'), was probably situated, or imagined, slightly north of Smedmore Hill. Creech Barrow is also on the parish boundary. Steeple today remains a tiny somnolent place, amalgamated ecclesiastically with Church Knowle.

Encombe House, so prominent in *The Hand of Ethelberta*, is a graceful eighteenth-century mansion in a fairy-tale setting, built for one of the sons of George Pitt of Kingston Maurward and later acquired by the Eldons, who were in turn superseded. Disappointingly, although Hardy describes both house and grounds at considerable length, almost all his descriptive passages are spurious. Some features (see page 34) are perhaps borrowed, like the anecdote that 'Enkworth's' original brick was faced with stone at the insistence of George III, from Kingston Maurward. But Beatty believes that Hardy simply devised for this mansion all that he disliked in interior decoration.

Kingston ('Little Enkworth'), whither the brougham was brought for Ethelberta's flight, stands on a typical Purbeck ridge, and is distinguished for G. E. Street's cathedral-like church of 1880. The old church (1838) is now used as a village hall. About three miles south, the coast pushes out to form St Aldhelm's or St Alban's Head, mentioned in the poems 'At Lulworth Cove a Century Back' and 'Days to Recollect'. The latter well evokes the atmosphere of the huge grassy headland, round which one may now walk by the Dorset coast path. The ancient chapel that once carried a light to guide seamen, and the coastguard station at the base of the promontory, were both there in the *Ethelberta* period; new are the quarters of the small RAF unit at Worth Matravers and the group of radar masts between that village and the point.

At the south-east corner of the Isle of Purbeck is Durlston Head, the 'old cliff' to which Hardy addressed himself in the poem 'To a Sea-Cliff'. Since 1975 the old wilderness behind the headland has become Durlston Country Park, an area of outstanding natural beauty and special scientific interest, and one of the most bizarre nature sanctuaries in Britain.

Swanage ('Knollsea') looms large in *The Hand of Ethelberta*, and the poem 'Once at Swanage' splendidly describes a rough sea witnessed here by Hardy and Emma not long after their marriage. The sea wall has been extensively rebuilt, in particular near the piers. The old pier remains in evidence, though reduced now to an irregular column of piles with a few cross-beams and planks. The 'new' pier, a magnificent piece of late Victoriana built in 1897, is close by. It still caters for excursion craft and in the summer there is still a regular service to Bournemouth ('Sandbourne'), but it is many years since steamers for Cherbourg called.

Architecturally Swanage has come in for some justifiably harsh strictures, but it has retained its pre-resort nucleus intact, even to the old lock-up, the 'stone chimneys' mentioned by Hardy, the millpool, and several footways still paved with the original slabs. The church underwent Victorian restoration, but despite extensions in 1908 is still in keeping with its mellow surroundings. The tower with the unembattled parapet that impressed Hardy has been preserved.

Captain Flower's tiny cottage 'on a high slope above the townlet' is modelled not, as Lea states, on Durlston Cottage, but on West End Cottage, one of a pair at the end of a short cul-de-sac off Seymer Road. Here Hardy and Emma stayed early in their married life, the real owner being Captain Masters, first coxswain of the Swanage lifeboat. The cream, slate-roofed pair of cottages are still occupied and in good repair, and their tiny gardens survive, though without 'The Lodging-House Fuchsias' hanging over the path. In contrast the 'orchard of aged [apple] trees' on the slope in front—the orchard garden of the Royal Victoria Hotel—fell to the developers in the mid-1960s, and is now covered by a congeries of flats and bungalows that dismally limit the view of the sea from West End Cottage. The 'grange scenery' included in the old view must refer to the grounds of the Grove, the mansion that preceded the Grosvenor Hotel down by the shore. Below the seaward side of this lay the sheltered stretch of shore known as Down-under-wall.

The 'brilliant variegated brick and stone villa' to which Ethelberta and her sister moved was probably one of the houses in Park Road. Swanage began to be 'discovered' around 1880, after the period of the novel. The first visitors were authors, artists, and people in need of rest and quiet, whom the inhabitants were glad to lodge in their own cottages. Only some years later were the first few hotels and true boarding-houses erected—just in time, perhaps, for the miserable honeymoon on which Raye and Anna were setting out at the end of the story 'On the Western Circuit'.

'Enkworth Court' (Encombe House), familiar to readers of *The Hand of Ethelberta*, seen from the neighbouring downs in its beautiful ravine that leads down to the sea west of St Aldhelm's Head. The house, of Purbeck stone throughout, was designed in the early eighteenth century by an unidentified architect.

The coast looking westward from Swyre Head above 'Enkworth Court'. The deep inlet is Kimmeridge Bay; the large building near the centre, Smedmore House.

The 'sinister ledge of limestones ... like a crocodile's teeth' (*Ethelberta*), to avoid which steamers southbound from Swanage had to steam east at first, refers to the rocky ledge off Peveril Point, at the southern tip of Swanage Bay. On the northern side of the bay the white cliffs, followed close in-shore during good weather by the Bournemouth steamers, are those between Ballard Point and Handfast Point; and at Ballard Point, still unbuilt on—indeed, currently the scene of agricultural experiments—one can see the vertical cliff 'rounding off at the top in vegetation, like a forehead with low-grown hair', as it is described in the novel. This is the 'Bollard Head' of the poem 'The Brother'. The great white cliffs are more than ever 'hollowed into gaping caverns', and the two famous pillars, Old Harry and his Wife (described but not named in the novel), have suffered a fatality, though whether it is Old Harry or the Wife who has collapsed into the sea depends on whether you accept the verdict of Swanage or of Studland.

When Ethelberta rode her donkey from Swanage to Corfe ('Corvsgate') Castle, she started along the shore and then climbed to 'the lofty ridge which ran inland', Ballard Down. From here, on a fine day, the views so graphically limned by Hardy are hard to match, particularly northward across Poole Harbour. In the foreground, including the harbour, they have changed little, save for the line of cars snaking towards the Sandbanks ferry. But the middle-distance scene is as different from what Ethelberta saw as the ferry-bound cars are from her donkey: to the left of Brownsea Island—still exhibiting 'fir-trees and gorse' and now jointly administered by the National Trust and the Dorset Naturalists' Trust—the giant power-station chimneys and great square blocks of industrial Poole ('Havenpool'); to the right of the isle, the tall cliff-top hotels and apartment blocks of Bournemouth ('Sandbourne'); and behind both, the residential spread stretching toward Wimborne and Verwood.

Ballard Down is continued westward by Nine Barrow Down, given its own name in *Ethelberta*. Although from the Swanage–Corfe Castle road the tumuli make the ridge look like the back of a prehistoric monster, they are less numerous here than on some of the coastal heights farther west, and do not justify Hardy's epithet of 'a huge cemetery'. As one nears Corfe, the 'brilliant crimson heaths' (in season) round the head of the 'many-armed inland sea' become increasingly evident; and because their sandy base is pale, the paths that cross them still gleam white, in contrast to the tarred roads. Hardy does not exaggerate when he suggests that the more sombre climate south of the ridge encourages darker vegetation than to the north; nor have the agricultural advances of later times materially affected the contrast. Today the land south of Poole Harbour includes bird sanctuaries, nature reserves and, in remarkable but reasonably discreet contrast, Britain's most productive land-based oil wells at Wytch Farm.

Corfe Castle stands on a high knoll in the only gap (apart from that of Ulwell, close to the coast), in the long chain of Purbeck Hills. This celebrated place is noticed by Hardy only in *Ethelberta* and 'Old Mrs Chundle'. Since the castle's partial demolition in the Civil War it has remained uncommonly static. Squat towers that lean at crazy angles over the valley and look as if the next storm will send them crashing down can be seen leaning at exactly the same angles in Hutchins's 200-year-old engraving.

The moat and first gateway remain as described by Hardy, and despite the tread of tourists beyond number the 'green inclines' are green still. No genuine dungeons are in sight, but one or two lower rooms with barrel roofs may include the 'dungeon' entered by Ethelberta and the others, particularly since the rooms are 'partly open to the air overhead'. Owned since 1635 by the Bankes family (one of whom, Lady Bankes, defended it most spiritedly against Cromwell, and was vanquished only by treachery). It was in 1982 that Corfe Castle was made over to the National Trust, but not before the last Bankes owner had done much to preserve the ruins from any further deterioration.

Corfe Castle village is almost too pretty, as though constructed expressly for the summer coachloads. The only building identifiable in the novel is the Castle Inn, a small inn as stated. Situated on the highway to Swanage, it is unspoilt except for the presence of two petrol pumps. The 'village inn' elsewhere referred to is more likely to be the Greyhound or the Fox, both larger and more central—and also outwardly unspoilt. This absence of intrusive modern building caused Corfe Castle to be preferred to Dorchester for 'Casterbridge' in the 1970s TV serialization of *The Mayor of Casterbridge*.

Wareham and Lytchett Minster have already been dealt with in other sections (pages 68 and 57). Upton House, on the edge of Poole, is the prototype, in situation only, of 'Wyndway House' in *Ethelberta*. Neither the 'marble bas-relief of some battle-piece' nor the 'gilded and chandeliered salon' is to be found in the building; but the grounds do border a 'sheet of embayed sea', namely Holes Bay, a large lagoon (now bisected by the railway) at the back of

'Corvsgate' (Corfe) Castle, goal of the excursion in *The Hand of Ethelberta*. First built before the Conquest, it was steadily enlarged throughout the centuries. After its capture by the Cromwellians those charged with 'slighting it' found it so sturdy that the attempt to blow it up was only partially successful. 'Corvsgate' was the original Saxon name.

Poole Harbour. Except on this side, they are hemmed in today by the town's suburbs. During the 1960s the house, which belongs to Poole Corporation, was the home of an exiled Rumanian prince.

The 'paved wharf-side' of Poole Harbour is the scene of that almost unbearable poem 'The Mongrel'. But Poole itself, although touched upon once or twice, is used as a setting only once, in the short story 'To Please His Wife'. In this, adopting a practice unusual with him, Hardy uses four surnames all of which, with minor spelling variations, are to be found on the walls of the parish church, St James. With its pillars of Newfoundland pine, St James is a charming example of its period, completed in

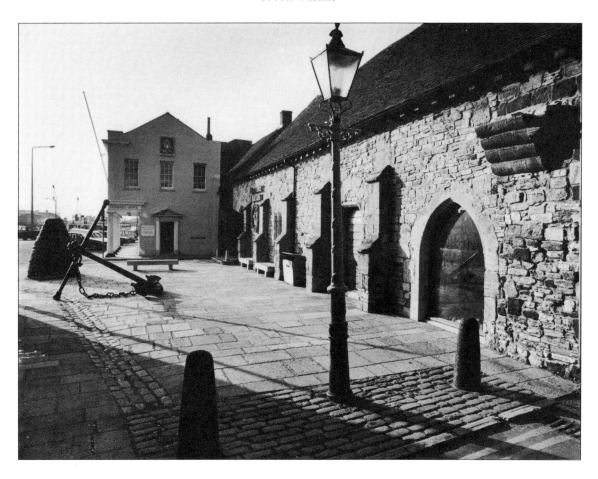

1820 and unmodified since. The 'Town Hall' from which Jolliffe escorted Emily Hanning home is the Old Guildhall, occupying an island site in Market Street and still structurally intact, in spite of having been converted into public baths before becoming a museum. The Town Cellars on the quay remains one of Poole's show pieces, with church-like buttresses and Gothic doorway and windows.

'Sloop Lane', in which stood the Hannings's stationery shop, does not appear in the annals of Poole, nor on Hutchins's town map. In the *Thomas Hardy Year Book* no 2 H. V. F. Johnstone argues credibly for Hardy having had in mind Bull's Head Lane (now Prosperous Street), close to which there used to be a little stationer's (Woodford's) that admirably fitted Hardy's description, even to the step down inside the

Among 'Havenpool's' (Poole's) historic buildings preserved after official indifference had allowed many to be destroyed are these two on the Quay. On the left, the Harbour Office, 1822. On the right, the fifteenth-century Town Cellars, now the Maritime Museum. Until 1788 the Cellars were twice as long, the big arch in the foreground marking the centre.

Opposite:
Somewhat misleadingly named The Mansion House, this agreeable late eighteenth-century residence in Thames Street, 'Havenpool', used to be the home of the real Lesters, though whether it was the home of Mr Lester in 'To Please His Wife' is subject to speculation on whether Hardy was introducing one of his familiar precautionary deceptions by stating that the house 'faced directly on the High Street'.

entrance. Mr Lester's home was a 'large, sub-stantial brick mansion' which 'faced directly on the High Street'. There are several houses, in particular Beech Hurst or Beechurst (built 1798—now offices) and Sir Peter Thompson's House (1749)—that answer to this description, and inevitably Lea identified the 'right' one. On the other hand the former home of the real-life Lesters, now the Mansion House Hotel & Club in Thames Street some way from the High Street, is also an exquisite red-brick Georgian house, splendidly kept today as a private hotel and diners' club.

The 'long, straight road' that ascended 'east-ward to an elevated suburb where the more fashionable houses stood' is likely to mean Parkstone Road; the 'elevated suburb' is Park-stone, still the most elegant part of Poole. In the mid-nineteenth century, when Poole was smal-ler, Bournemouth was still so tiny that a fair stretch of heath separated them; today, though utterly unlike, they form a single urban mass.

In addition to a noteworthy arts centre, much industrial and residential new building has come to Poole, some of it, like the Poole Pottery establishment on the quay, in the very heart of the oldest quarter. Nevertheless, the place re-mains rich in old buildings, ancient alleys and quaint corners, despite the tardiness of the corporation in perceiving its duty to preserve them. Even Master John Horseleigh and his Edith, who lived here with her brother in the 1540s, would recognize more than a few scenes.

10 UPPER WESSEX
HAMPSHIRE

I joined in a jolly trip to Weydon-Priors Fair:
I shot for nuts, bought gingerbreads, cream-cheese...

A LAST JOURNEY

Southsea ('Solentsea') was where the Imaginative Woman and her husband ousted the poet Robert Trewe from Coburg House. Except for sundry new houses and flats, the seafront terraces are still predominantly Victorian. Of the several terraces and parades, St Helen's Parade displays unmatching houses with steps up to their entrances and small front gardens, but none particularly suggests Coburg House. Opposite the houses, trim public gardens with a bandstand have replaced a wild common. The excursion steamers used to tie up at Clarence Pier, completely rebuilt in 1961. The cemetery in the story was probably the one in Highland Road.

'The fashionable town on the island opposite' is Ryde, Isle of Wight, which in the last forty years has doubled its population and halved its exclusiveness. Bonchurch, adjoining Ventnor on the south-east coast, is the scene of 'A Singer Asleep', verses in tribute to Swinburne. This small, steep resort also remains predominantly Victorian, and Swinburne's house and remarkably hideous tomb are in good preservation.

Portsmouth receives few mentions by Hardy; its most illustrious showpiece, HMS *Victory*, well described in *The Trumpet-Major*, was renovated some years ago, and now, of course, competes in interest with the recently salvaged *Mary Rose*. Southampton is alluded to more often, but is never used as a setting.

Bournemouth ('Sandbourne') Pier, mentioned in *Ethelberta*, was the old wooden pier opened in 1861, partly swept away six years later, and replaced by the present iron pier in 1880. The plural allusion to 'piers' in *Tess* takes account of Boscombe and Southbourne piers, both built in the 1880s, of vhich Boscombe, rebuilt after severe Second World War damage, survives. Bournemouth pier has also been restored since the war. The groves of pines—authentic remnants of the heath—the promenades, the covered gardens, are more than ever a feature of this 'city of detached mansions' (*Tess*), which themselves have largely given place to huge blocks of flats. It was in one of the then new houses among the pines—or firs, as Hardy calls them—that in *The Hand of Ethelberta* the Chickerells made their last home, Firtop Villa. In Tess's day the population was 18,000; in 1961 151,000, but in 1981, surprisingly, below 145,000. A mile inland from the houses it is difficult to credit the proximity of a large town.

'The Herons' being imaginary, we do not know the starting-point of Tess's last independent journey; nor is the fugitives' route very clear. Angel walked from one of the Bournemouth stations—probably the western—toward the next one 'onward', that is westward, for he crossed a valley (the Bourne?) in that direction and was overtaken by Tess after turning north into the fir wood just beyond it. The couple continued north through the firs that 'here abounded for miles' but have now mostly given way to buildings as far out as Hurn Forest. The inn near which they stopped to eat seems to have been in the Hurn–St Leonards area. Afterwards they went on 'into the depths of the New Forest' to 'Bramshurst Manor', an empty house that stood 'behind a brook and a bridge' and has been identified with Moyles Court, north of Ringwood. Correctly defined as 'an old brick building of regular design and large accommodation', the ancient manor had by 1860 decayed to a mere shell. Today, fully restored, it is a preparatory school for girls and boys. The brook and bridge are easily recognizable, despite the presence of a new concrete bridge nearby.

The New Forest ('the Great Forest') is the subject of the poem 'Throwing a Tree'; and inevitably the Trampwoman and her friends included it in their territory. It is not easy to say how different it looked then, or even at the later day when Tess and Angel passed through it. Roads, for instance, have increased in busyness but scarcely in number. Holiday-makers strow parts of the forest with caravans, but so did the gypsies. Its extent has remained roughly the

Outside 'Wintoncester' (Winchester) Cathedral, inside which the story of 'Lady Mottisfont' opens. Not many years ago the foundations of the original Saxon minster were discovered just beyond the gaunt trees on the right.

same for the past 300 years, and the number of trees has actually increased since Hardy wrote. The verderers' courts and most of the old forest laws persist, though the Forestry Commission took over management of the timber in 1923.

Almost in Tess's and Angel's path lay Hurn Court, the 'Rookington Park' of *Ethelberta* and today a boys' school. The unchanged frontage (last modified in 1840) still looks on to a large 'expanse of green grass', near which are majestic vestiges of the once-plentiful 'fine old timber'.

Although no longer a lonely town 'hardly modified' by 'years of steam traffic', Ringwood is unmistakably the 'Oozewood' of 'Master John Horseleigh, Knight'. It retains picturesque features, but motor transport has succeeded where steam (now departed) failed: the population has jumped by seventy per cent in the last few years, and most of the consequent new building is humdrum. The Walls' house is untraceable, as is the 'Black Lamb', though a plain Lamb (rebuilt) stands near the disused station.

The 'Noble Dame' story, 'Lady Mottisfont', is laid mainly in two mansions near Romsey. 'Deansleigh Park' is Broadlands, a buff-toned classical building in a gracious park on the town's outskirts. This was the birthplace and for long the home of Lord Palmerston, later becoming the seat of the Mountbattens. Hardy's reference to a 'pool fed by a trickling brook' is puzzling, for the River Test, which flows before the house, was broad even before its enlargement to form a lake. The other mansion, 'Fernell Hall', is the former Embley House, two miles to the west. Here for many years, whenever she could escape from London, lived Florence Nightingale; but the house was almost wholly rebuilt in the late 1960s, and is now yet another boys' school.

'Lady Mottisfont' opens in Winchester ('Wintoncester') Cathedral, inside which the changes since Hardy wrote have been few. Outside, however, where the cathedral green lies to the north of the nave, excavations have revealed the complex foundations of the old minster—the Saxon cathedral—and below these part of the Roman forum. Nor is the site the only one in the city where ancient Winchester is being unearthed; yet, in contrast, so many new buildings have been put up that Angel Clare and 'Liza-Lu would have difficulty in recognizing some areas, though not the gaol. A new wing has been added to this, the various frontages facing the road have been rendered and painted white, and no flagstaff now rises from the octagonal tower; but the other Hardy features, even to the 'yews and evergreen oaks' on their high bank above the roadside wall, are all present still. Only the white wicket through which the two visitors slipped out has gone, having been bricked up in the interests of safety.

Farther up the hill the first milestone on the

Above:
A deal of argument has been expended over whether Angel Clare and Liza-Lu could have really seen the tower of 'Wintoncester' Gaol from beside this milestone on the Romsey road. Of course the trees were much smaller, the houses still to be built, and yet . . . However, I am assured by someone who has carried out expert research that it would have been possible – just.

Opposite above:
The 'Great Forest' (New Forest) figures incidentally in a number of Hardy's prose and verse writings, but is a major setting only toward the close of *Tess* and in the poem 'Throwing a Tree'. Unlike the 'heath-croppers' on 'Egdon Heath', the famous New Forest ponies are nowhere mentioned.

Opposite below:
'Rookington Park' (Hurn Court) in *The Hand of Ethelberta* lies just behind 'Sandbourne' (Bournemouth), disquietingly near to Hurn Airport. Nevertheless, some at least of the 'fine old timber' survives to adorn the grounds of what is now a boys' school.

Romsey road continues to stand, legible if no longer white, on the 'green margin of the grass', near a bus shelter. It is hard to believe that even without the multiplication of buildings and trees that today obscures the view, Angel and 'Liza-Lu could ever have seen the gaol tower and panorama of the city from beside the milestone. But I am indebted to the careful researches of Miss Josephine Dool, of Winchester City Museum, for the opinion that the spectacle might just have been possible; and there is the fact that Hardy afterwards took his friend Florence Henniker to the spot without that forthright lady recording any denial.

North-east of Winchester there stood, until its demolition in the 1960s, Herriard House, Pinion's suggestion for the prototype of 'Icenway House' in 'The Lady Icenway'. Lea postulated Marwell Hall: but this is so nearly due south of Winchester as to seem hardly consistent with Hardy's statement that from 'Heymere

Map of the Principal Towns and Villages of UPPER WESSEX

BASED ON THE WORKS OF THOMAS HARDY

Key to the Map of Upper Wessex
Hardy's names in italics.

Bramshurst Manor	Moyles Court
Chaseborough	*Cranborne*
Deansleigh Park	Broadlands
Farnfield	Farnborough
Fernell Hall	Embley House
Ingpen Beacon	Inkpen Beacon
Melchester	Salisbury
Oozewood	Ringwood
Quartershot	Aldershot
Rookington Park	Hurn Court
Sandbourne	Bournemouth
Solentsea	Southsea
Stoke Barehills	Basingstoke
Weydon Priors	Weyhill
Wintoncester	Winchester

MID-WESSEX

Melchester

Arrowthorne Lodge

SOUTH WESSEX

Chaseborough

Bramshurst Manor

Oozewood

GREA

Rookington Park

Sandbourne

Fer

NORTH WESSEX

Ingpen Beacon

...*ton Priors*

Old Basing House

Stoke Barehills

Icenway House?

Farnfield

Quartershot

Wintoncester

...*eansleigh Park*

Southampton

Portsmouth

Solentsea

Ryde

THE ISLAND

Bonchurch

Scale in Miles

0 ½ 1   2   3   4   5

'Wintoncester' (Winchester) Gaol, where Tess was hanged for murder. The portion on the left of the picture was not built by then, but rising behind it is the tower above which Angel and Liza-Lu saw the black flag raised at the hour of execution.

The burial-ground on Old Chapel Hill, 'Stoke Barehills' (Basingstoke) was originally created for funerals outside the town walls during the Papal Interdict imposed on all England during the reign of King John. A Chapel of the Holy Ghost was erected, to which a chantry was added in 1542. Some remnants survive, and are alluded to in *Jude*.

House', between Bristol and Exeter, 'Icenway' lay 'beyond Wintoncester'—unless we assume 'Heymere' to have been very near Bristol indeed. However, neither Herriard nor Marwell possesses any records showing a connection with the events in the story, nor do their churches hold a clue. Marwell Hall, built in 1816, was severely damaged by fire in 1969. It now adjoins a wildlife park.

Creeping toward Herriard village is that rapidly developing industrial town Basingstoke ('Stoke Barehills'). Hardy's 'old town of nine or ten thousand souls' is now an overspill centre for many times that number, and has been completely redesigned; so that it is surprising to find all the features described in *Jude* surviving with minimal alteration, except for the site of the 'Great Wessex Show'. This was the once-celebrated Royal Counties Show, which began in 1854 as the Basingstoke Root and Stock Show and acquired its later name in 1861. Though its offices were always at Basingstoke, the show moved from town to town, the last being held at

Thanks to the interest shown by the building firm that now owns the area, a surprising number of relics from 'Weydon Priors' (Weyhill) Fairground have survived. Here are two booths, one open, one shuttered, still looking much as they would have done when Henchard, the future Mayor of 'Casterbridge', visited the Fair and sold his wife to sailor Newson.

Kingsclere in 1966. The Basingstoke showground occupied the area of the present cricket ground alongside Bounty Road.

Both the railway routes mentioned by Hardy continue to operate, and the two westbound highways whose rival merits were debated have become the A30 and B3400. Their 'point of reunion' is by Andover. Much of the refashioning of central Basingstoke has taken place just south of the station, immediately north of which you may still see the 'cemetery standing amid some picturesque medieval ruins'. The ruins are those of the thirteenth-century chapel of the Holy Ghost and the sixteenth-century guild chapel of Holy Trinity, both now freed of ivy and protected against further deterioration. The cemetery is no longer used as such except for an occasional burial in a family vault, but is rather perfunctorily maintained as a kind of public park. The chapels mentioned by Hardy were two flint ones, now demolished.

Where even Basingstoke's 'new red brick suburb' appears mellow amid the steel and concrete, the ancient parish church seems undeserving of the adjectives 'gaunt, unattractive'. It is unaltered except for the south aisle, rebuilt after a fire in the 1930s.

Barely separated now from Basingstoke is Basing; Old Basing House is the 'House of Long Sieging' in the poem 'My Cicely'—an allusion to the Royalists' four-year defence of it during the Civil War. In the 1960s army experts, using geiger counters, made an unsuccessful attempt to locate the large sum of money reputedly hidden in the grounds.

'Arrowthorne Lodge' in *Ethelberta* is probably imaginary, but from the references to road and rail would have stood in about the position of Breamore House, north of Fordingbridge. 'Farnfield' in the same novel, the park with a knacker's yard in place of a mansion, was evidently pictured near Farnborough, on the Surrey border.

Weyhill ('Weydon Priors'), west of Andover, where Henchard sold his wife at the fair, Hardy depicts as shrinking; and it is still shrinking, consisting of little more than a church, two inns, and a handful of cottages. Yet Weyhill Fair was among the great ones, and did not finally expire until 1947. Its site is roughly commensurate with the premises of A. J. Dunning & Sons, building contractors, thanks to whose enlightened policy many of the fair booths have survived, including the two rows shown by Lea, in which hops and the once-famous Wiltshire cheeses were sold; even today the rows are referred to as the 'hop lines'. The nearest inn, the Star, preserves upstairs the two rooms once occupied by the drovers and their dogs, though the drovers' room no longer has 'DR' on the door.

11 NORTH WESSEX and CHRISTMINSTER

Berkshire and Oxford

Though the College stones
Are stroked with the sun,
And the gownsmen and Dons
Who held you as one
Of brightest brow
Still think as they did,
Why haunt with them now
Your candle is hid?

EVELYN G. OF CHRISTMINSTER

Jude and Sue spent a considerable time in Reading ('Aldbrickham'). It then had 60,000 or 70,000 inhabitants: in 1981 the figure was 130,891. Twentieth-century houses encircle the original town, and there is much redesigning of the centre, where even the two railway stations have become one. Yet a fair if shrinking amount of old Reading remains, including the George Hotel, where the couple first stayed and where Jude had spent his night of reconciliation with Arabella. The George is still one of the leading inns of the town.

Jude and Sue lodged for most of their sojourn in a little lane far from the station and 'almost out in the country'. This can be placed with near-certainty in the area of small streets and Victorian two-storey red-brick terrace houses west of Southampton and Whitley Streets. There is no 'Spring Street' on the nineteenth-century maps, but there is a Spring Gardens, off which leads Spring Terrace. These were still in existence as recently as the early 1970s, but have given place today to a more elegant residential quarter. However, terrace houses of exactly the same style are still (so far) to be seen in nearby East Street, and (again so far) there is still open country not far away. The inn, the 'Prince', in which Arabella stayed, vanished earlier.

The region is part of St Giles parish, the clerk of which from 1871 to 1885 lived and worked at 66 Horn Street. Jude and Sue wished to marry in a 'Superintendent Registrar's office', yet went to 'the office of the district'. There were two of these, the nearer and likelier being at 24 Southampton Street on the corner of Mundesley Street—another street that, if it has not yet actually disappeared, has been bereft of every building on either side and even its name-plates. Mundesley Street could well be the 'unfrequented side alley' up and down which the couple walked after Sue's courage had failed her. The church where they saw a wedding would be St Giles itself (restored 1873).

Reading too was where Sam Hobson in 'The Son's Veto' bought his greengrocery business, and somewhere near was 'Gaymead', a 'pretty village, with its church and parsonage', where he and Sophy had formerly lived. We are told of a white gate to the parsonage garden, trees in the vicinity, and a glebe. The church had communion-rails, a roof held by tiebeams, and a 'fine peal of bells'. Several prototypes have been suggested (as well as that there was none), and selection might be easier if one could identify the 'church out by Gaymead' of the Devil and Ten Commandments legend related in *Jude*. This

Above:
The little streets in 'Aldbrickham' (Reading), typical of 'Spring Street' where Jude and Sue lived after she had left Richard Phillotson, are disappearing with bewildering rapidity. Here is one characteristic but almost certainly doomed terrace.

Left:
Interior of the surviving church (there were formerly two) at Sulhampstead Abbots, according to one credible but unconfirmed account Hardy's model for 'Gaymead' in *Jude the Obscure* and the unpleasant short story 'The Son's Veto'.

cautionary tale, however, seems to have been borrowed by Hardy from another part of the country. The Wessex Edition map, showing Gaymead in the position of Theale, can scarcely be accurate, since Theale meets none of the descriptive points: nor does Shinfield, Lea's identification, despite his lengthy description.

The most probable prototype is Sulhampstead or Sulhampstead Abbots, about three miles south of Theale. I am told by one

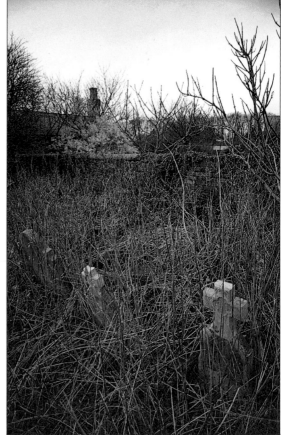

The composer of hymns who played the organ in 'the large church' at 'Kennetbridge' (Newbury) in *Jude* is clearly based on Henry Godding, commemorated by this memorial window in the north aisle. St Nicholas is a Late Perpendicular building of 1509–33, though giving little sign of its age after the familiar Victorian over-restoration.

The abandoned burial-ground at 'Marygreen', formerly the churchyard of the old church whose replacement so annoyed Hardy.

who knew her that a certain Sulhampstead lady, long dead now, was once introduced to Hardy at a social gathering, and that on learning where she lived, he said that he had put her village into one of his stories as 'Gaymead'. I have so far been unable to obtain corroboration of this claim, but at least it is true that although Sulhampstead is scattered and not notably attractive, and its fine church possesses only three bells, in other respects the church corresponds more nearly with Hardy's brief description than does any other in the area.

Inkpen ('Ingpen') Beacon, named in the poem 'Wessex Heights', and in fact England's loftiest point south of the Cotswolds and east of the Mendips, is today a popular, but so far unspoilt, viewpoint for motorists, especially from nearby Newbury ('Kennetbridge'). This, like Reading, is a fast-growing industrial town in the heart of which one can nevertheless still find the remnants of an older place justifying Hardy's phrase 'a quaint old borough'. To Newbury came Jude, seeking the composer of the new hymn he had heard near Salisbury. The hymn appears to be

The new church at 'Marygreen' (Fawley Magna) – admittedly of unusual appearance for an English village – on which Hardy poured such scorn in the opening pages of *Jude*. The architect who so earned censure was the eminent G. E. Street. Curiously, a sketch of the old church by Hardy himself shows it to have been even more unorthodox.

imaginary, but for the composer Hardy probably had in mind Henry Godding, organist from 1865 to 1894 at the parish church of St Nicholas ('I think he plays in the large church there') for which he composed several chants. He had no known connection with Oxford, but the Goddings did own a shop, though not a wine business. Today there is a memorial window to the organist in the church, which stands behind a trim sward amid the shops.

The Jack and the Chequers, at either of which Anny would rather have stayed than at the (untraceable) temperance hotel, can both be seen: the Chequers still as a hotel, the Jack as a modern fashion-shop, retaining, however, a first-floor Tudor room with a fine oriel window looking on to a side alley. The new chapel, to see the laying of whose foundations Arabella came

to Newbury, was the Baptist chapel opened in 1859 (somewhat postdated by Hardy). It stood in Northbrook Street not far from the Jack, on the spot now occupied by Richard Shops, and has been rebuilt at St Mary's Hill, some distance away.

When Arabella and Anny left for Wantage they must, to pass within sight of Jude's birthplace, Great Fawley ('Marygreen'), have taken what are now the B4000 and A338. At Fawley Hardy alludes to cottages pulled down,

Key to the map of North Wessex
Hardy's names in italics.

Aldbrickham	Reading
Alfredston	Wantage
Christminster	Oxford
Cresscombe	Letcombe Bassett
Ingpen Beacon	Inkpen Beacon
Kennetbridge	Newbury
Lumsdon	*Cumnor*
Marygreen	Fawley

trees on the green felled and the old church replaced by a new one, all prior to the start of the novel. These changes seem to have exhausetd the local capacity for innovation; modern Fawley is an unattractive little village, its green a lumpy grass waste, its roofs flaunting great stretches of corrugated iron, its new buildings few and ugly, like the new classroom tacked on to the Victorian school in the wrong-coloured brick, or the uninspired stabling of the only important newcomer, the Fawley Stud. Ironically, by far the most striking feature is the church 'of German-Gothic design, unfamiliar to English eyes . . . erected . . . by a certain obliterator of historic records [G. E. Street] who had run down from London and back in a day'. Its construction was begun, as a tablet on the wall testifies, in 1863, once more upsetting Weber's chronology, which places the opening of the story in 1855.

Immediately north of 'Marygreen' lies the 'wide and lonely depression' in which the small Jude was employed to scare the rooks – at the time the field was bearing grain. Across the expanse runs the path to the 'Alfredston' (Wantage) road.

The vicarage, no longer a church property since the amalgamation of the parish with Chaddleworth, dates, like the school, from the 1860s. There used to be two wells, one, photographed by Lea but now vanished, near the house today optimistically called Jude Cottage, the other, near the cemetery, beside the main approach to the village. This well has long been covered by what appears to be the lid of a tomb—not without a certain relevance, if the rumour is true that the shaft contains many skeletons of sheep and pigs. From which well the boy Jude is supposed to have drawn water we do not know. The old graveyard is now a small, melancholy area of rank grass, out of which

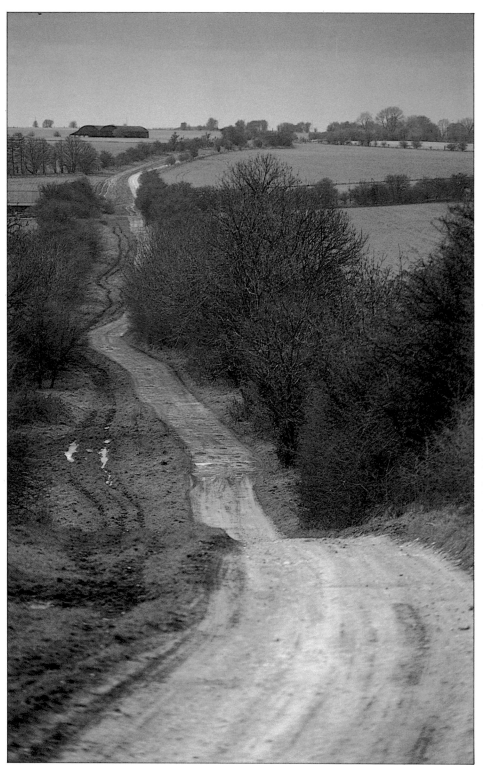

Part of the Oxfordshire – in Hardy's day 'North Wessex' or Berkshire – stretch of the ancient Ridgeway west of the site of the 'Brown' (Red) House barn, from whose thatched top the boy Jude gazed so longingly at 'Christminster' (Oxford).

enough gravestones protrude to excite speculation on how many were really 'obliterated' and
replaced by those 'ninepenny cast-iron crosses
warranted to last five years'. The crosses have all
duly vanished. A short distance north of the
cemetery lay the pond (now filled in) where,
according to Jude's great-aunt, the young Sue
had so impudently paddled.

Just opposite the graveyard, on the edge of
the green, there used to stand, well within living
memory, a pair of thatched cottages of which
one was the old village bakery and in all
likelihood the prototype of Great-Aunt
Drusilla's home, though this cannot be proved. I
have seen a photograph of the cottage, which
does not show the diamond-leaded window
described in *Jude*; but this might well have had to
be replaced, and in favour of the building there is
a lean-to at the end of it that could have been old
Drusilla's 'great fuelhouse'. The claim of the old
bakery would be greatly helped if we knew that
Mary Head, Hardy's grandmother, who spent
thirteen of her early years (from 1772) at Fawley,
had spent them under this roof.

Close to the site of the vanished building
stands a terrace of nineteenth-century brick
cottages, the farthest of which has long been the
village store and post-office. Whether Hardy
thought of this as the Widow Edlin's home we
cannot tell, but between 1854 and 1876 the
storekeeper-postmaster was a Charles Edlin.

The 'great meadow', scene of Jude's bird-
scaring, remains wide and lonely, and the path
across it later taken by him to visit Arabella is
still in use. Their nuptial cottage, near the
junction of this path with the Wantage road, was
either pulled or burnt down at the turn of the
century; a little thicket projecting into the field
from the roadside hedge used to mark the site of
its garden, but was uprooted when pipes for
North Sea gas were sunk beside the hedge
during the 1970s. The 'unhealthy fir-trees' near
by vanished soon after the garden. The pond in
which Jude tried to drown himself, but could
not break the ice, lay in a fold of the 'open down'
about 350 yards west of the path. Some thirty-
five feet in diameter, it was filled in many years
ago.

The former 'hedgeless highway' to Wantage
now has substantial hedges along much of both
sides nearly all the way from the Fawley turning.
At the crest of the hill, where the Ridgeway
crosses the road, a pair of twentieth-century
cottages stand behind a small lawn, and a few
dozen yards west stand two more, rendered.
Between the pairs is the site of the Red ('Brown')
House, of which no trace is left. Hardy errs in
identifying the Ridgeway with the 'Icknield
Street and original Roman road'. Both roads are
long pre-Roman, and the Icknield Way traverses
the northern escarpment at a lower level, along
the line of the A417 and B4507. The Ridgeway,
described in *Jude* as green, is today gravelled
along this reach. The 'circular British earthbank'
just north of it, where the courting Jude and
Arabella walked, is Segsbury Camp or Letcombe
Castle, a grassy fort still undisturbed apart from
the lane across its centre, and that was already
old in Jude's time.

'Cresscombe' is Letcombe Bassett, a valley
village mainly notable for the watercress beds
(now disused) that occupy much of its centre.
Alongside these stands a detached, elegantly
kept thatched cottage locally known as
Arabella's; but its identity is open to considerable doubt, for it is not isolated, and its position
at the bottom of the dip and on the same side of
the stream as the road is wholly incompatible
with Hardy's precise account of Jude's and
Arabella's first sight of one another. Nor can it
be easily reconciled with Jude's route from
Fawley, which Lea (who initiated the claim of
the cottage) professes to have followed.

The gibbet that Drusilla said used to stand
where the 'Fenworth' (also spelt 'Fensworth')
road left the highway by a handpost, was
situated where the Letcombe Regis road
branches off opposite the track over Furzewick
Down. Although 'Fensworth' suggests Furzewick, the name probably stands for Letcombe
Regis. The handpost has been supplanted by a
modern sign.

Nearby stood the celebrated milestone on the back of which the Oxford-besotted youth was said by Hardy to have carved his inscription. Removed during the 1939 anti-invasion measures, the stone was subsequently believed lost but in 1969 it turned up and has now been reinstated.

When Arabella walked back to Wantage after meeting Phillotson on the Fawley road, she 'practised dimple-making ... from where the pollard willows begin to the old almshouses in the first street of the town'. The willows, unpollarded, are today hardly recognizable, and badly smothered by creeper. They are faced across the road by new houses. The seventeenth-century almshouses, of red brick and cream-painted stone, are splendidly maintained.

In the town itself, an uninspiring place, the only identifiable *Jude* building is the Bear Hotel, from which Sue took a 'little car' to return to Fawley. The Bear stands back from the Market Place, its interior pleasantly modernized behind a frontage that Sue would have no difficulty in recognizing. She had travelled by train to Wantage Road ('Alfredston Road') station— opened in 1863, demolished just over a century later—and had covered the two miles into the town by steam tram. This vehicle, called the Grantham Car, was the first of its kind in England; there is a model of it in the Science Museum, South Kensington. It had supplanted a horse-tram in 1876, this date reinforcing the evidence of Fawley Church and Hertford College (see page 173) that the action of *Jude* should be placed at least a decade after the dates suggested by Weber. In time the Grantham Car was superseded by a somewhat senile train, which continued to carry passengers until 1925 and freight until 1946, when it made a last dramatic journey, tearing up the track behind it.

Just before the road from Wantage reaches Oxford it skirts Cumnor ('Lumsdon'), the village to which Jude and Sue walked to call on Phillotson. Cumnor was then separated from Oxford by a stretch of 'prettily wooded country'. Today the route is bordered by houses on both sides; but they are detached, and stand in large, well-timbered gardens. Cumnor church tower is 'embattled', as stated, but there is no turret, nor ever was. There is a large new school, but the premises of the old one provide play-group facilities; the 'homely little dwelling' in which Phillotson lived is still occupied. The 'old house across the way' that sheltered Sue also survives. Cumnor, much extended, is now one of Oxford's wealthiest residential suburbs.

New building of a more industrial sort is in evidence when one crosses out of 'Wessex' and enters the city through Botley and Osney, but there is far less here than to the south-east where the Nuffield car-building empire sprawls. In 1928 Cowley and several other districts were brought within the city bounds, so that with still later additions academic Oxford has been reduced to a tiny nucleus. Not that it did not know the pains of expansion long before; in 1887 complaints were already being made about the increasing barrier between city and countryside, one of the areas involved being the so-called Jericho ('Beersheba'), after Jericho Road (now Walton Street), its chief artery. There are still a Jericho Street and a Jericho Inn—the latter very smart, a good example of the change that is beginning to overtake more and more buildings in this once entirely (and still mainly) working-class quarter of two-storey red-brick terrace houses, very similar to the Spring Gardens quarter of Reading.

Here Jude had his first lodgings, and almost his last meeting with Sue. Hardy wrote a key to many of his 'Christminster' names, identifying Jericho positively with 'Beersheba'; so why did he describe the view from that first room of Jude's as though the house were on the southern edge of central Oxford instead of the north-western? The 'raw and cold air from the Meadows' came from Port Meadow, and the church of 'St Silas' is St Barnabas, designed by Hardy's one-time employer. A. W. Blomfield. As high-church (up to the time of writing) in fact as in fiction, it still has a large cross suspended above the chancel steps, though the design

Below:

The milestone on the 'Christminster' road, on the back of which the young Jude carved the word THITHER, with his initials and a fist pointing toward the city of his dreams. Years later, dying, his dreams long since shattered, he rested against the same milestone after his last visit to 'Marygreen'. There is, of course, no carving on the back of the stone; but it is a strong-minded reader of *Jude* who can visit it and forbear a look.

Above:

This attractive and well-kept cottage at 'Lumsdon' (Cumnor), just outside Oxford, is the one in which Sue Bridehead in *Jude the Obscure* lodged while assistant teacher to Richard Phillotson. The former school buildings, and his own 'humble lodging', are opposite across the lane.

Right:

Port Meadow, the great dreary expanse on the north-western side of 'Christminster', the 'raw and cold air' from which sent a chill through Jude's first lodging and his heart, setting the tone for his relationship with the city.

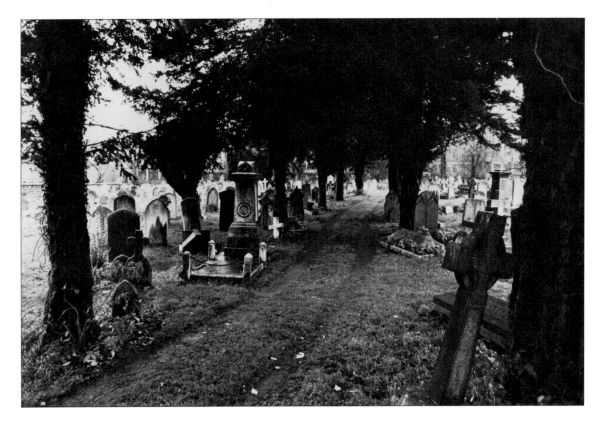

Though unnamed in the novel, there can be little doubt that the strange cemetery of St Sepulchre, hidden away off Walton Street in the 'Beersheba' (Jericho) quarter of north-west 'Christminster', is where Jude's children were buried. The entrance is today further obscured by a cottage astonishingly erected outside it.

differs somewhat from the cross in *Jude*.

During the Fawleys' family visit to Oxford Sue and the children occupied lodgings that looked toward where, 'at some distance opposite, the outer walls of Sarcophagus College— silent, black and windowless—threw their four centuries of gloom, bigotry and decay into the little room'. The restricted view included the 'outlines of Rubric College beyond the other' and the tower of a third. If we are to take all this literally, 'Sarcophagus' was a fifteenth-century foundation near to Brasenose, and it is tempting to think Hardy had in mind All Souls, especially since the name itself has some affinity with a

sarcophagus. But if the suggestion is correct, he must have imagined the windowless walls: unlike several of its neighbours, All Souls exhibits none. The inn where Jude slept, and also 'Mildew Lane', are not identifiable. The cemetery where the children were buried was surely St Sepulchre, reached by a short path between the houses of Walton Street. The burial-ground, virtually disused since 1954, lives on as a peaceful public garden, crossed by a winding path between trees that in summer form a green tunnel.

The most striking innovation in the university area is the cleaning of the older stonework. By 1970 most colleges, the Bodleian, the Sheldonian Theatre, and many other landmarks were exhibiting details that had been masked for generations. Prior to the cleaning, most of the alterations to the older colleges had been effected (under Gilbert Scott) just before the *Jude* period, and the greatest change following it had been the

Broad Street, 'Christminster', showing in the foreground the cross in the roadway marking the spot where Bishops Ridley and Latimer were burnt at the stake in 1555. Here Jude arranged his first rendezvous with Sue.

past nine on the great bell in Tom Tower, it was still rung by hand. In our own lazier age it is operated electrically.

His first rendezvous with Sue was near the cross in Broad Street marking the spot where the martyrs were burnt at the stake; and, despite resurfacing, the road is still so marked. The 'singularly built theatre' into whose lantern he climbed was the Sheldonian, and the great library before it the Bodleian, now eclipsed by the New Bodleian at the corner of Broad Street and Parks Road.

The Sheldonian was also the focus of attention when Jude, Sue and the children stood in the rain to watch the procession on 'Remembrance Day'—the Commemoration or Encaenia. The family had come from the railway station, at that time one of a pair side by side: the Midland Region station has now been abandoned. At Carfax ('Fourways') Jude led the way along the High Street ('Chief Street') as far as the 'church with the Italian porch, whose helical columns were heavily draped with creepers'—St Mary the Virgin, now cleaned and creeperless—where they 'turned in on the left'—up Catte Street—and came to the 'open space' between the Sheldonian Theatre and 'the nearest college'—Hertford—where the crowd were gathered. It is Hertford College that displays the carved frieze (a stag motif) and the Latin motto that Jude explained to his fellow-bystanders: *Ad fontes aquarum sicut cervus anhelat*—'As pants the hart for cooling streams'. He is stated to have studied the carving 'years before', but in fact this part of Hertford was not built until 1887.

Of Oxford's more famous inns, several are changing their function as the colleges that are their landlords cast about for extra accommodation. Thus the Mitre ('Crozier') retains its restaurant (now a steak-house) and bars, but has turned over its hotel quarters to Lincoln. The 'low-ceiled tavern' where Jude recited the creed in Latin, and which on his return to Oxford he found had become an enlarged, modernized and fashionable rendezvous, is the Lamb and Flag, adjoining its landlord, St John's College. The

construction of the New Foundations, succeeded in the present century by the addition of still more buildings (some very striking in design) to meet the ever-increasing pressure on accommodation. Nor has the process ended: for the 1970s saw the start of a massive programme of new faculties, museums and libraries.

Among Hardy's code-names not already quoted are 'Cardinal'—Christ Church; 'Biblioll'—Balliol; 'Crozier'—? Oriel (but according to Lea, Merton); 'Old Time Street'—Merton Street or Oriel Street. The 'Cathedral-church of Cardinal College' is Oxford Cathedral, still accessible across the vast green quadrangle of Christ Church. When Jude heard the 101-stroke curfew that sounds every evening at five

Boathouses on the banks have now replaced the 'gay barges' of the college rowing clubs that bordered the Isis in Jude's time, but here, seen appropriately from Folly Bridge, is an old vessel such as Arabella might have set eyes on when she went to watch the races while Jude lay dying.

The view across 'Chrisminster' from the 'octagonal chamber in the lantern of a singularly built theatre' – the Sheldonian – to which Jude climbed after finding every college barred to him.

Flam, as the students call it, has been further enlarged and altered a number of times, in keeping with changing tastes. The typical gin-palace of Jude's later visit has therefore disappeared; but the 'low-ceiled tavern' remains easily recognizable in the central section, much frequented for down-to-earth evening meals. When this low part was the whole tavern, entry was made a short distance up the adjoining alley—the 'court' or 'lane' of the novel—across the mouth of which the St Giles Street frontage extends to form an arch. With the enlargement, a second doorway became available under the arch itself, and it must be this that Hardy called a 'spacious and inviting entrance'.

Carfax ('Fourways'), with its ancient St Martin's Tower, is still a popular rendezvous. The High, as the university calls it, remains broad and reasonably undisfigured, a street of many shops and some interesting taverns. South and west of Carfax, on either side of St Aldate's, lies what little remains to justify Hardy's vivid picture of obscure alleys, jutting porticoes, oriel windows, and florid doorways. Today reconstruction has left little of the 'rottenness' which formerly made it 'impossible that modern thought could house itself in such decrepit chambers.' West again lies more rebuilding.

In *Jude*'s closing pages Arabella goes to 'Oldgate' College, entering under an archway and walking 'along the gravel paths and under the aged limes'. Although the most celebrated limes at the time were in the grounds of Trinity, the allusion to the archway establishes 'Oldgate' College as New College; not only is the entrance arched, but an arch spans New College Lane just outside. Limes grow in two parts of the gardens; those in the nearer are recent replacements; but at the far end of the remoter garden there is still a row of older trees.

The lodging in which Jude died, that house so wistfully and vainly sought by Lea, remains as elusive for us as for him. After Jude's death Arabella and her friends made their way down St Aldate's to Folly Bridge and thence 'passed by a narrow slit down to the riverside path'. The bridge is the same today, and the steps and slopes down to the two towpaths are bordered by the iron railings that bordered them then. Nor has Christ Church Meadow ('Cardinal Meadow'), having escaped a project to drive a sunken road across it, materially altered. It is the banks of the river that are changing, as the 'gay barges' of the boat clubs are steadily replaced by modern boathouses.

Hardy denied that 'Christminster' was to be wholly equated with Oxford. Outside *Jude* and *The Life* the city is hardly mentioned, and always under its real name. In the only Oxford poem, from which the lines at the head of this chapter are taken, 'Evelyn G.' is Mrs A. D. Godley (*née* Gifford, Emma's cousin and the wife of the Public Orator). She died in 1920 at Arlington House, today known simply as 27 Norham Road. Situated near the Parks, the yellow-brick Victorian house is now converted into flats.

12 MID-WESSEX

Wiltshire

The grey Cathedral, towards whose face
Bend eyes untold, has not met yours;
Your shade has never swept its base,

Your form has never darked its doors,
Nor have your faultless feet once thrown
A pensive pit-pat on its floors.

IN A CATHEDRAL CITY (SALISBURY)

Win Green ('Wingreen'), already mentioned (page 70) in relation to Tess's journey with Alec, is also touched upon in the poem 'The Vampirine Fair'. The hill is part of the Wiltshire area of Cranborne Chase that when Hardy knew it had been redeemed from a wilderness and turned into farmland. As such it was much affected by the lean times of the mid-nineteenth century and again by those of the 1920s and 1930s. In the period of *Tess* Win Green and its surrounding coombs must have looked very much as they did in our own century before Rolf Gardiner of Fontmell Magna restored large tracts of the reverted land and clothed the bare hills with forest.

The 'Manor Court' of 'The Vampirine Fair' is Rushmore, a large early nineteenth-century mansion south-west of Win Green, former home of the remarkable General A. H. Lane Fox Pitt-Rivers. This house, shabby but outwardly unmodified, has now become a boys' preparatory school. Primroses still border the long drive. The 'churchyard home' of the poem is at Tollard Royal, where the church still bears a 'steeple-cock'.

Hardy and Emma stayed at Rushmore during the 1890s, and paid a visit to the most fantastic of the general's enterprises, the Larmer Gardens: an experience later used for the poem 'Concerning Agnes'. General Pitt-Rivers had laid out these grounds as a place of public recreation. An ornamental pool was dug, a 'temple' built, a caretaker's house, bandstand and theatre erected. 'Quarters' were constructed—wooden picnic houses, in various Indian styles, about a large lawn for dancing. The whole was approached by a broad avenue of magnificent trees festooned with lamps, the 'faery lamps' of the poem. At the peak of the venture 24,000 people visited the Larmer Gardens on a single Sunday. But the enterprise had the evanescence of all faery things, and after the general's death the gardens fell into increasing decay. Mr Michael Pitt-Rivers has now restored the scene as much as may be, although the bandstand and two of the fragile 'quarters' were past redemption; but in the current economic climate any hope of regularly reopening the grounds remains in abeyance. They are, however, occasionally opened in aid of charity.

Not surprisingly, the Wiltshire scene most frequently met with in Hardy's work is Salisbury. He had a great affection for the cathedral, despite his rejection of its creed in the poems

Map of the Principal Towns and Villages of MID-WESSEX

BASED ON THE WORKS OF THOMAS HARDY

Key to the map of Mid-Wessex
Hardy's names in italics.

Hardy's name	Real name
Devil's Door	Devil's Den
Falls	Mells
Ingpen Beacon	Inkpen Beacon
Leddenton	Gillingham
Manor Court	Rushmore
Marlbury	Marlborough
Melchester	Salisbury
Old Melchester	Old Sarum
Shaston	Shaftesbury
Stourton Tower	Alfred's Tower
Weydon Priors	Weyhill

OUTER WESSEX

R. Avon

Bath

Shockerwick House

Chipp. Sta

G R

Falls

Boyton Station

Stourton Tower

Wardo Castle

Leddenton

Wingr.

Shaston

Mano.

SOUTH WESSEX

NORTH WESSEX

R. Thames

RIDGEWAY

RIDGEWAY

MARLBURY DOWNS

Devil's Door

Marlbury

Shakeforest Towers?

Ingpen Beacon

E

PLAIN

Weydon Priors

Stonehenge

R. AVON

R. BSS

UPPER WESSEX

Old Melchester

Melchester

ASE

Scale in Miles

0 ½ 1 2 3 4 5

Above:
'Wingreen' (Win Green), touched upon in *Tess* and in the poem 'The Vampirine Fair', is the highest point in 'Mid-Wessex' (Wiltshire), and from its upper slopes one gets this magnificent view over 'The Chase' (Cranborne Chase).

Left:
The 'Temple' in the unique and dream-like Larmer Gardens at Tollard Royal. The poem 'Concerning Agnes' commemorates Hardy's meeting here in 1895 with Mrs (later Lady) Agnes Grove, one of the succession of beautiful women of literary bent who stirred his romantic feelings.

'The Impercipient' and 'A Cathedral Façade at Midnight'. It figures prominently in *The Hand of Ethelberta*, in one passage of which Christopher plays the organ while Ethelberta inspects the 'sallow monuments'. The monuments are the same today, with a minor addition or two, but the organ was replaced in 1876, a few years after the action of the novel: Christopher would have played the instrument presented by King George III in 1792. This is still in use in Salisbury, for it was re-erected in the church of St Thomas were converted into very expensive flats. Hardy's 'ancient edifice of the fifteenth century, once a palace'—the King's House—which had been the School headquarters, is now the new home of the Salisbury and South Wiltshire Museum. The garden still runs down to the Avon, and in front of the house the courtyard survives, with its wall much lowered. Beyond the lane 'trees of emerald green' shade the sward as they did in 'The High-School Lawn'. The Theological College, also mentioned in *Jude*, a large seventeenth-century building on the north side of the Close, remains virtually unaltered, though it now incorporates the former Wells Theological College.

Another visitor to the 'damp and venerable Close', a few years later than Ethelberta and her friends, was Louis Glanvill (*Two on a Tower*). His goal was the Bishop's Palace, which has now become the Cathedral School. The trees in the palace grounds, and the rooks that nested in them, were both said by Hardy to seem 'older, if possible, than those in the Close'. Some of the trees near the palace are certainly very old, but others have died and been replaced. The rooks have died and not been replaced.

The description of the city of Salisbury in *Jude* hardly applies today: '... a quiet and soothing place, almost wholly ecclesiastical in its tone; a spot where worldly learning and intellectual smartness had no establishment'. Perhaps the change was already beginning when Hardy wrote, for he made Sue say that the centre of life had moved from the cathedral to the railway station. Now it has moved again, to the central car-park.

On market days the focus was probably always the Market Place. Round this, inevitably,

of Canterbury, the scene of Sue's wedding with Phillotson. Following the controversial eighteenth-century work by Wyatt on 'the fair fane of Poore's olden episcopal see' ('My Cicely'), Gilbert Scott carried out further restoration in the 1860s and 1870s—work used by Hardy to provide Jude with his term as mason—and in 1939 the upper part of the spire was strengthened. It is now surmounted at night by a red warning-light. The cathedral is floodlit nightly.

The Close remains unspoilt except on the west side, and there is no more spacious or gracious setting for a cathedral in western Europe. But on the west the Teachers Training College ('Melchester Normal School'), attended so ingloriously by Sue and rather more successfully by Hardy's sisters, was greatly enlarged, mainly after the Second World War, by the addition of uninspired red-brick blocks that ruin the harmony of this side of the Close. In the late 1970s the School was closed down and these blocks

Left:
Few buildings are floodlit so rewardingly as 'Melchester' (Salisbury) Cathedral, islanded amid its huge dark sward. The building, except the spire (one of the two or three tallest in Europe), was completed in 1220 to replace Old Sarum. Despite the floodlighting, the poem 'A Cathedral Façade at Midnight' remains valid, for by then the lighting has been switched off.

Opposite:
The north-east corner of 'Melchester' Market Place on a non-market day. The Harnhams' house in 'On the Western Circuit' would seem to have been either that on the extreme left of the photograph or the house on the far corner behind the lamp-standard.

various twentieth-century structures have appeared, but many highly diverse buildings from earlier epochs remain, among them, fairly certainly, the original of the Harnhams' house in 'On the Western Circuit'. The 'dignified residence of considerable size' stood at the 'remotest corner' from that nearest to the cathedral, that is at the north-east angle. The most likely candidate is the *second* Georgian house along Blue Boar Row from Endless Street. A modern shop-front now spans the ground-floor, otherwise the house is unaltered.

Markets are still held twice a week, though livestock is now sold in a new market a few streets away. On three October days each year the square teems, by ancient right, with a fun fair, as in the story. At the south-east corner stands the Guildhall ('the Town Hall') where Ethelberta and the others attended Christopher's concert in 'a large upstair assembly room' (the Banqueting Room). Concerts

are still held there, but two courts of justice maintain the official character of the building, from which the city corporation transferred its deliberations in 1927.

When Ethelberta and Picotee left the Guildhall they made their way up 'a long street' (Fisherton Street) to the railway station. Jude, too, must have known this thoroughfare, though the 'street leading from the station' in which he found a temperance hotel may have been Mill Road. The 'town bridge' that he crossed was Fisherton Bridge, rebuilt in 1961. Fisherton Street today consists mainly of small shops in rather mean buildings dating from before the *Jude* period, interspersed now with two or three larger interpolations in red brick.

The unnamed 'junction' where the whip incident occurred in *Two on a Tower* is not identified as 'Melchester' because this would not at all have suited certain aspects of the story, nor would Salisbury's busy twin stations have per-

'Melchester Town Hall' – the late eighteenth-century Guildhall in Salisbury Market Place – was where Christopher in *The Hand of Ethelberta* gave the concert to which Lord Mountclere escorted Ethelberta and Picotee. He performed in this first-floor Banqueting Hall, still frequently the scene of musical events.

mitted the episode to take place without attracting a large crowd. But Hardy's data concerning the 'junction's' relationship to 'Welland House' (Charborough) are so explicit that Salisbury is the only possible location. After stating (correctly) that 'Warborne' (Wimborne) station lay five miles from 'Welland House': and 'the next station above that nine miles' (again correctly), he continues: 'They [Swithin and Viviette] were bound for the latter: their plan being that she should there take the train to the junction where the whip accident had occurred . . . and return . . . as if from Bath'. Since Wimborne is east of Charborough, the 'next station' can only be

farther east, and was in fact at West Moors, where the Salisbury & Dorset Junction Railway (opened in 1866) branched off from the London & South Western, to run north and join another of the L & SW lines two miles outside Salisbury.

The words quoted above make it plain that West Moors itself was not the 'junction'—and in any case passengers from Salisbury to Wimborne did not have to change there. Coming from Bath, the only change necessary was at Salisbury, which therefore was the real 'junction' behind Hardy's careful veil. This, too, is where Viviette's brother would have changed on his journey from London—though in practice he would have been more likely to have travelled to Wimborne direct through Southampton. Today the little S & DJR line has long been closed and the track torn up. Salisbury is still a junction for other routes, but the old GWR station has long been closed and converted into a depot.

On returning from the station, Ethelberta and her sister booked in at the Red Lion, which has a George IV façade, but the original fourteenth-century nucleus inside the courtyard. Here, too, Phillotson stayed before his marriage, and nearly a century and a half earlier the First Countess of Wessex (*A Group of Noble Dames*) had secret appointments with her own husband. Ethelberta's Lord Mountclere stayed further south at the White Hart, where in the story 'A Committee-Man of the "Terror"' Madame V— had left the coach. The White Hart is an eighteenth-century hostelry that has retained much of its original appearance.

Both Jude and Charles Raye, in 'On the Western Circuit', had lodgings in the High Street, a relatively short thoroughfare that has managed to remain old-world at the North (or Close) Gate end while becoming wholly twentieth-century at the other. A stone's throw from the modern end stands the church of St Thomas of Canterbury, already mentioned. The Phillotson–Sue wedding preceded by only a few years the discovery over the chancel arch of a 'doom', a mediaeval mural portraying the Last Judgement (an omen that would have been a gift to Hardy), which had lain hidden under white-wash since 1573. In other respects St Thomas's continued much as at the time of the novel until the 1960s, when most of the stonework of the large Perpendicular windows was replaced and an extensive programme of restoration begun.

The Market House in which Jude told Sue of his marriage to Arabella stood from 1859 until the early 1970s on the west side of a small extension of the Market Place called the Cheese Market, and was a lofty affair of stone and much ironwork. Used in its last years for exhibitions, it has now been replaced by the new City Library, but most of the façade has been retained. The adjoining covered pedestrianway to the car-park used in Jude's day to house a spur of the railway.

The 'cemetery on the hill' where Jude first worked is on the eastern outskirts, bordering London Road. A hundred years ago it looked upon open meadows, many of which have now been built over. Also on the city outskirts stands Old Sarum ('Old Melchester'), until well into the present century heavily overgrown, swarming with rabbits, its deep ditch choked with trees and shrubs: a worthy setting for Anna's seduction in 'On the Western Circuit'. Today the whole area is in the trim condition one expects of properties in the care of the Department of the Environment. The ruins of the castle and the ground-plan of the razed cathedral are well signposted, and in 1954 Salisbury City Corporation acquired some forty-four acres adjoining, in order to keep the site clear of building encroachment.

Close to Salisbury is Wilton, a small town living mainly on its memories. Lea and Pinion both give Wilton House, seat of the Earls of Pembroke, as the scene of the principal events in 'The Marchioness of Stonehenge'. Certainly Hardy's meagre clues suggest this. But neither the most authoritative account of the Pembrokes, Tresham Lever's *The Herberts of Wilton*, nor the researches of the late earl—no mean authority on the history of his family—have produced evidence that the story concerns any real occupants of Wilton.

Salisbury was the starting-point of Mr George Crookhill's strange journey, the adventurous part of which, as we have already seen (page 69), began as he toiled up 'Bissett' (Coombe Bissett) Hill (still rural, now part of the A354). Tess and Angel also went through the city on the journey that ended at Stonehenge, and few Hardy passages so accurately evoke the spirit of a place as his description of their arrival at the monument in the dark. Today, after a period as the private property of the local lord of the manor, it is administered by the Department of the Environment; the land immediately outside the circle, on the other hand, is in the jurisdiction of the National Trust. In 1969 the Trust put the car-park and other amenities below ground level, but controversy continues over what should be done both to show off the monument to best advantage, and to preserve the site from the deterioration caused by an excess of visitors.

Since the *Tess* episode (about 1889) there have

The description of Tess and Angel identifying Stonehenge in the dark is Hardy at his descriptive best. Night is certainly the most rewarding time to approach this sadly over-visited monument; the ideal visit – to be achieved only with great luck – is during a nocturnal thunderstorm; then Stonehenge really comes into its own.

been several changes in the great circle itself. In 1899 two monoliths in the outer circle keeled over. In 1901 the upright of the central trilithon, which for centuries had been tilting inward, was straightened. In 1958, at the end of half a century of skilled archaeological work, many of the fallen stones were correctly replaced. The surrounding ditch, too, has been partly excavated during this century; and just inside it a ring of blocked-up pits, the Aubrey Holes, has been incompletely dug out. Less than a mile north of Stonehenge lie Larkhill camp and its artillery ranges, and in 1981 the excavation programme was extended to the intervening downland,

resulting in evidence of a Late Bronze Age settlement.

For their excursion from Salisbury to Wardour Castle Jude and Sue took the train to, presumably, Tisbury (the line is still in operation), from which the walk is about two miles. In discussing the project Sue had confused the 'new' Wardour Castle with the old. The later building, Palladian in style, was finished in 1776 for the 8th Earl of Arundell, and its beautiful circular central gallery did in fact become the home of a fine collection of paintings by the masters Hardy names. But after the death of the last earl in 1944 the mansion began to fall into disrepair, and one by one the pictures were sold off. The Arundells finally sold the castle to a religious order for conversion into a seminary; but 'conversion' included stripping out the decorated ceilings and wall-panelling, followed by a proposal to pull down the mansion altogether! Luckily the secular authorities were able

The exquisite circular gallery in which hung the paintings that Jude and Sue went to see at Wardour Castle; even the massive doors in this circle are constructed on a curve. The picture collection was later dispersed.

to intervene, and Wardour Castle, repaired and with the survival of its remaining decoration assured, has since 1960 been occupied by the Cranborne Chase School for Girls.

On leaving the castle Sue and Jude walked across the 'open country, wide and high' to a station on another line, 'about seven miles off' to the north. This was evidently Boyton (now closed) on the Warminster line. All this region of Wiltshire continues to be one of the least spoilt parts of the county, with vast views. The walkers crossed the 'old road from London to Land's End'—not the A303, but the older B3087 through Chilmark and Hindon. The shepherd's cottage where they were accommodated for the night is probably fictitious. Another 'mid-Wessex' railway station is mentioned in *A Pair of Blue Eyes*. This is Chippenham (still in service), where Knight and Smith saw the waggon bearing Elfride's coffin attached to their train.

North of Salisbury Plain (the 'Great Plain') are the Marlborough ('Marlbury') Downs, scene of 'What the Shepherd Saw'. The focus of the tale is an arch of three stones, the Devil's Den ('Devil's Door'), standing in a shallow culti-vated valley, Clatford Bottom, immediately north of the Bath road (A4) two miles west of Marlborough. The stones, with two more, recumbent, formed part of a Stone Age tomb. Hardy describes the arch as it is today—two uprights bridged by a horizontal. They stood thus when Bradley wrote in 1907, but later one of the uprights developed a crack, and the cross-stone was in grave danger of falling until repairs were carried out in 1921. Hutton's description of the monument in *Highways and Byways in Wiltshire* (1917) is incorrect.

What the youthful sheep-minder in 'What the Shepherd Saw' did see at the 'Devil's Door' (Devil's Den) was the concealment of a newly murdered body; but he might have seen even worse, for legend has it that at midnight this ancient cromlech on the 'Marlbury' (Marlborough) Downs is liable to be visited by the Devil himself driving eight white oxen with which he tries in vain to drag the stones apart, while on the top one a white rabbit with burning coals for eyes sits watching and mocking.

'Lambing Corner', where the shepherd boy had his hut, had a real existence, but for many years now has been just part of the rolling farmland. This has become much more domesticated in appearance notwithstanding lingering tracts of furze and a vastly diminished number of sheep. The duke and duchess lived at 'Shakeforest Towers', a name unmistakably suggested by Savernake Forest; and indeed 'the old park entrance . . . now closed up and the lodge cleared away', close to the 'great western road', is a reference to the gate (now open again) leading into Savernake's Grand Avenue from the A4. The 'ancestral trees' are no doubt the avenue's famous beeches, many of which having lived their allotted span, are now being felled and replaced. But the house itself must have been suggested by Clatford House, immediately across the A4 opposite Clatford Bottom. This extraordinary building is a gabled farmhouse of brick and tile on three sides, but the side facing the highway is of stone, Georgian in design, and extended upward to form a dummy top storey, with painted-in windows to hide the gables. The house is privately owned.

In the heart of Savernake Forest stands Tottenham House, for long the seat of the Marquesses of Ailesbury and today yet another boys' preparatory school.

> Well: when in Wessex on your rounds
> Take a brief step beyond its bounds,
> And enter Gloucester . . .

This invitation introduces 'The Abbey Mason', Hardy's account in verse of the legendary invention of the Perpendicular style by the mason in charge of rebuilding at the abbey church, Gloucester, which later became the cathedral. No one knows the degree of truth in the story; but in a much changed and uglified city the unknown mason's 'petrified lacework' stands intact.

13 OUTER WESSEX
Somerset

Beneath us figured tor and lea,
From Mendip to the western sea—
I doubt if finer sight there be
    Within this royal realm.

A TRAMPWOMAN'S TRAGEDY

One brief scene in *The Dynasts* is laid just on the Somerset side of the border with Wiltshire, at Shockerwick House, now the seat of the Dukes of Newcastle. A previous occupant had become a close friend of the painter Gainsborough, and William Pitt the Younger was visiting Shockerwick from Bath to see the mansion's Gainsborough paintings when the news of Austerlitz reached him. Hardy combined the receipt of the news with Pitt's famous injunction to roll up the map of Europe, although in fact that remark was made while he was being conveyed, seriously ill, back into his own home at Putney. But the tradition that the incident took place at Shockerwick persists there to this day.

Of Hardy's allusions to Bath the most familiar is the description given by Bathsheba Everdene's young farmhand, Cainy Ball. It was not until afterwards, in 1878, that the Roman baths, the most extensive outside Italy, were disinterred, discoveries continuing far into the twentieth century. The water 'ready boiled for use' flows hot as ever. The city remains an elegant shopping centre, but the prototypes (if any) of the shops named by Cainy defy identification. The 'clock with a face as big as a baking-trendle' may have been the abbey's, though the

dial is not really large. The abbey, featured in the poem 'Aquae Sulis', was last restored extensively between 1864 and 1871, so that it remains very much as when Hardy wrote, with the exception of a covered cloister added to the nave in 1923 as a war memorial.

In *Far from the Madding Crowd*, *Two on a Tower* and 'The Marchioness of Stonehenge', weddings take place at Bath, but none of the lodgings and only one of the churches is specified. Sergeant Troy married Bathsheba at St Ambrose's, and it has been suggested that Hardy had in mind the fashionable St Andrew's in Julian Road, dedicated just before he visited Bath in 1873. If so, he took the liberty of setting it back into the period of the novel. The church was destroyed by enemy action in 1941. The poem 'Midnight on Beechen, 187–' evokes a panorama of Bath on a night in mid-June. This high bluff just south of the railway has wooded flanks, and near its summit runs a footpath from which the view is now almost hidden in summer, except at two points, by the growth of Cainy's 'old wooden trees'. Apart from the riverside in the foreground the spectacle has not so far lost too much of its period character; but there is, nevertheless, a steady erosion, for the author-

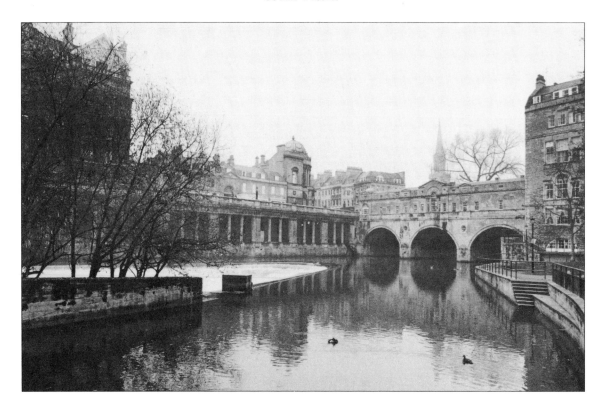

ities, though ready enough to protect individual buildings, seem unable to grasp that it is the homogeneity of the eighteenth-century whole that makes Bath unique.

From Bath it is a natural transition to the other half of the see, Wells ('Fountall'). Here Maumbry, in 'A Changed Man', and the Halborough brothers in 'A Tragedy of Two Ambitions', studied at the Theological College in the close, old Halborough was sentenced, and the cathedral 'by Mendip east of Dunkery Tor' saw the attempted robbery recalled in the poem 'The Sacrilege'. Today even the eighteenth-century thief would find cathedral and close very little different. Several years ago a vast project was embarked upon to restore the scores of stone figures adorning the cathedral's west façade.

There used to be a small prison behind the Guildhall, but it was never more than a remand gaol for prisoners awaiting trial; in real life old Halborough would have served his seven days at Shepton Mallet. Since the reorganization of the court system the Wells building, no longer a prison, is used as a storeroom for legal files. But it retains the bars across the windows.

Some miles east of Wells, and next to a hamlet with the improbable name of Vobster, is Mells ('Falls'), the home of Squire Dornell (really Horner), whose daughter became the First Countess of Wessex. The Horners held Mells until 1917, when the building was all but destroyed by fire. The present mansion, designed in 1923 by Sir Edward Lutyens, was built for another owner.

Mells Park, however, continues to be graced with many fine trees that in their youth must have shaded Squire Dornell, though the long avenue of beeches that he compared favourably with the Melbury Park oaks had to be uprooted some years ago as the result of age and disease. But the ride itself, asphalted now, is still the drive to the house.

Glastonbury (Glaston), a graceful town de-

Above:
'Midnight On Beechen, 187–' depicted Bath spread below on 'a night of mid-June, mute and dry'. This photograph shows the city on a night in mid-February, dark and damp, and yet unquestionably brighter than the lighting of the 1870s could have made it. The vantage-point here is not Beechen: a path still runs along the top of that hill, but the trees on its flank now obscure the panorama even in winter.

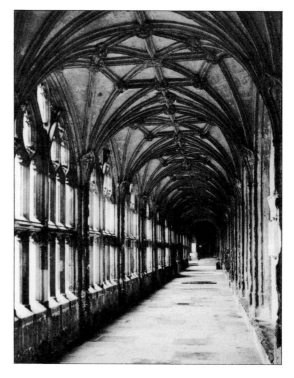

Opposite:
Hardy wrote several poems about Bath, caused a number of characters in his novels to be married there, but never made it a principal prose setting. Here, on a winter's day, are the Avon and renowned Pulteney Bridge.

Right:
With the Mendip Hills to the north and the watery moors to the south, 'Fountall' (Wells) was until even after the railway era subject to a difficulty of access that has kept it very small for a cathedral city. The extensive cloisters were added to the Cathedral in the mid-fifteenth century.

Map of the Principal Towns and Villages
of
OUTER WESSEX
BASED ON THE WORKS OF THOMAS HARDY

Key to the map of Outer Wessex

Hardy's names in italics.

Camelot	Cadbury Hill
Clyfton Horseleigh	Clifton Maybank
Dunkery Tor	Dunkery Beacon
Estminster	Yetminster
Falls	Mells
Fountall	Wells
Glaston	Glastonbury
Ivelchester	Ilchester
Ivell	Yeovil
Leddenton	Gillingham
Marlott	Marnhull
Markton	Dunster
Millpool	Milborne Port
Mountislope House	Montacute House
Narrobourne	West Coker
Sherton Abbas	Sherborne
Stapleford	Stalbridge
Stourton Tower	Alfred's Tower
Toneborough	Taunton

Bath

Shockerwick House

MENDIP HILLS

Priddy

Binegar

Fountall

Falls

POLDEN HILLS

EDGE

R

Glaston

Marshall's Elm

Stourton Tower

MID-WESSEX

R. PARRET

R. YEO

Long Load

Ivelchester

Pill Bridge

Camelot

Leddenton

Millpool

Marlott

Stapleford

Ivell

Montislope House

Sherton Abbas

Narrobourne

Clyfton Horseleigh

Estminster

SOUTH WESSEX

Kings Hintock

Winyards Gap

spite its growth, is briefly mentioned as the place where the Trampwoman's friend, Mother Lee, died. This little company faced 'the gusts on Mendip ridge', and it was in certain Mendip caves that the adventures in Hardy's only children's story, 'Our Exploits at West Poley', took place. West and East Poley, and 'Nick's Pocket' and 'Grim Billy' caves, are imaginary; but Priddy, at whose annual fair the unhappy protagonist of 'The Sacrilege' 'snatched a silk-piece red and rare' is a true Mendip village. The fair is still held, and it is not just a fun-fair; sheep and a few cattle change hands. A Mendip village that has lost its fair is Binegar, to whose revelries old Halborough and his new wife went after visiting Joshua. The field near the church in which a horse fair was held until the 1950s is still pointed out.

Wills Neck—the 'Wylls-Neck' of 'Wessex Heights', and the highest point in the Quantocks—has escaped desecration except by stag-hunting, which continues undiminished

Above:
'Wylls-Neck' (Will's Neck), at 1261ft the highest point in the Quantock Hills and one of Hardy's 'Wessex Heights' –

'shaped as if by a kindly hand
For thinking, dreaming, dying on . . .'

Opposite above:
'Glaston' (Glastonbury) deserves far more attention from Hardy than it gets, which is simply a brief mention in 'A Trampwoman's Tragedy' that her friend Mother Lee died there. A landmark for miles around is St Michael's Tower on Glastonbury Tor, an isolated conical hill from which this photograph was taken on a day of mist. Close by is the spot at which St Joseph is said to have buried the Holy Grail.

Opposite below:
A view over Dunster, the 'Markton' of *A Laodicean*, from the Castle hill. Hardy wrote most of the novel while lying seriously ill at Tooting, London, and in consequence it lacks his customary local colour.

Marshall's Elm, the former inn at the eastern end of the Polden ridge, where according to Hardy the murder described by the Trampwoman took place. The ballad is loosely founded on facts known to him, he claimed, for many years. The real Trampwoman's name was Mary Ann Taylor.

between the castles of fact and fiction—even less than Hardy indicates in his preface. Beatty has made out a very plausible case for contending that Hardy, forced to dictate *A Laodicean* from a London sick-bed, modelled Stancy on Corfe Castle (page 148) and took its paintings from Hutchins's list for Kingston Lacy. Today a National Trust property, Dunster Castle, thrusting its complex lineaments, the colour of a Golden Russet apple, high above the trees, retains an agreeable touch of fairyland; the Trust has lately made extensive repairs. Below the hill the village has been very carefully protected from anything out of harmony: perhaps too carefully, making it a little precious.

'Toneborough Deane' in 'The Sacrilege' is Taunton Deane, a first-class dairying region. At Taunton ('Toneborough'), in *A Laodicean*, Somerset's rival Havill had his office, and Captain de Stancy was quartered in the cavalry barracks. In 1879 these were demolished and replaced by infantry barracks, from which the last combatant troops departed in 1959; their quarters became offices for the Army Pay Corps and other units. The small military museum later established there as well has now been incorporated in the County Museum. At 'Toneborough' too the Honourable Laura (*A Group of Noble Dames*) was secretly married in the church of St Mary, notable today for the resplendent colours of its interior where all the painted woodwork was recently restored.

As to Exmoor and Dunkery Beacon, respectively 'Exon Moor' and 'Dunkery Tor' in 'The Sacrilege', Dunkery, like Wills Neck, has been spared twentieth-century embellishments; but Exmoor is the subject of some concern because of the steady conversion of marginal areas into farmland.

From one meaning of 'moor' to another: 'sad Sedge-Moor' was 'skirted' by the Trampwoman's party, and 'Sedgemoor' is mentioned in 'Molly Gone'. In the days before skilled drainage turned it into pasture, enough of the moor was marshland for many parts to need 'skirting'. The drainage was begun centuries

(except in areas bought by organizations that prohibit hunting), more than half a century after Hardy sent a message of encouragement to a Taunton gathering of the League for the Prohibition of Cruel Sports. Much of the range now belongs to the National Trust. Beyond the Quantocks lies Dunster, the principal setting of *A Laodicean*. The evidence that, in situation at least, Dunster Castle is 'Stancy Castle' and Dunster village 'Markton' is provided by Hardy's Wessex map and also by the similarity of 'de Stancy' to de Lancy, the name of a family with a seat near by. But there is no resemblance ago, but even now a wide strip on either side of King's Sedgemoor Drain is covered only by the coarsest grass and sedge, its appearance probably differing little from what it was in the Trampwoman's day.

Like a backbone along these fenlands runs the narrow ridge of the Polden Hills. It was while the Trampwoman and her friends were climbing 'toilsome Poldon [*sic*] crest' that the teller of the tale began her fatal flirtation. They were making for the spot where the tragedy was to occur, the inn 'far-famed as Marshall's Elm', almost at the eastern extremity of the range. Marshall's Elm became a farmhouse before the turn of the century; today, in that it offers bed and breakfast, it has returned in some measure to its original function. There appear to be few alterations inside, but there is no visible evidence that it was ever an inn. Hardy referred in a footnote to the former 'fine old swinging sign'. This was still recalled locally when Lea wrote; now it is not even a memory. Near the house its occupants today run a small camp and caravan site during the summer.

In the jail at 'Ivel-chester' (Ilchester) the Trampwoman's lover was hanged. Hardy sup-

plies a footnote referring to the terrible conditions in the jail, which he describes as demolished. It was not entirely pulled down, however, for half-hidden today behind a petrol station (itself due for demolition now that Ilchester has a bypass) there was still standing in 1983 a low building with odd cross-shaped windows, until recently used as a storehouse, which was once part of the boys' prison quarters. Behind this again are two semi-detached stone houses, still known as Goal Cottages, which were in fact the prison bakery and wash-house. On the other hand, according to J. Stevens Cox, the tall, narrow building by the river Yeo popularly believed to be the 'hanging chamber' (and photographed as such by Lea) is nothing more than a garden summer-house built after the demolition of the prison.

A few miles west of Ilchester the Yeo passes under a humped bridge that unites the villages of

Gaol Cottages (not the most felicitous of addresses) at 'Ivelchester' (Ilchester). Outside this singularly ill-run prison the Trampwoman's fancy-man was supposedly hanged, and the horse-thief Blue Jimmy also mentioned in the ballad was certainly so.

'Toneborough' Deane from the slopes of 'Wylls-Neck'. In
the poem 'The Sacrilege', based on an early nineteenth-
century gipsy tale, a fickle girl tempts a professional thief
to do the one thing from which he has always held back –
rob the Cathedral. He is caught and hanged, but his
brother shadows the temptress 'from Toneborough Deane
to Dunkery Tor', and eventually murders her.

St Mary Magdalene, 'Toneborough' (Taunton), where
'The Honourable Laura' was secretly married. The large
and splendid early Tudor church began its career as a
chapel-of-ease for Taunton Priory.

A 'rhine' (pronounced 'reen') or drainage-channel on
King's Sedgemoor, the Trampwoman's 'sad Sedge-Moor'
– sad, possibly, to Hardy because it was the scene of the
last battle on English soil, when James II's forces defeated
the simple peasants who joined the rebel Monmouth. But
Hardy also named it in 'Molly Gone', his lament for his
adored sister Mary (d. 1915), among the places to which
they had enjoyed excursions.

Long Load and Little Load. On the Little Load side the mouth of a tributary stream has been widened to make a bay for a barge, and this is the spot referred to in the introductory note to the poem 'Vagg Hollow'. Here, and at a now vanished wharf on the Long Load side, barges from the Bristol Channel off-loaded into waggons that carried their merchandise 'inland', that is to Yeovil and Sherborne. The waggon route, however, was by Ash and Tintinhull, and did not pass through Vagg Hollow. It therefore seems likely that 'Load Bridge' was a slip for Pill Bridge, which still spans the river Ivel midway between the Loads and Ilchester, and where barges also unshipped. From Pill Bridge (itself too narrow for vehicles) a road, still partly in evidence, led into Ilchester, after which the waggons would have travelled, as Hardy says, down 'the old Roman Road' (now the A37) as far as the Halfway Inn. Here today the A37 swings east, but the old road ran straight on toward Preston Plucknett, and indeed continues to do so as a little-used lane, surprisingly verdant in an area fast becoming a Yeovil suburb. Vagg Hollow is a very deep depression just north of the intersection with the route from Tintinhull. Hallucinations are still occasionally experienced there. The poem 'On Martock Moor' refers to a flat expanse; now rich pasturage, a few miles west of Ash. 'Weir-Water' was probably a weir on the River Parrett.

To some extent the suburban atmosphere has spread to Tintinhull, a straggling village noted for the presence of Tintinhull House (or The Mansion), the 'manor' of 'The Flirt's Tragedy', 'Embowered in Tintinhull Valley / By laurel and yew'. Today it belongs to the National Trust. The garden (redesigned in 1900) still boasts a fine old yew. Close at hand is Montacute ('Montislope') House, familiar to readers of Llewellyn Powys. Hardy is on record as having told Lea that Montacute was 'Elm-Cranlynch' in 'The First Countess of Wessex'. But Hardy was confusing two branches of the Phelips ('Phelipson') family. The Phelipses indeed held Montacute from the Dissolution until the early 1930s,

and *Richard* Phelips whose daughter Edith married Sir John Horsey ('Horseleigh') belonged to Montacute, which is therefore the 'Montislope' of 'Master John Horseleigh, Knight'. But *Charles* Phelips, the Charles 'Phelipson' of 'The First Countess', belonged to a lesser branch that had been banished in some disgrace in 1587 to the family's small manor at Corfe Mullen near Wimborne, and it is this manor that is 'Elm-Cranlynch' (see page 76).

Montacute, a National Trust property now, is a big, curiously impersonal house—perhaps because the furniture is an assemblage of gifts made to the Trust and never formed a home. A feature of great interest to Hardy readers is a plaster frieze in the hall, depicting a sixteenth-century version of the skimmington ride (*The Mayor of Casterbridge*). In the time of Sir John Horsey the present house did not exist; it was begun only in the 1590s by the nephew of the Edith Phelips who married Sir John. Nearly two hundred years later, when Edward Phelips of Montacute was planning his modifications, he bought the drawing-room chimneypiece, some windows, and the whole of the ornamental stone façade of Clifton Maybank (see page 111) for re-erection. There is a reference in 'Molly Gone' to 'Montacute Crest'. This is St Michael's Hill, the conical tree-clad eminence immediately west of the house.

Between Montacute and Clifton Maybank lies West Coker, the 'Narrobourne' of 'A Tragedy of Two Ambitions'. 'Narrobourne House' is described as a 'gloomy' manor house with a conservatory, a gravel terrace on the east side, and a view across the meads to a point where the local stream encounters a weir with a footbridge over it, then narrows to 'pass under a barrel arch or culvert constructed for waggons to cross into the middle of the mead in hay-making time'. There are trees round about, and a footpath leading past the weir from a point on the main road between the village and Hendford Hill—the real name of a hill leading south-westward out of Yeovil ('Ivell').

Several manor houses adorn the Cokers, and

--- field boundaries
------ footpaths

To Hendford Hill
and Yeovil

church

Manor

WEST COKER

lake

Coker Stream

HOLYWELL

Forester's
Arms

Skinner's
Hill
Farm

sluice etc
(see inset)

mill

Holywell
House

To East Coker

footpath

cattle bridge
over culvert

backwater

lane to
Forester's Arms

footbridge
and sluice
(weir)

mill
pool

mill

mill

Above:
To illustrate 'A Tragedy of Two Ambitions'.

Below:
Though this frieze is situated in Montacute House,
Somerset, it is highly pertinent to *The Mayor of
Casterbridge*, for it depicts a Skimmington or 'Skimmety'
Ride in progress.

Below:

Pill Bridge over the River Yeo, an interesting example of a bridge long enough to require two large stone arches, but too narrow to take even a small vehicle or laden pack-animal. The road still visible at this end led via 'Ivelchester' (Ilchester) to the sinister 'Vagg Hollow' of the poem so named.

Above:

'Narrobourne' (West Coker) Manor seen from near the point at which old Halborough was drowned in the 'Coker Rill' in the story 'A Tragedy of Two Ambitions'. The neighbouring village of East Coker is closely associated with the poet T. S. Eliot, who is buried there.

The new bridge over the Coker stream, replacing the old waggon-bridge and narrow culvert that for so long hid Halborough's body. On the right, the 'weir'—i.e. sluice—controlling the inflow from the mill backwater.

many weirs used to serve mills along the stream. But only one locality meets virtually all Hardy's points. In the hamlet of Holywell, between West and North Coker, there stands a disused mill, now renovated in part as a private house; and in the former watermeadows behind it there lay until 1970 a combination of sluice, footbridge, culvert and narrowing stream so closely resembling Hardy's picture that identification is unavoidable. In 1970 the culvert and waggon-bridge were replaced by a stone and concrete structure carrying the drive to the house; and to my great regret the opportunity for recording the old bridge in a photograph was lost.

Close to the site grow trees through which the brothers could have seen the lights of West Coker Manor along the mead upstream. The modest size of the 'Coker Rill', as it is called in the poem 'The Pat of Butter'—a 'narrow

bourne' in truth—makes it hard to find spots where even a drunken man in the dark could drown; but here the channel is so deep and steep-sided that with the brook in spate, as we are told it was, the episode becomes entirely credible.

There are minor objections. 'Narrobourne' church had three bells; both Coker churches have eight. The weir had 'hatches', whereas there is really only one (making the structure technically a sluice). The drowning man's cry, if it reached Rosa in the manor, must have been audible in the millhouse and in Holywell House. But these are small points, reminders that Hardy saw no reason why he should not take liberties in a piece of fiction. That he took some in this tale is evidenced by his references to the 'stile by a bridge' past Hendford Hill, for none is traceable. Possibly Hardy 'moved' the manor: it was stated to be close to the footpath.

Suburbia has encroached from Yeovil in this direction too; bungalows come to within a few yards of the weir. Yet West Coker remains a pretty place. The manor, cheerful enough now and delightfully modernized within, could well have had a 'gloomy' appearance in Victorian times. There is neither trace nor recollection of a conservatory (except at St Juliot all Hardy's conservatories seem untraceable), but the 'broad gravel path' can be recognized. The church, little changed, is chiefly of interest for the name of a former rector: Halberton, significantly like Halborough.

Yeovil itself, the sprawling helicopter- and glove-making town, bears little resemblance to the place where old Halborough proposed to stay at the (fictitious) 'Castle Inn', and Mr Cope ('For Conscience' Sake') lived in 'St Peter's Street' and was a curate at 'St John's Church'; both of these are real names—St John's, in fact, is the parish church, of some prestige. Apart from it, the few old buildings look over-whelmed.

A dozen miles west, beside the tree-lined A30 that here runs along a 700ft ridge, stands Windwhisle Inn, yet another 'lone inn' favoured by the Trampwoman and her friends. Until the 1950s this was still a rough public house, with benches and scrubbed tables, not much changed from the tramps' and highwaymen's haunt of old. Now it has been made elegant and com-fortable, and it is only for those with a romantic and quite impractical love for the squalid past that a spell is broken. Nevertheless, Windwhistle retains a more antique appearance than, say, the Horton Inn; and there is a woman's ghost seen from time to time on the road outside, even by those who have not yet imbibed within.

Windwhistle lies between Chard and Crew-kerne. The poem 'Growth in May' bears the footnote 'Near Chard', the country around which is the rich pasture-land described in the poem. Tracts of 'elbow-high green' that cause even the hedges to 'make a mean show as a fence' have not entirely vanished, praise be. Crewkerne is mentioned in the poem 'At Wynyard's Gap'.

Today, despite the presence of a shopping precinct and large cheese factory, it is still old-world; these small Wessex market centres do not change much with the decades, or even with the centuries. In the same poem there is also an allusion to Pen Wood. This is a large, irregular-shaped tract on the slopes of Birt's Hill a few miles east of Crewkerne, with the Dorset–Somerset boundary across its middle. Its main distinction, and the reason for its remaining unspoiled, is that at no point is it touched by even a minor road.

Corton Hill is one more of the landmarks listed in 'Molly Gone'. Corton Ridge and Corton Hill are two steep heights, grassy and gorse-strewn, about four miles north of Sherborne, forming part of the western edge of the uplands that here bound the plains of the Yeo. A little to the north is Cadbury Castle, a circular hill supporting an earthwork that is the 'Camelot' of the poem 'Channel Firing'. In the late 1960s extensive excavations were made there in an attempt to establish a historical basis for the Arthurian association, but results were incon-clusive. The same poem alludes to 'Stourton Tower'; this is Alfred's Tower, a late eighteenth-century brick landmark on the wooded heights dividing Somerset from Wilt-shire. Now a National Trust property, the tower is in good repair.

Hemmed in on all sides but the north by the Dorset boundary is Milborne Port ('Millpool'), once among the properties of the squire in 'Squire Petrick's Lady' (see page 97). Today the little town, if no longer what it was, is far from moribund, and its attractive old houses are surrounded by much new development.

Where the road from Bristol to Poole (A357) crosses that from London to Land's End (A30) stands Henstridge Ash. In a note to 'By Hen-stridge Cross at the Year's End' Hardy refers to 'this centuries-old cross-road'. Originally the poem bore the name 'Mellstock Cross', but the four arms are in any case symbolic. The 'white handpost' has given place to traffic lights.

14 LOWER WESSEX

Devon

A very West-of-Wessex girl
As blithe as blithe could be,
Was once well-known to me,
And she would laud her native town,
And hope and hope that we
Might sometimes study up and down
Its charms in company.

THE WEST-OF-WESSEX GIRL

The only Hardy work in prose or verse to have a North Devon setting is the Noble Dame story 'The Honourable Laura'. From his own map it is not difficult to didentify 'Cliff-Martin' with Combe Martin, and to place the (imaginary) Prospect Hotel in the region of Woody Bay. The waterfall in the story, though not corresponding in detail, is based on the Hanging Water that cascades down the wooded slopes into this inlet. To suit his tale Hardy narrows the flanks, increases the final drop and eliminates the trees that might have checked Northbrook's fall. He may also have invented the rock-hewn steps; today the descent is by a broad gravel path that zigzags across the stream. But the cascade remains spectacular. The shore is boulder-strewn, but probably displayed enough sand to make it suitable for a duel. The Woody Bay Hotel, however, cannot be identified with the 'Prospect', which lay some way inland near the turnpike road. The 'nearest railway town' was Lynton, on the Barnstaple & Lynton Railway.

Coombe Martin, straggling inland along North Devon's only coastal road, has never made up its mind whether or not to become a full-blown resort. Barnstable ('Downstaple'), also mentioned, may be defined as an industrial growth round a beautiful and historic centre; in the late 1960s it was unsuccessfully suggested as an 'overspill' town for London.

In South Devon the 'Silverthorne Dairy House', home of the milkmaid of the 'Romantic Adventures', was (according to Hardy's supplementary information to Lea) 'probably' near Silverton, north of Exeter ('Exonbury'), in a still superbly lush dairying area. At Exeter, in 'For Conscience Sake', Mr Milborne discovered his former betrothed and their daughter running a dancing-school in a 'central and open place'; he took rooms opposite. Since much of the city centre was damaged beyond repair by Second World War bombing, the odds are against the survival of any particular buildings Hardy may have had in mind. But old houses are still to be seen, sometimes where least expected: one of the charms of contemporary Exeter is that antique corners are to be found hiding amid sadly unimaginative post-war reshaping.

The allusion in 'The Carrier' to 'Sidwell Church and wall' refers to St Sidwell's in the north-east sector of the city, and suggests Cullompton as the carrier's destination. The church seen today is new, its predecessor having been destroyed in the air raids; but the churchyard walls are the old ones.

The carefully-pinpointed route of the rider in

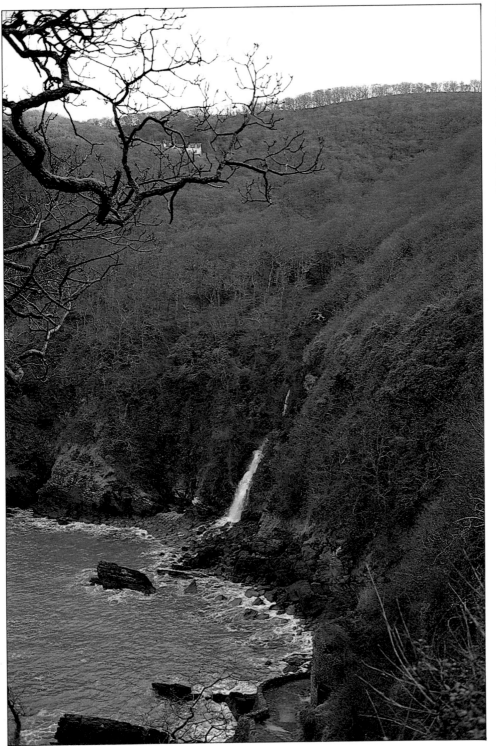

Left:
Few reaches of even the North Devon coast are more grandiose than Woody Bay, the unnamed setting of most of the action in 'The Honourable Laura'. The Hanging Water, the waterfall of the story, is conspicuous; the building near the summit is the modern Woody Bay Hotel.

Opposite:
In his decidedly sub-standard story 'The Romantic Adventures of a Milkmaid' Hardy causes Baron Xanten to moor his yacht off 'Idmouth' (Sidmouth). Today largely a geriatric refuge for former administrators of Britain's vanished Empire, the resort has recently, by contrast, gained fame as the scene of an annual international folk festival. This photograph shows the unspoilt elegance of the mainly 1820–30 sea-front.

'My Cicely' ended at a 'graveacre' in or near 'Exonbury' (Exeter), 'Where Exe scents the sea'. Bailey suggests, very plausibly, that the poem is a highly fanciful record of a genuine journey made by Hardy after Tryphena Sparks, now Mrs Gale, had established herself in the hotel run by her husband at Topsham, on the fringe of Exeter, and that the occasion of his trip was the news of her mother-in-law's death, which he took to refer to her own. That the 'graveacre' is Topsham churchyard is indicated by Hardy's tailpiece illustration to 'My Cicely', which shows the twin towers of Exeter Cathedral as seen from the Topsham direction. The identity of the 'Lions-Three' is more puzzling, since there is no record of a Three Lions at the time anywhere in Devon; but at Honiton—on the A30, fifteen miles from Exeter—one of the old coaching inns is called the Three Tuns. The present narrow stuccoed frontage on the main street—relatively peaceful since the coming of the by-pass—conceals an old building that rambles back to a

great depth. Alternatively the inn could be fictional, its name suggested by the three lions in Dorchester's coat-of-arms (Bailey).

Some five miles west of Honiton along the 'Highway' one comes to Fairmile Hill, one of the two possible locations for 'The Dear', though the haughty maiden of this poem may have been encountered in Dorset (see page 100). In favour of the Devon hill is the fact that 'my dear' is a much commoner Devonian than Dorset form of address. But the damsel would have had to be brave as well as haughty to have risked a walk amid the traffic on Devon's Fairmile Hill today.

On the coast to the south stands Sidmouth ('Idmouth'), the resort near which Baron Xanten's yacht was moored in 'The Romantic Adventures of a Milkmaid'. The short but charming Victorian seafront is still much as Hardy knew it. In 'A Mere Interlude', 'Tor-upon-Sea' is Torquay, the now much-enlarged South Devon coast resort.

That scenes should have altered since Hardy

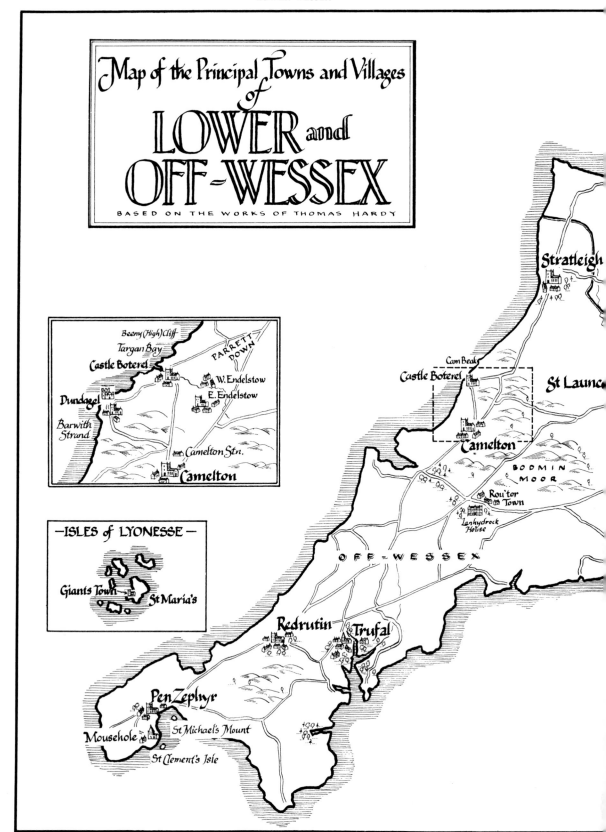

Map of the Principal Towns and Villages
of
LOWER and
OFF-WESSEX
BASED ON THE WORKS OF THOMAS HARDY

Stratleigh

Beeny (High) Cliff
Targan Bay
Castle Boterel
W. Endelstow
E. Endelstow
Dundagel
Barwith Strand
PARRETT DOWN
Camelton Stn.
Camelton

Cam Beak
Castle Boterel
St Launce
Camelton
BODMIN MOOR
Rou'tor Town
Lanhydrock House

OFF-WESSEX

-ISLES of LYONESSE-
Giants Town
St Maria's

Redrutin
Trufal

PenZephyr
Mousehole
St Michael's Mount
St Clement's Isle

Key to the map of Lower and Off-Wessex
Hardy's names in italics.

Barwith Strand	Trebarwith Strand
Castle Noterel	Boscastle
Camelton	Camelford
Cliff Martin	Coombe Martin
Dundagel	Tintagel
Dunkery Tor	Dunkery Beacon
Exonbury	Exeter
Exon Moor	Exmoor
Idmouth	Sidmouth
Isles of Lyonesse	Isles of Scilly
Markton	Dunster
Pen Zephyr	Penzance
Port Bredy	Bridport
Redrutin	Redruth
Rou'tor Town	Bodmin
St Launce's	Launceston
Silverthorne	Silverton
Stratleigh	Bude
Targan Bay	Pentargon Bay
Trufal	Truro

Scale
in Miles
0 2 4 6 8 10

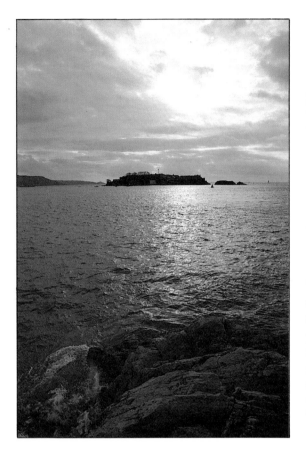

Winter sky over Plymouth Sound, with Drake's Island in the distance. Hardy constantly renewed his promise to Emma to accompany her on a visit to the town in which she had spent her first twenty years, but he never did so. Only after her death did he try to make amends in this, as in so much else.

described them is to be expected, but Plymouth had already undergone great alteration between the time when Emma was brought up there and her visit in 1890 following her father's death. This is made clear in the poem 'Lonely Days'. But the tramlines and 'electric ropes' have vanished as though they had never come, and the 'duller and dingier tone' of the house-fronts has been countered by the bright freshness of so much new building since the devastation of the last war. The 'Three Towns' of 'Places'— Plymouth, Devonport and Stonehouse—were amalgamated in 1914, since when nine other territories have been engulfed. The Hoe as known to Hardy was not very different from the Hoe today, although in Emma's childhood, the period conjured up in so many of the Plymouth poems, it was still a bluff of crude rock, with no promenade. The latter and the various paths and roads have been asphalted since Hardy wrote, and inevitably new monuments have appeared. Across the Sound the Breakwater, afer the lapse of a century, would occasion no surprise to Stephen (*A Pair of Blue Eyes*), but farther out the present Eddystone Lighthouse was put up in 1882, and the one he saw has been re-erected on the Hoe.

A recent addition to the Hoe is the Hoe Theatre, in which the band now 'booms' in summer instead of in the open as in 'The Marble-streeted Town'. The 'marble' was limestone paving that when worn smooth looked like marble, especially during rain. There is still some in service. West Hoe Pier, from which the suitor rowed to Cremyll in 'The Second Night', continues to extend its crab-claw arms below Grand Parade. (For Cremyll and Edgcumbe see page 212).

St Andrew's church, the premier church of Plymouth, was gutted by fire-bombs, only the shell and tower, with its splendid carillon and chimes of ten bells, surviving. The church has been fully restored, but its churchyard with the 'multifarious tombstones' noticed by Stephen has given place to a gracious terrace bordering Royal Parade, the wide new avenue that has replaced Plymouth's chief pre-war thorough-fare, Bedford Street (also noted by Stephen). St Andrew's bells, said in 'Places' to chime 'the quaint old Hundred-and-Thirteenth tune ... Night, morn, and noon', really played fourteen tunes, a new one each day for a fortnight, every four hours. This has been discontinued (it must have driven nearby residents nearly mad at night), but the bells are often rung by hand, and one day in 1969 a Dorset visitor heard them playing another of Hardy's favourites, the Sicilian Mariners' Hymn.

St Charles church was also gutted, and its shell has been kept as a permanent memorial of those fearful nights. It stands, nearly inaccessible, on the centre island of a busy roundabout. At night the interior is floodlit. Here, Hardy states in *The Life*, Emma long wished to be buried in the Gifford vault, until on attending her father's funeral she found the sepulchre had been 'broken into, if not removed' to improve the church entrance.

Most of the houses in which she passed her childhood have also now disappeared. Several of them can be identified in the Plymouth poems. Her birthplace, alluded to in the opening stanza of 'Places', was 10 York Street, a thoroughfare that suffered so much in the air raids that it has been swept away in the replanning. The 'room by the Hoe' in the following stanza was in her next-but-one home, 9 Sussex Street. On her manuscript of *Some Recollections* Hardy set a query by the number, but 'John Gifford, Solicitor' is entered for number 9 in Brendon's *Directory* for 1852. Close to the Hoe Park, Sussex Street is a short road now closed at the northern end, but formerly linking Saltram Place (Citadel Road) with Princess Place. Again the air raids annihilated most of the houses, including the Gifford residence, which stood on the east side, at what has now become the top of the cul-de-sac. Its garden, already destroyed by a new road (Sussex Place) when Emma wrote *Some Recollections*, is the scene of the second and third stanzas of 'During Wind and Rain'. The 'high new house' in the last stanza, to which the family moved from Sussex Street, is 9 Bedford Terrace, an even shorter cul-de-sac off Tavistock Road. This little backwater survived the war, and still conforms in almost every detail to Emma's own description. No 9, the last house in the row, was until a few years ago a smart private residence, but is now a hostel and, sad to say, very shabby. It was probably this building to which Hardy pictured Emma returning late in life and hearing the dancers 'through the party-wall' as recorded in 'Lonely Days'.

15 OFF-WESSEX
Cornwall

Does there even a place like Saint-Juliot exist?
Or a Vallency Valley
With stream and leafed alley,
Or Beeny, or Bos with its flounce flinging mist?

A DREAM OR NO

For Hardy Cornwall remained almost exclusively the county of his courtship. Even Cremyll, already mentioned in connection with Plymouth (page 210), is linked by Bailey with this, for he believes that 'The Second Night' was inspired by a detour Hardy made to Plymouth, where Tryphena was then headmistress of a school, during the return from one of his visits to St Juliot. Cremyll has altered little, but at Mount Edgcumbe (the girl in the poem was an 'Edgcumbe lass') the glorious Tudor mansion—now partly rebuilt—was ruined by the bombing of 1941.

St Juliot ('West Endelstow') is the focal point of Hardy's Cornish writings; and precisely because it was of such personal moment, he disguised much of the topography in a way that even now we cannot entirely rectify. One scene, however, that he described with complete fidelity in *A Pair of Blue Eyes* is the rectory ('vicarage' in earlier editions), and his description fits almost as well today. The house stands in a 'little dell like a nest', and traces of a quarry are still visible in the vicinity. 'A thicket of shrubs and trees' still encloses a lawn—now very small—and the conservatory, subject of 'The Frozen Greenhouse', has been restored. The french window that figures in both the novel and the poem 'At the Word Farewell' (in which the lawn also appears) continues in being, but the verandah is no more, although its floor still extends along the south wall. Gone too is the subject of 'The Sundial on a Wet Day'; it stood a little way out from the south-east angle of the house. Below the grounds, the field in which Hardy noted the 'old horse pulling a harrow' that forty-five years later formed the motif for his poem 'In Time of the "Breaking of Nations"', is a field still, though no longer visible from the garden. In the poem 'A Duettist at her Pianoforte' Emma, by then Mrs Hardy, is looking back on the duets she used to play with her sister, Helen Catherine Holder, in the rectory drawing-room. The house is the 'dwelling' of 'The Seven Times', and is the theme or setting of several other poems that do not touch upon individual features. Grey-roofed, grey-walled, with deep blue woodwork, it displays only minor architectural modifications—the 'inner lobby of the front entrance' has had one wall removed, opening it into the adjacent study, and early in this century the drawing-room was given a new fireplace—but is no longer a rectory, tiny St Juliot having been amalgamated with no fewer than six other parishes under Boscastle ('Castle Boterel').

When we leave the rectory grounds the verisimilitude of the picture ends; for the novelist represents the village as being much nearer the sea than it is, which explains why he says of the churchyard that 'not a tree could exist up there', although the trees that today ring it were there when he wrote, as Emma's sketch (now hanging in the church) proves. Other trees make it impossible to see the church from the rectory. (According to Lea, the position of 'West Endelstow' is a mixture of those of St Juliot and Forrabury. It is Forrabury, for instance, that provides the view of the sea 'to a width of half the horizon'.) Emma's picture shows the graveyard indeed 'serrated with the outline of graves and a very few memorial stones'. Since then the number of headstones has increased, although the 'monotonous grey-green grass' is still unkempt.

The 'tower owning neither battlement nor pinnacle' is shown in Emma's pre-restoration sketch to have owned both; nor does the new tower differ. The 'six-and-thirty old seat-ends' that Hardy saw decaying in an aisle were removed during the restoration, but another sketch now in the church shows what they looked like. The west gallery was also removed. The most interesting feature of the present church is the two tablets on the north wall, one recording that Emma laid the first stone of the rebuilt aisle and tower and directed the church music, the other testifying to Hardy's supervision of the restoration in 1871. There is a third tablet in memory of Emma's brother-in-law, the Reverend Caddell Holder. The tablet to Emma is the subject of the poems 'The Marble Tablet' and 'The Monument-Maker'.

The principal original of 'Endelstow House' (*A Pair of Blue Eyes*) is Lanhydrock House (now a National Trust property) in the Fowey valley south of Bodmin. Here one may identify the 'spacious court', the many-mullioned windows, the 'ancient gatehouse of dun stone' (spanned, however, by a rounded arch, not 'high-shouldered Tudor'), the avenue of sycamores beyond, and the long, barrel-vaulted picture-gallery described in the novel. The gallery and the wing it occupies are in fact the only remnants of the mansion as seen by Hardy; in 1881 the central and southern blocks were destroyed in a fire and replaced by exact replicas.

Lanhydrock, however, is not the only model for 'Endelstow House'. The latter had mullioned dormer windows, surmounted, like the gables, by grotesque figures; tall 'octagonal and twisted' chimneys, surpassed in height, however, by the trees behind them; polygonal bays in the angles of the court, their surfaces 'entirely occupied by buttresses and windows'; and over the main entrance a 'far-projecting oriel springing from a fantastic series of mouldings'. None of these features appears at Lanhydrock, or elsewhere in Cornwall. But in Dorset, within a few miles of his home, was a mansion Hardy had several reasons for knowing intimately* and which displayed all the missing features— Athelhampton, already considered in an earlier chapter (page 55) as the prototype of 'Athelhall'. Here are the mullioned dormers and roof-gables with the grotesque finials; the tall (but not twisted: a slip?) chimneys overtopped by the trees behind, a polygonal bay, all buttress and window; and when a gatehouse stood to the south of the present frontage, above the gate (which had a 'high-shouldered Tudor arch') projected a magnificent oriel supported on a truly 'fantastic series of mouldings'.

'Endelstow Park' is probably based on that of Lanhydrock. The Smiths' cottage and its little bridge correspond accurately with the appearance (as it would have been then) of the National Trust-owned cottage called Newmill or New Mills beside the Valency, over which there is a footbridge flanked by a ford. The 'faint outline of ditch and mound' indicating the site of an earlier house appears to be an allusion to Prideaux Castle, an ancient earthwork five miles south of Lanhydrock above the Luxulyan valley

---

* His father had worked on the restoration; he himself had sketched it in water-colour in 1859 (the painting is now in the Dorset County Museum); and he had written an article on the new church for the *Dorset County Chronicle*.

Left:
St Juliot Rectory –
today yet another ex-
rectory – mirrored
with minute accuracy
as 'West Endelstow'
Rectory in *Blue Eyes*.
Here in 1870 Hardy
first met Emma and
immediately fell in
love. Very few changes
have overtaken either
the house or the
garden in the
intervening years.

Opposite above:
Newmill or New Mills,
in the Valency Valley,
the probable original
of the Smiths' cottage
in Hardy's one Cornish
novel. The footbridge
and the ford beside it
are part of a once-
frequented route
between the two
'Endelstows' (see page
216).

Opposite below:
Looking across the
'Vallency' (Valency)
Valley from 'East
Endelstow'
(Lesnewth). In the
distance is the lonely
church of 'West
Endelstow' (St Juliot),
which for *A Pair of
Blue Eyes* Hardy
'moved' much nearer
the coast.

'Camelton' (Camelford) railway-station had a relatively short life. In 1870 the line still ended at 'St Launce's' (Launceston); by the close of the action in *Blue Eyes* it had been extended to Padstow, with a station at 'Camelton'; but in the drastic curtailments following the Second World War it was an early casualty. At present 'Camelton' station buildings are used as offices and store-rooms.

that provided Hardy with the name Lord Luxellian.

'Endelstow house' was situated at 'East Endelstow'—Lesnewth, a village even smaller (if possible) than St Juliot, and in reality not east but south of it, across the valley. Because Hardy placed St Juliot nearer the sea, the contrast in scenery between the two 'Endelstows' is purely fanciful. 'East Endelstow' church (the scene, according to Hardy's own note, of the poem 'The Young Churchwarden') reflects aspects of those at both Lanhydrock and Lesnewth. 'Not

forty yards from the mansion' accurately places Lanhydrock church in relation to the house, but 'in a little dell' relates to Lesnewth, for Lanhydrock church stands on a small rise. Today neither graveyard is demarcated by square boundary-stones. Yews are not conspicuous round either church. The 'Luxellian vault' is another Dorset importation, being based on the tomb of the O'Briens in Stinsford Church (see page 30).

'East Endelstow', we are told, lay on two sides of a ravine, the halves being united by a bridge from which a steep ascent led to 'West Endelstow'. Lesnewth parish is indeed divided by a ravine running south from the Valency valley, and the road referred to can still be followed, although it has long ceased to be a principal link between the two villages. It descends eastward from Lesnewth church, crosses the picturesque stream at the bottom of the ravine by a concrete bridge built about 1960 to replace a stone one destroyed by a flood, then breasts the ridge carrying Treworld Farm. From here a lane drops down to the bridge over the Valency beside Newmill, but remembering Hardy's *imaginary* position for St Juliot, he was probably thinking of the other lane, to Minster and Forrabury.

The route by which Knight and Stephen followed the hearse from Camelford ('Camelton') station to Lesnewth church is mainly imaginary—inevitably so, if Hardy was to maintain his fiction that St Juliot lay much nearer than Lesnewth to the sea. But there are still one or two people who recall the smithy in which, in the novel, the two men took shelter. It is not named on the 25 in OS map (which marks most smithies), although it was still functioning when the first edition was published; but those who knew it remember that it stood east of Lesnewth church, where the track from Helset joins the St Juliot road by Trewannion. It ceased operations around 1904, when the smith left to join a colleague at Tresparrett Posts. The 'Welcome Home' inn, by contrast, never existed. Camelford station has now become an agricultural store. Camelford itself remains a small, most attractive townlet, in which the 'Luxellian Arms' was probably a pseudonym for the Darlington Hotel. The railway has long forsaken the station.

Somewhere along the Valency valley lies the waterfall in which, as recorded in the poem 'Under the Waterfall', Emma and Hardy lost a tumbler during a picnic. But despite his sketch of her trying to recover the fugitive, and a claim by Phelps to have identified the fall, it could in fact have been any one of a score along the picturesque stream.

The 'Manor House' or 'The Crags' has no counterpart in or near St Juliot; but the feature from which it took its name, the 'jutting angle of a wild enclosure . . . which almost overhung the valley' has several possible models farther down the northern flank of the Valency gorge, notably the first to be encountered—or rather, seen above one—on entering the valley-mouth. The precipitous field immediately above this would then become the site of Elfride's and Knight's parting in Chapter 34. This beautiful and thickly wooded ravine figures in a number of poems. It runs just west of St Juliot, between interleaving hills, at the foot of which the river purls along, as pretty to the ear as to the eye; and the footpath so prominent in the novel is still walkable, albeit with certain stretches often under water. Much of the woodland on the south side of the valley is now National Trust property. Newmill is part of an isolated group of several cottages, one of them in ruins; but which, if any, are we to pick for Mrs Jethway's house? When she is found crushed under the fallen church tower at 'West Endelstow', Knight wants her to be carried to the 'nearest house', the rectory; but Lord Luxellian suggests that since a surgeon will have to be summoned from Boscastle, it would be better to carry her to the first house in that direction; and when they do so, it proves to be her own home. In reality the rectory, Newmill, and the cottages mentioned above all lie in the direction of Boscastle from the church; but Hardy's shifting of St Juliot blurs all such realities. Mrs Jethway's home was rather large, had a set of rock-cut steps leading to the water, where there was a hollowed-out basin, and stood alone under 'a row of scrubby oaks'. None of these features, even the standing alone, belongs to any of the real cottages. The indefatigable Lea settled for the easternmost, Rose Cottage; perversely, perhaps, I favour the westernmost, if only because it has a few rock steps and stands most apart. The whole scene is somewhat marred today, however, by the construction (still incomplete) of a set of large rectangular concrete basins by the river for breeding trout.

While still at quite a distance from its mouth the Valency valley widens out, and the river disappears behind the houses to flow at last into Boscastle harbour. This little haven, where Stephen landed from Bristol, is now a National Trust property wholly given over to small pleasure-craft and fishing-boats; but there are

Beeny High Cliff, or Buckator, plays a leading part in *Blue Eyes* and, because
it was the scene of many of Hardy's earliest activities with Emma, is also the
setting for a large number of the love-poems composed after her death.
Though slightly lame, Emma was a brilliant horsewoman, and struck awe
into the locals by her equestrian exploits on these mighty slopes.

One of many waterfalls along the Valency Valley that could have been the scene of the incident of the lost picnic-glass recorded in the poem 'Under the Waterfall' and in Hardy's sketch of Emma trying to rescue it. An obstacle to exact identification is the constantly varying relationship between rock and water, according to the rainfall.

The graceful waterfall that carries the 'upper stream', north of the Valency, to its destination in 'Targan' (Pentargon) Bay. This fall too is the setting for several of the poems inspired by Emma's death.

many people in the hill-girt town who can recall when, before the days of proper roads, the port took in much of their coal and general supplies.

Boscastle has not had many additions: the inevitable car-parks, a wider bridge, new buildings on the fringes, souvenir shops. All too often 'the drizzle bedrenches', as in the poem 'At Castle Boterel'; and in winter 'Upon Boterel Hill, where the waggoners skid' as Hardy wrote in 'Places', the motorist sometimes fares little better, although an easier route now bypasses the terrifying 1 in 3 gradient that he and Emma knew.

The north-east road out of Boscastle arrives in due course at Bude, the 'Stratleigh' of the novel, no longer 'a small watering-place' but a major resort. Long before this the route passes near two cliffs prominent in novel and verse. One is the cliff to which Elfride rode, with Stephen accompanying her on foot, and where, in a natural alcove, they exchanged their first kiss and she lost her ear-ring; she returned much later to this same cliff with Knight and found the ear-ring still in the alcove. Let us call this cliff A. Cliff B is the cliff that Elfride reached on foot by crossing a hill behind the rectory and following a stream until it ended in a waterfall with the cliff on the right; here she met Knight, and after they had seen the *Puffin* steaming to Boscastle with Stephen aboard, they experienced the terrible adventure that nearly cost them their lives.

Hardy describes cliff A and its approach by saying that to reach it Elfride and Stephen left the lane and crossed some fields. They then followed an irregular path that eventually ended in a flat ledge passing round the face of the 'huge blue-black rock' about halfway up. Here they found the alcove and sat down. Below them, gulls screamed on detached rocks. Only when referring to Elfride's second visit, this time with Knight, does Hardy suddenly give the cliff a name, 'Windy Beak', and calls it the second-highest along the coast, with the popular reputation of being the highest of all. Elfride mentions that it is farther from St Juliot than the cliff of their misadventure.

Now to cliff B. After describing the stream followed by Elfride as 'smaller than that in her own valley' and at a higher level, flowing past a green carpet at the bottom of a shallow bush-lined trough, Hardy remarks that toward its mouth the ridge to the left of it 'dwindled lower and became insignificant', while that to the right rose steadily higher until it ended in a clearly defined edge. Presently the bed of the stream reached a similar edge, and the stream tumbled to its death in a cascade. The cliff was 'visible like a concave wall', and consisted of 'blackish-grey slate, unvaried in its whole height by a single change of shade'. A grassy path 'wound along inside a bank, placed as a safeguard for unwary pedestrians' to the top of the cliff, and thence inland. The height of this cliff was locally believed to be 700 feet, but was actually 650. Perpendicular 'from the half-tide level', the rampart formed no headland, but one wall of an inlet, with a promontory at a lower level on either side. In the novel this cliff is referred to as the 'Cliff Without a Name', but in his Preface of 1895 Hardy admitted that it had one, and later still he allowed it to be identified with Beeny Cliff, so marking it on his own map.

This is where the confusion starts. All the attributes, except the height, of cliff B, the scene of Knight's near-tragedy, belong not to Beeny Cliff* but to a very similar one nearer to Boscastle, forming the north wall of Pentargon ('Targan') Bay. This cliff, too, is black, sheer, concave in horizontal section, and curving toward the left of anyone looking seaward. To it belong the summit path, the protective bank, the waterfall, with its miniature meadows near the base, and the stream that has its source in the shallow vale north of the Valency. Even the freak air currents that Knight was demonstrating are familiar to local people. Beeny High Cliff, while sharing many of these features, never had a bank protecting the path over its top, and

---

* More often known locally as Beeny High Cliff or Buckator. The OS map marks the whole stretch between the Pentargon and Beeny inlets as Beeny Cliff. There is also a High Cliff, *tout court*, a mile north of Beeny High Cliff.

though there is a small waterfall beside it, this wells out of the ground a few yards from the drop; there is no stream.

Now let us consider cliff A, 'Windy Beak', the scene of the lost-and-found ear-ring. The loss of the ear-ring is based on a genuine experience of Emma's at Beeny High Cliff. 'Windy Beak', moreover, has all the characteristics of Beeny: it is black, sheer, locally believed to be the highest rampart on the coast but is actually the second-highest, and it is confronted by an isolated dome in the sea called Gull Rock. In short, cliff A *is* Beeny. But Beeny having been subsequently mis-identified as the scene of Knight's folly, 'Windy Beak' had to be assigned either an imaginary status, or a prototype elsewhere: hence the identification with the Strangles (Lea), which is not sheer, and Cam Beak (several writers), which is not black. Nor had either of these ever been considered the highest cliff in the district. If only Hardy had admitted that his 'Cliff Without a Name' was the Pentargon cliff, to which he had given Beeny's height, and that Beeny was 'Windy Beak', all would have been plain.

Phelps suggests that the seat and alcove are to be discovered in the vestiges of former quarry workings on the *north*-west face of Beeny High Cliff, citing in support the exact coincidence of the view from there with Hardy's description—a view that is wholly hidden from the *south*-west face. In that context the 'distant lightship' seen after the recovery of the ear-ring would be the lighthouse on Lundy Island, there being no light*ship* within range at the time. But the north-west face is a very long and arduous walk from the south-west, it is not black but brown, and Hardy unequivocally states that the ledge leading to the seat 'passed round the [concave] face of the huge blue-black rock'. One explanation could be that the real loss of an ear-ring (i.e., by Emma) did take place among the quarry workings, but that for the novel Hardy transferred the episode, together with the ledge and seat, to the more dramatic face, either forgetting or not caring to alter the description of the view. If

there were ever an actual ledge and seat on the south-west face, they have long disappeared in the numerous rock-falls to which these cliffs are prone.

The 'shallow, bush-lined trough' of the stream that Elfride followed to Pentargon Bay has become so thickly overgrown, in addition to having its banks blocked by stone walls, that progress along it is now all but impossible, even in the upper reaches above St Juliot, but the path giving access from the rectory can still be made out. Perhaps the route was never practicable outside Hardy's imagination, for Emma records that he and she normally approached the bay by the (still used) path from Boscastle harbour.

Bay and waterfall appear in several poems, including 'Best Times' and 'After a Journey'. Hardy made rough sketches here, and also at the lovers' other picnic site beside Beeny High Cliff. The 'Figure in the Scene' describes one sketch, and 'Why did I Sketch?' looks back on it. 'Where the Picnic Was' may be set here or in Dorset (see page 132). 'If You had Known', 'The Phantom Horsewoman', the lilting, exquisite 'Beeny Cliff': these are but a few examples of the spate of poems that hark back to this strip of coast or to St Juliot.

'A Man was Drawing Near to Me' depicts Emma's feelings as she awaited the young architect's first visit to the lonely rectory. He passes Hallworthy, Otterham, Tresparrett Posts, Hennett 'Byre'. Of these, Otterham is still a very drowsy village, deprived now of its railway station; Hennett, a magnificent old stone-built farm with some modern additions near St Juliot church; Hallworthy a village yet, though at a busy road junction; and Tresparrett Posts, though at an even busier junction, has altered little from the portrait of it in 'Where Three Roads Joined'. Between Tresparrett village and Posts lies Tresparrett Down, the 'Parrett Down' of *A Pair of Blue Eyes*. It remains open pasture, but where the main road skirts the village many bungalows have recently appeared.

At most seasons Bodmin Moor today fully lives up to the dreary picture that met Stephen

Above:
St Benet's Abbey, Lanivet, home of Emma's friends the Serjeants, and the destination of Hardy and herself on the walk which included the eerie experience recorded in the poem 'Near Lanivet, 1872'. In a now vanished summerhouse in the sadly derelict garden seen here, Hardy that same year wrote part of *A Pair of Blue Eyes*.

Opposite above:
Near the seaward end of the only road down to 'Barwith' (Trebarwith) Strand, another *Blue Eyes* setting. During modern summers tourists beset the hamlet like greenfly on an unsprayed rosebush, but the old coastguard cottages, though they became a hotel and are now a pub, remain outwardly their old selves.

Left:
Far more impressive than the Valency's little waterfalls, if less important in Hardy annals, is the cascade near St Nectan's Kieve. The glen below has been the scene of strange experiences. For example, the nineteenth-century novelist Wilkie Collins was walking up it when he met two ladies who said they lived near the Kieve as recluses. But when he enquired, no one had ever heard of them.

In 1870, Hardy, then still an architect, was despatched by his employer to St Juliot to see about restoring the crumbling church. His first activity was to drive over with his hosts to order roofing-slates from quarries near Penpethy – an expedition that inspired the poem 'Green Slates'. Some quarries are still worked, others – including this one – not. The tin mine engine-house has been restored.

on his drive from Launceston ('St Launce's'). In the poem 'St Launce's Revisited' the 'Castle and keep uprearing' (where in *A Pair of Blue Eyes* Mrs Smith as a girl had looked for owls' feathers) still 'uprear' above a plethora of 'quaint gables and jumbled roofs'. Opposite the castle bailey, now laid out as a small park, stands the town hall built in 1881; its predecessor, in front of which the young lawyer removed Mrs Smith's bramble, was the curious building still to be seen between the main part of St Mary Magdalene church and its tower.

In the valley north of the town is the now passengerless railway station, beyond which the old packhorse bridge continues to carry pedestrians across the river, while wheeled traffic thunders over a newer bridge close by. Up the hill again, the 'Falcon' where Elfride changed her clothes is the White Hart, a pleasant inn on the Market Place which is also the 'inn / Smiling nigh' of 'St Launce's Revisited'. 'Hill Street' in *Blue Eyes* is a fictitious name, but the shop once kept by the versatile seller and player of 'flutes, and fiddles, and grand pianners' occupies the angle between Church Street and High Street. It was run by one Hayman, who not only sold and played instruments but manufactured his own 'pianners', which enjoyed a wide reputation. After his death his shop and studio became a clothier's, and are now a garden shop. But over a doorway in High Street you may still see the stone-cut likeness of two musicians.

In a dell off the Launceston–Halworthy road snuggles St Clether ('Cleather'), scene of 'The Face at the Casement'. The poem commemorates a real death, that of William Henry Serjeant, the son of the curate, who died at the vicarage on 26 January 1872, at the age of twenty-three, and was buried in a still identifiable grave in the churchyard. We know that the Serjeants knew the Holders, because William's father preached at the rededication of St Juliot church. It is therefore easy to believe that Emma and Hardy (with or without the Holders) drove over during Hardy's third Cornish visit in May–June 1871 to enquire after the young man's

health. If, as they left, Hardy glanced back in time to see the invalid turn away from his window, the incident would have been all he needed to engender his narrative. Today the vicarage is a private cottage, for the parish has been combined with Tresmeer and Laneast, where the present vicar lives. The building stands opposite the entrance to the church, and according to the present occupants the window was the bay one on the ground floor.

In the early 1870s Emma stayed with friends near Lanivet, a large village on the Bodmin–St Austell road (now A391). Hardy visited her here, and during a walk they experienced the curious incident related in 'Near Lanivet, 1872'. There are several junctions where the handpost, which Hardy noted as 'on the St Austell road', may have stood; but they seem unlikely to include the one suggested by Bailey. Most of the old posts have been replaced by international-style metal signs. The subject of the poem 'By the Runic Stone', has been variously identified. Miss Evelyn Hardy believes it to be the Grecian cross, bearing a ninth-century inscription, now to be seen in the front garden of the Wharncliffe Arms at Tintagel, having been rescued from serving as a gatepost at Trevillet Farm, above St Nectan's Kieve. Hardy and the Gifford sisters would have passed Trevillet on their way to the Penpethy quarries in March 1870, and St Nectan's Kieve is referred to (as 'Nietan's Kieve') in Hardy's verse play *The Famous Tragedy of the Queen of Cornwall*. Phelps, while not rejecting Miss Hardy's theory, proposes as an alternative a large inscribed stone at Slaughterbridge, one mile north of Camelford, commemorating the death of a Briton in a battle with the Saxons (and unconnected with King Arthur, as popularly believed). Finally Pinion opts for the Celtic cross by the south stile of St Juliot churchyard.

St Nectan's Kieve is a spectacular waterfall at the head of Rocky Valley, a beautiful and verdant ravine descending to the sea from a point between Boscastle and Tintagel. Hard by the Kieve the Saint built his oratory. A tablet

The exceptionally handsome shop-front at 'St Launce's' that once belonged to Hayman, a piano-maker and instrument-seller introduced into *A Pair of Blue Eyes* as the vendor of 'flutes, and fiddles, and grand pianners'. After many uses, the shop is now a horticulturalist's.

St 'Cleather' (Clether), one of the tiniest villages even in Cornwall, is the scene of the events behind the poem 'The Face At the Casement'. The former vicarage is seen here from the churchyard gate. According to the present occupants, the dying youth's window was the projecting one on the ground floor.

proclaims that the ruins of this have now been rebuilt, but all that is immediately apparent is a modern shack-café. One mile to the south-east, at the highest point of the hills hereabouts, stands Condolden Barrow—a very lonely spot—the 'Condol's crown' mentioned in *The Queen of Cornwall*. At the seaward end of Rocky Valley lies Bossiney, scene of the poem 'The Self-Unconscious' and today famous for its magnificent cliff scenery but also for its sands and safe bathing.

Whether Bossiney or Boscastle is the 'Bos' of other poems is open to argument. A few miles inland Rough Tor, a 1300ft peak on Bodmin Moor, is the 'Rou'tor' of 'I Rose and Went to Rou'tor Town'. The 'town', nevertheless, is not nearby Camelford but Bodmin; the subject of the verses is the displeasure of Emma's father, then living at Kirland Manor, near Bodmin, at her engagement. The Manor, shorn now of creeper and with different windows in half its southern façade, remains in other respects unchanged.

Tintagel castle, in which Hardy and Emma were once trapped, is much better cared for than a century ago, the Department of the Environment having equipped it with plenty of paths, staircases and lawns. Hardy set *The Famous Tragedy of the Queen of Cornwall* in the Great Hall, but neither text nor stage directions offer descriptive matter. Not far away on the cliffs stands Tintagel's large church, restored since Emma sketched it but before Hardy and Florence had the unhappy experience there recorded in *The Life*.

Trebarwith ('Barwith') Strand, a rectangular bay three-quarters of a mile in breadth, to which the Swancourts and Knight drove 'along a road by neutral green hills', accurately fits Hardy's picture. Seen from its north-western extremity, the whole expanse of cliff and shore (now owned by the National Trust) reveals no sign of humanity except a glimpse of white buildings in the south-east angle. In reality, the cleft through which the only road descends contains a moderate colony of bungalows and small hotels, and is bordered by a significantly large car-park. In Hardy's day the white buildings mentioned above were coastguard cottages. Later converted into a hotel, they are now a public house named after Port William, the tiny landing-place just round the southern tip of the cleft. The little cottage cited in *Blue Eyes* is probably Surf Cottage, near the sea; a snack bar now adjoins one end, and a shop partly obscures the front, but the cottage itself has not been altered.

A short way inland along the Trebarwith road are cliffs of a far more bizarre appearance, formed by the slate-quarrying near Penpethy. Hardy's visit to see about materials for St Juliot church is commemorated in the poem 'Green Slates'. The quarries worked then are now abandoned, but others in the group remain in vigorous operation.

Still further down the coast from Tintagel, nearly at Padstow, Pentire Head, boasting one of the loftiest completely sheer cliffs even on the north Cornish coast, is the 'Pen-Tyre' mentioned in *The Queen of Cornwall*.

We are left with Hardy's one Cornish setting, in prose or verse, that is not associated with Emma. This is the scene of the story 'A Mere Interlude', which takes place further west than the other 'Off-Wessex' localities. Using an assortment of real names and his own modifications, Hardy alludes to Truro ('Trufal'), Mousehole and St Clement's Isle, St Michael's Mount and Redruth ('Redrutin'); but the main action is laid in Penzance ('Pen-Zephyr'), which is perfunctorily sketched, and in the Scillies (the 'Isles of Lyonesse'), which are not described at all beyond the mention that they include St Mary's ('St Maria's') and its town, Hugh Town ('Giant's Town').

Thus, at the extreme end of 'Off-Wessex', we also come to the end of this survey. But though the book is at a close, its subject is not. New clues continue to come to light, upsetting old beliefs, solving old mysteries. Perhaps all the keys to Hardy's Wessex will never be found. And that, if galling to us, is how Hardy would have preferred it.

NOTE ON
A GROUP OF NOBLE DAMES

The degree of historical truth in these stories has been the subject of argument ever since they were published. At the one extreme the eminent W. R. Rutland derides the notion of any reality underlying 'such far-fetched tales'—including, presumably, those based on Hutchins; at the other there are Hardy's own statements and the rather over-dramatic testimony of Sidney Heath. Three times at least Hardy declared the tales to be substantially true: in a letter to Edward Clodd, in which he said 'most' of the stories were 'founded on fact'; in a letter offering the American serial rights to Harper's, in which he included the parenthesis 'names disguised but incidents approximating to fact'; and, according to Weber in *Thomas Hardy and the Lady from Madison Square*, in conversation with Rebekah Owen.

Sidney Heath was the author of an apparently unpublished article under the title 'How Thomas Hardy Offended the County Families of Dorset' (1906), of which the typescript is now in the Dorset County Museum. Written somewhat in the vein of a *chronique scandaleuse*, the article declares *all* the stories to be no less than a 'transcript of official documents put into the form of fiction'. These documents are said to have been found, interspersed among deeds, by H. Moule during his curatorship of the museum, and to have been copied out by Hardy, who took the copies to Max Gate. The article recounts how some of the heads of the families involved reacted to publication of the tales, one ordering all Hardy works in his house to be burnt in the courtyard, another threatening with dismissal any employee found bringing a book by Hardy on to the premises, a third forbidding the local bookseller to stock the Wessex novels. Heath of course gives no names, though it is evident they

were all in the documents. But when Professor Bailey recently looked for these they had disappeared, perhaps not entirely by accident; and Hardy's copies would beyond doubt have been destroyed. One intriguing aspect of the article is that Heath makes no reference to the fact that several of the stories are set in other counties; on the contrary, his implication is that each tale refers to a Dorset seat. Are we to infer from this that the non-Dorset locations are just part of Hardy's method of concealment? This is hard to believe of 'Lady Mottisfont', but it could explain why the present owners of several of the conjectured sites in the 'outside' counties have, at my request, searched their family papers without finding anything to suggest the source of Hardy's material.

My impression is that in at least one or two cases—perhaps those in which he felt the discovery of the real protagonists would be most damaging—Hardy adopted a double disguise, fictionalizing a setting that, even if identified, would be found to have nothing to do with his *dramatis personae*. The most interesting of the mysteries involves 'The Duchess of Hamptonshire', not only because it contains the most detailed topographical description, but because Hardy seems to have been so deeply impressed by the realities behind it that he wrote the tale three times, under different titles and for different magazines (see Weber, 'A Masquerade of Noble Dames', *PMLA*, June 1943). In the other versions the 'Batton Castle' of 'The Duchess' becomes 'Stroome Castle' and 'Croome Castle'. Now, 'Batton' is very like a Hardy substitution for Badminton, and Badminton is very near Castle Combe. The 'Batton' mansion does not resemble either the present or former Badminton House, but the fictional park could pass for that of Badminton. 'Emmeline', the heroine's name in all three story versions, is not found in the church there, but 'Emily' appears on a number of memorials. I am assured by the family historian that Hardy's tale has nothing whatever to do with the Beauforts, who own Badminton;

but did Hardy use this area as the basis of his topography, doubly hiding the fact that the true happenings he found so interesting had been enacted somewhere much nearer home? Or is this theory itself a red herring?

BIBLIOGRAPHY

This list includes the great majority of books most likely to help the topographical student, and all the works to which reference has been made in the text. Apart from the principal biographies, the many studies concerned primarily with Hardy's life and place in literature have had to be omitted. Nor has it been possible to cover the great array of local histories, ranging from large volumes to pamphlets, many of which have proved invaluable in the preparation of this volume. For these, readers are recommended to the public reference libraries in the appropriate areas.

Biographies

Gittings, Robert. *Young Thomas Hardy* (London, 1975).

Gittings, Robert. *The Older Hardy* (London, 1978).

Gittings, Robert. *The Second Mrs Hardy* (London, 1979).

Hardy, Evelyn. *Thomas Hardy: a Critical Biography* (London, 1954).

Hardy, Florence Emily. *The Life of Thomas Hardy*. Originally published as *The Early Life* (1928) and *The Later Life* (1930). Now recognized beyond dispute as Hardy's own handiwork, edited and completed by his second wife.

Kay-Robinson, Denys. *The First Mrs Thomas Hardy* (London, 1979).

Millgate, Michael. *Thomas Hardy: a Biography* (Oxford, 1982).

Weber, Carl J. *Hardy of Wessex* (New York and London, 1965, revised).

Books of major topographical interest (in order of publication)

Hutchins, John. *The History and Antiquities of the County of Dorset*. (1st ed 1774; 2nd ed 1796–1815; 3rd ed, corrected, augmented and improved by William Shipp and James Whitworth Hodson, 1861–73. Reissued Wakefield 1973.) Hardy's principal historical source. The engravings differ in each edition; the Dorset County Library (reference room) contains a pamphlet tabulating the variations.

Windle, B. C. A. *The Wessex of Thomas Hardy*, with illustrations by E. H. New (1902. Reprinted Wakefield 1978). Almost the earliest key to Hardy's settings, and in many respects the most charming. Some bad mistakes, offset by surprising accuracies.

Harper, C. G. *The Hardy Country* (London, 1904). Windle without the charm, and New without the grace. Nevertheless, a fuller picture at nearly as early a date, with some interesting engravings.

Treves, Frederick. *Highways and Byways in Dorset* (1906. Reprinted 1981). Treves was the surgeon who performed a secret operation on King Edward VII just before his coronation. His book contains many references to Hardy's works, and is adequately illustrated.

Lea, Hermann. *Thomas Hardy's Wessex* (1913). Reprinted as *Highways and Byways in Hardy's Wessex* (1925). Reprinted in facsimile, Guernsey, 1969. Reprinted (London) 1978. Despite its reputed infallibility, Lea's now almost legendary book contains a number of mistakes (as well as some curious gaps) which cannot be glossed over by maintaining that because he obtained his information direct from Hardy (who also corrected the proofs), error is impossible. Hardy's own memory in later life was not immune to lapses, and the closer one studies Lea *in the field*, the deeper grows the suspicion that during the two men's strenuous journeys Hardy's concentration sometimes wavered, leaving the questioning topographer to take for assent a silence that was merely, in the phrase of one of my helpers, a quiet failure to disagree. Nevertheless, Lea disseminated much fascinating information, and his photographs remain the fullest pictorial record ever made of the Hardy scene.

Purdy, R. L. *Thomas Hardy: a Bibliographical Study* (London, 1954). The origins of Hardy's prose and verse.

Douch, Robert. *Dorset: a Handbook of Local History*, with additions and corrections to 1960 (Bristol, 1962). An indispensable guide to the local histories, including pamphlets.

Lea, Hermann. *Thomas Hardy through the Camera's Eye*, edited by Cox, J. S. (Beaminster, 1964). Supplementary information dictated by Hardy, covering the stories collected in *A Changed Man* and in the verse volumes *Satires of Circumstance* and *Moments of Vision*. One or two blunders in identification again show that Hardy did not always recollect accurately.

Pinion, F. B. *A Hardy Companion* (London, 1968). Contains a long alphabetical list of virtually every character and place in Hardy's prose and verse, with a full key to the Wessex nomenclature including some identifications not previously offered. Information much condensed but of great usefulness. A few inaccuracies.

Bailey, J. O. *The Poetry of Thomas Hardy: a Handbook and Commentary* (N Carolina, USA, and London, 1970). Includes the sum-total of knowledge to date about the topography embodied in Hardy's verse, with special attention to the present condition of the scenes. A very few minor errors and one or two very odd judgements, but indispensable.

An Inventory of the Historical Monuments in Dorset: West Dorset (1952. Reprinted 1975), South-East Dorset (1970. Reprinted 1975), Central Dorset (1970), North Dorset (1972), East Dorset (1975). To date, this is the only county in Hardy's Wessex fully surveyed by the Royal Commission; also useful are the volumes on the City of Oxford (1951. Reprinted 1967) and the City of Salisbury, Vol I (1980) dealing with the City outside the Cathedral Close.

Beatty, C. J. P. *The Part Played by Architecture in the Life of Thomas Hardy (with Particular Reference to the Novels)*. PhD thesis, London University, 1963; available on microfilm in Dorset County Library. Exhaustive and in general reliable on the scenes it covers. Some original identifications.

Cox, J. S. (general editor). *Thomas Hardy; materials for a Study of his Life, Times, and Works* and *More materials* ... (St Peter Port, Guernsey, 1968 and 1971). Originally published as 72 separate monographs, now collected into two volumes. The interest for the topographical student varies according to subject.

The Thomas Hardy Year Book (Guernsey, 1970 and at steadily lengthening intervals since). A most valuable publication in which Hardy scholars set forth their latest views and report the results of the latest researches. Ten issues had appeared up to spring 1983.

Pevsner, Nikolaus (and others). *The Buildings of England*. All the relevant counties have now been covered in this famous series, the Dorset volume (1972) being the last to appear.

O'Sullivan, T. *Thomas Hardy: an Illustrated Biography* (London 1975). A splendid collection of pictures and maps of different dates, including many of the scenes that appear in Hardy's works.

Phelps, Kenneth. *The Wormwood Cup* (Padstow, 1975). Deals only with Hardy in Cornwall, but within that limit outstandingly informative.

Burnett, David. *A Dorset Camera 1855–1914, A Dorset Camera 1914–1945*, and *Dorset Before the Camera* (Stanbridge, Dorset, 1974, 1975 and 1982 respectively). Valuable collections of Dorset pictures showing many scenes of interest to the student of Hardy topography. The same author and publisher have produced a similar trilogy dealing with Wiltshire; a companion on Somerset is in preparation.

Hyland, Paul. *Purbeck: the Ingrained Island* (London, 1978). Excellently told and wonderfully detailed on every aspect of this small piece of country, which nevertheless contains a number of Hardy settings.

Pinion, F. B. (editor) *The Thomas Hardy Society Review*. Annual publication comparable with the *Year Books*, but unillustrated. First number 1975. Frequent topographical subjects.

Enstice, Andrew. *Landscapes of the Mind* (London, 1979). The imaginary social and physical milieu in which Hardy's characters move, contrasted with the reality. Unusual and fascinating.

Hawkins, Desmond. *Hardy's Wessex* (London, 1983). Photos by A. Kersting. Informative and thoughtful.

Some books of minor topographical interest (alphabetically listed)

Adlam, Brian. *The Book of Dorchester*; Gibb, J. H. P. *The Book of Sherborne*; Short, Basil, and Sales, John. *The Book of Bridport*. All in the Barracuda Books series (Buckingham, 1980–81). In preparation, *The Book of Wimborne*.

Beatty, C. J. P. (editor). *Thomas Hardy's Architectural Notebooks* (Dorchester, 1966).

Björk, Lennart A. (editor). *The Literary Notes of Thomas Hardy*: 2 vols (Göteborg, Sweden, 1974).

Cochrane, C. *The Lost Roads of Wessex* (Newton Abbot, 1969).

Deacon, Lois, and Coleman, Terry. *Providence and Mr Hardy* (London, 1966).

Edwards, Anne-Marie. *Discovering Hardy's Wessex* (Southampton, 1982).

Gant, Roland. *Dorset Villages* (London, 1980).

Goode, Ronald. *The Old Roads of Dorset* (Bournemouth, 1966 [revised]).

Hardy, Emma Lavinia, ed. Evelyn Hardy and Robert Gittings. *Some Recollections* (written 1911, ed. and pub. London, 1964).

'Holland, Clive' (C. J. Hankinson). *Thomas Hardy, O.M., the Man, His Works, and the Land of Wessex* (London, 1933).

'Holland, Clive' (C. J. Hankinson). *Thomas Hardy's Wessex Scene* (Dorchester, 1948).

Irvine, Peter. *Victorian and Edwardian Dorchester from Old Photographs* (London, 1977).

Maxwell, Donald. *The Landscape of Thomas Hardy* (paintings) (London, 1928).

Millgate, Michael. *Thomas Hardy: his Career as a Novelist* (London, 1971).

Parker, W. M. *On the trail of the Wessex Novels* (Poole, 1924).

Pinion, F. B. *Thomas Hardy: a Commentary on the Poems* (London, 1976).

Pouncy, John. *Dorsetshire Photographically Illustrated* (Dorchester, 1857).

Purdy, Richard L., and Millgate, Michael (editors). *The Collected Letters of Thomas Hardy* (Oxford, vol. I 1978, vol. II 1980, vol. III 1982; other vols to follow).

Sherren, Wilkinson. *The Wessex of Romance* (London, 1902).

Tyndale, Walter; text by 'Clive Holland'. *Wessex* (paintings) (1906).

Although, as already stated, pamphlets on topographical subjects are too numerous to be listed here, mention may be made of the series of fifteen 'Tour Pamphlets', by various authors, published by the Thomas Hardy Society. Unavoidably somewhat superficial, and, perhaps equally unavoidably, not always one hundred per cent accurate, these are nevertheless inexpensive and useful guides, offering practical information for both the motorist and the pedestrian exploring Hardy's 'Wessex' for the first time. They also have the merit of being kept up to date by frequent revision.

TITLE-BY-TITLE INDEX

Title-by-title index to the Wessex places in Hardy's prose fiction, together with
The Dynasts and *The Queen of Cornwall*. In alphabetical order of volumes.
Short stories in the order in which they appear in the volumes.

GENERAL INDEX

Place-names are shown in capitals: Hardy place-names in italic capitals.
Poems are listed under that heading. Names of Hardy characters are not indexed, but references
are covered under the titles of the appropriate works.
Page numbers in italic type refer to illustrations.

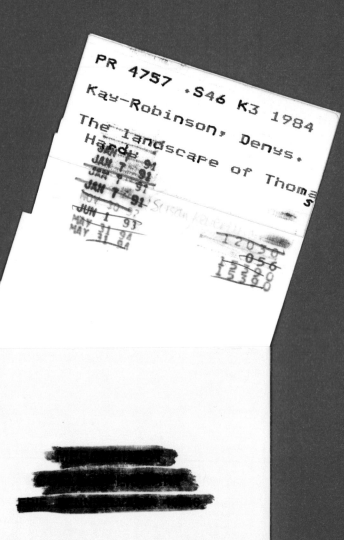